THE MOST OFF-KEY, OUT-OF-TUNE, AND AWFULLY HARD-TO-BELIEVE ROCK 'N' ROLL TOUR EVER!

"'It's just not fair,' Stephen King blurted one night after the show. 'Dave Barry got the whip jammed into his mouth *two* nights in a row! When's it going to be *my* turn?'"
—Amy Tan, on props

"This is the nadir of western civilization. Right here, in our show."   —Al Kooper, on the Critics Chorus

"Don't play so loud." "Don't play at all." "I don't think we should do this song." —Dave Barry, on Al Kooper's insightful and nonjudgmental musical advice

"It took a year to figure out all the metaphysical stuff. In the beginning, I was stymied by the words to 'Da Doo Ron Ron.'"
—Tad Bartimus, Wanton Siren

"I never intended to become known for cross-dressing."
—Dave Marsh, in white taffeta

"There's no such thing as bad publicity. I think."
—Matt Groening, reviewing Don Henley reviewing the Remainders

"I used to be able to *whistle* through my navel, but that was before the sinus operation."
—Roy Blount, Jr.

Mid-Life Confidential

MID-LIFE Confidential

THE ROCK BOTTOM REMAINDERS
Tour America with Three Chords and an Attitude

DAVE BARRY

TAD BARTIMUS

ROY BLOUNT, JR.

MICHAEL DORRIS

ROBERT FULGHUM

KATHI KAMEN GOLDMARK

MATT GROENING

STEPHEN KING

TABITHA KING

BARBARA KINGSOLVER

AL KOOPER

GREIL MARCUS

DAVE MARSH

RIDLEY PEARSON

JOEL SELVIN

AMY TAN

**EDITED BY
DAVE MARSH**

**PHOTOGRAPHS BY
TABITHA KING**

Ⓟ

A PLUME BOOK

PLUME
Published by the Penguin Group
Penguin Books USA Inc., 375 Hudson Street, New York, New York 10014, U.S.A.
Penguin Books Ltd, 27 Wrights Lane, London W8 5TZ, England
Penguin Books Australia Ltd, Ringwood, Victoria, Australia
Penguin Books Canada Ltd, 10 Alcorn Avenue, Toronto, Ontario, Canada M4V 3B2
Penguin Books (N.Z.) Ltd, 182–190 Wairau Road, Auckland 10, New Zealand

Penguin Books Ltd, Registered Offices: Harmondsworth, Middlesex, England

Published by Plume, an imprint of Dutton Signet,
a division of Penguin Books USA Inc.
Previously published in a Viking edition.

First Plume Printing, August, 1995
10 9 8 7 6 5 4 3 2 1

 REGISTERED TRADEMARK—MARCA REGISTRADA

The Library of Congress has catalogued the Viking edition as follows:

Mid-life confidential: the Rock Bottom Remainders tour America with
  three chords and an attitude/edited by Dave Marsh.
    p.   cm.
  ISBN 0-670-85234-1 (hc.)
  ISBN 0-452-27459-1 (pbk.)
  1. Rock Bottom Remainders (musical group). 2. Authors, American—
Journeys—United States. I. Marsh, Dave. II. Rock Bottom
Remainders (musical group).
ML421.R6M5 1994
781.66'092'273—dc20
[B] 94–2073

Printed in the United States of America
Original hardcover design by Charles Kreloff

January 1993

Dear Band,

    The funeral for Dave Marsh's daughter Kristen, twenty-one, was held in an enormous Episcopal cathedral that was filled with several hundred people as selections from Kristen's favorite music were played. The last song before the ceremony began was "No Woman, No Cry." I had never heard that fine song so thoroughly before, and I don't think I'll ever hear it again without thinking of Kristen and Dave and Barbara and my own children and my friends, including you all.

    A year or so ago, at Dave's insistence, I inscribed something to Kristen. They trusted then that her rare cancer would be cured, but nine weeks ago it came back, and she went down fast, physically but not in spirit. The thing I inscribed was a sportive article I'd written in Self *magazine of all places (watch out what you write— you might wind up inscribing it to somebody's daughter), about why men don't like condoms. I advised her to study hard so that someday she, too, could write about rubbers for money. Dave said she would like that fine. That was the closest I came to meeting Kristen, but I felt good about having her out there as a reader, and her funeral—she was eulogized movingly by Dave, by Jon Landau, and by two of her friends—evoked her so vividly that I cried over the loss of her and felt grateful for all the things I haven't lost. I wish you all could have heard the things that were said about Kristen and Dave and Barbara, and their other daughter, Sasha: a household, evidently, of enviable closeness, liveliness, and fondness. Bruce Springsteen and Patti Scialfa sang a song of his, "If I Should Fall Behind," and the Boss remembered that when Kristen traveled with him she would give him a wink before he went on stage that "made me feel kind of foolish in a nice kind of way. It said, 'Hey, Mr. Big Rock Star—you better be yourself if you're going to be around me.'"*

    It was a beautiful service, and I told Dave so from all of us. I move that we dedicate our book to Kristen, and that we take time, whenever we go on stage, to wish we were good enough for her to wink at us.

Roy

Acknowledgments

The Remainders thank:

The spouses and kids who let us do this and mostly didn't even laugh too hard when they read Don Henley's review, listened to us practice, and observed our costume changes; Peter Clifton, the first publishing professional to believe in the idea (and still manage to keep his job); George Gerrity, "spiritual adviser and guard dog," who shared his insight, experience, and every music industry resource at his disposal and led us to Bob Daitz; Bob Daitz, who taught us more than we thought we'd ever want to know about mustache grooming and many other things (and Van Halen for sharing him with us); Stephen Pillster, who booked our tour, a hard sell if ever there was one; Ron Heard and Randy Edwards, who performed CPR (Creative Production Rescue) on our video; and Tabitha King, who provided significant moral and medical support in addition to her fantastic photography.

Special thanks to our intrepid crew: Carole Eitingon, Lorraine Battle, the legendary Hoover, mythic Mouse, Jim England (Maine's best), and the hardest-driving men in show business, Bob Dannic and Dave Worters. Jerry Peterson and Josh Kelly weren't just ringers; they were good company and, better yet, good copy (writers know no greater praise).

Pam Dorman, our editor at Viking, took a chance on one of the unlikeliest projects ever to cross a desk and stuck with us through fear, loathing, and copy editing. Our other ace in the hole at Viking has been the wonderful Patti Kelly, a loyal and honorary Remainderette.

We would also like to thank: Audrey deChadenèdes, Judi Smith, Catherine Talese, and numerous other assistants who never bargained for amateur rock 'n' roll when they signed up; our legal department, including Susan Grode, Kathy Hersh, Bob Martis, and especially Frank Curtis, who also served us well as literary agent; Marcia Zwick, Cynthia Robins, Gloria Pass, and Susanne Moss, the Remainders' wardrobe and makeup auxiliary; our multitudinous crew volunteers, including panty-line policeman and Anaheim operations manager Jerry Pompili, Walter Mayes, Jim Foster, George McFadden, Suzanne Wickham, Jackie DeVal, Esther Levine, and David Wenger, and the many booksellers and media escorts who also chipped in; Ennis and David Dellca for the excellence of their stand-in crew work (and dancing) in Atlanta; Gretchen Schields, Robert Foothorap, Neal Preston, and Betty and Si Kamen, our art, photography, and graphics department; Jane Sharp for vocal coaching (we did *her* no favors despite what she did for us); and Keta Bill for remedial choreography beyond the point where all hope should undoubtedly have been abandoned. Also, the American Booksellers Association, for rolling with it;

Rock Medicine; Tomie dePaola; BMG Music Video; Robert Fulghum's anonymous donor; and Louis Chan and the Yet Wah Karaoke Bar.

Kathi Kamen Goldmark thanks Joe and Tony Goldmark, the Ray Price Club, and the Rhinestone Bolo Band.

Al Kooper wishes to thank all of the coauthors/heroes/heroines contained herein for treating me as an equal (I'm not worthy); my first band, The Artisto-cats, in whose mold I musically modeled the Remainders; Jimmy Vivino for giving of his talent, time, and spirit; and last but not least, my permanent family: father Sam, mother Nat, son Brian, and dog Daisy.

Amy Tan gives a great big kiss to Louie Louie for being the Leader of the Pack.

Tad Bartimus's Remainderheroes are: Dean Wariner, Ginni Chaffin, Gaby Benson, Jeff Hickson, Scott McCartney, Paula and Walt Steige, Ann and Greg Steiner, and Louis D. Boccardi.

Greil Marcus thanks Sally, Fred, Arthur B. Gallagher, all the guys at "Mom's," God, the late Otis Redding, you know who you are, and my agents.

Dave Marsh thanks Sandy Choron for flinging her underwear, Barbara Carr for guarding the gate, Lee Ballinger for moral support and political savvy, the rest of the band for not telling me not to, Don Henley because nobody else will, and *Vanity Fair*'s photographer for making a man of me.

Contents

Survivors of the Siege
(PERSONNEL)

DAVE BARRY, *lead guitar, vocals*

TAD BARTIMUS, *Remainderette*

LORRAINE BATTLE, *wardrobe, shop till you drop*

ROY BLOUNT, JR., *Critics Chorus and master of ceremonies*

BOB DAITZ, *tour manager, scapegoat, nonnavigator, Sammy you should see me now*

BOB DANNIC, *universal crew, driver*

MICHAEL DORRIS, *percussion (Anaheim and Bottom Line only)*

CAROLE EITINGON, *concessions, merchandising, life of the party*

JIM ENGLAND, *guitar technician, mysterious man from Maine*

ROBERT FULGHUM, *mandocello, vocals*

KATHI KAMEN GOLDMARK, *Remainderette and Founding Mom*

MATT GROENING, *Critics Chorus*

HOOVER (CHRIS RANKIN), *production manager, sound engineer, good shorts*

JOSH KELLY, *drums, best attitude in the biz (and the bus)*

STEPHEN KING, *rhythm guitar, vocals*

TABITHA KING, *tour photographer, shop till you drop*

BARBARA KINGSOLVER, *keyboards, vocals*

AL KOOPER, *musical director, guitar, keyboards, vocals, video expert*

GREIL MARCUS, *Critics Chorus*

DAVE MARSH, *Critics Chorus, Teen Angel*

MOUSE (DANNY DELALUZ), *keyboard/drum technician, lead flashlight*

RIDLEY PEARSON, *bass guitar, vocals, Designated Worrier*

JERRY PETERSON, *saxophone, "Check it out!"*

JOEL SELVIN, *Critics Chorus, lead scream*

AMY TAN, *Remainderette, Rhythm Dominatrix*

JIMMY VIVINO, *keyboards, vocals*

DAVE WORTERS, *bus driver, tour guide*

The Rock Bottom Remainders' 1993 "Three Chords and an Attitude" Tour Itinerary

May 16–19	Boston, Massachusetts	Rehearsals
May 20	Providence, Rhode Island	Shooters Waterfront Cafe
May 21	Northampton, Massachusetts	Pearl Street
May 22	Cambridge, Massachusetts	Nightstage (two shows)
May 22–23	Travel by bus to Washington, D.C.	Sleep if you can
May 24	Washington, D.C.	The Bayou
May 24–25	Travel by bus to Philadelphia, Pennsylvania	Do media all day
May 25	Philadelphia, Pennsylvania	Katmandu
May 25–26	Travel by bus to Atlanta, Georgia Barbara Kingsolver departs; pick up Jimmy Vivino as ringer keyboardist	Sleep if we ever arrive
May 27	Atlanta, Georgia Greil Marcus arrives	The Roxy
May 28	Travel by bus to Nashville, Tennessee	328 Performance Hall
May 29	Fly to Miami, Florida, at 6:30 A.M. Barbara Kingsolver returns; Jimmy Vivino departs; Matt Groening and Robert Fulghum arrive; all present for ritual torture by *Vanity Fair* photographer	Stay awake if you can
May 30	Miami, Florida	The Paragon
May 31	Points north and west	Fly home; sleep all you wanna

Song List 1993

"Mammer Jammer" (Ridley Pearson and Amy Tan, lead vocals)

"Teen Angel" (Stephen King)

"Gloria" (Dave Barry)

"(Sittin' on) The Dock of the Bay" (Barbara Kingsolver)

"Nadine" (Ridley)

"Money" (Dave B.)

"Take Out Some Insurance" (Kathi Kamen Goldmark)

"Wooly Bully" (Critics Chorus)

"634-5789" (Ridley)

"Caress Me Baby" (aka "Koresh Me Baby") (Al Kooper)

"Give Him a Great Big Kiss" (Amy)

"The Boy from New York City" (Remainderettes, Kingsolver)

"Susie-Q" (Stephen)

"Good Rockin' Tonight" (Ridley)

"Stand by Me" (Stephen)

"Louie Louie" (Critics Chorus; Joel Selvin, scream solo)

"You Can't Sit Down" (Kathi)

"The Last Time" (Dave B.)

"Who Do You Love" (Stephen)

"Land of 1,000 Dances" (Dave B.)

"Last Kiss" (Stephen)

"Leader of the Pack" (Amy)

"Double Shot (Of My Baby's Love)" (Critics Chorus)

"He Will Break Your Heart" (Dave B., Kathi)

"My Guy" (Tad Bartimus)

"Chain of Fools" (Tad)

"These Boots Are Made for Walkin'" (Amy)

"Endless Sleep" (Stephen)

"Midnight Hour" (Ridley)

"Short Shorts" (Critics Chorus; Remainderettes)

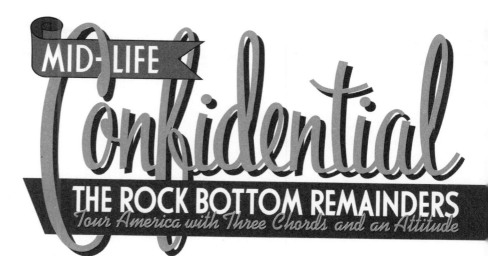

MID-LIFE

Confidential

THE ROCK BOTTOM REMAINDERS

Tour America with Three Chords and an Attitude

Do you hear what I hear? Nah, it's just the fax machine:

A DOCUMENTARY HISTORY OF THE ROCK BOTTOM REMAINDERS BEFORE THE TOUR

*I*t all started sometime in the fall of 1991 with a fax from Kathi Kamen Goldmark. No one on the receiving end doubts that it—the Remainders, our lives, the universe—will all end with one.

> *Dear Michael, Louise, Oscar, Dave, Dave, Barbara, Bob, Robert, Amy, Anna, Gita, Roy, Ridley, Tomie, Matt, and Doreen,*
>
> > *Well, I had this idea.*
> > *What would happen if, during the next ABA, a group of well-known authors got together, formed a rock band, and performed a benefit for children's literacy or some other nice, book-related cause? What would you think if I told you I'm trying to make this actually happen? How would you like to be in the band?*
> > *I am looking into renting a nightclub in Anaheim for the show. I'm even trying to call in some old L.A. favors and recruit a "celebrity" musical director/band leader to whip things into shape in a day or two. Rehearsal space and equipment needs are easy. I can drive down with my PA and some other stuff, and we can rent the rest. What I need to know is, can you be there, with or without your publisher's approval and sponsorship, for a couple of rehearsals and the show? Are you ready to rock? Can we even agree on a set list?*
>
> > *Your mission, should you choose to accept it:*
> > *_ fill out and return the enclosed questionnaire*
> > *_ practice, practice, practice*
> > *_ go see* The Commitments
> > *_ hope that Wilson Pickett writes a book this year.*

The key questions on the questionnaire in question were:

> *_ Yes, I would love to be in this band! Count me in!*
> *_ No, I'm far too important and dignified to do anything this silly.*
> *_ I'd love to, but I'm a little scared, and I might have to wash my hair that night. Let's talk more about it.*

By January 11, when Kathi wrote to Stephen King, inviting him to join, the group had a name: the Remainders, a name suggested by Michael Dorris, who also proposed calling ourselves the Blurbs, Hard Cover, Cheap Trade Edition, Seamless Prose, or Finally in Paperback. It's not hard to see why "the Remainders" won out by acclamation. But two weeks later, with King in the fold (and a few of those originally invited out), a legal search turned up a real band that already used that name. (God, we hope that none of the fans of *those* Remainders have picked up this book, thinking to read about their bar-band favorites, and gotten stuck with a tome about a bunch of writers *posing* as a bar band.)

That was as much business as we conducted that year. But on January 3, 1992, Kathi struck again, with the first of her truly hefty faxes. (Please remember that you are reading excerpts only.)

Hi, Campers!

Lots of news about the band, which is now officially called . . . THE ROCK BOTTOM REMAINDERS. So here goes:

I have booked a nightclub called Cowboy Boogie for the night of Monday, May 25. Cowboy Boogie is a half-mile from the convention center. The place holds almost 1,000 people, and I'm thinking we might want to do two shows, say at 9:30 and 11:30.

A flurry of business detail, followed by what may or may not have been the most important purpose of this missive:

One more thing, and I feel a little shy about this, but I would like to be in the band, even though I've never been a best-selling author. I can either

The Anaheim version. Shown are (in back row, from left) Gerry Peterson, saxophone "ringer"; Dave Barry; Barbara Kingsolver; Matt Groening; Kathi Goldmark; Al Kooper; Tad Bartimus; Robert Fulghum; Michael Dorris; (front row, from left) Josh Kelly, drums "ringer"; Stephen King; Roy Blount, Jr.; Joel Selvin; Ridley Pearson; Dave Marsh; Greil Marcus; Amy Tan.

play rhythm guitar and belt out a few lead vocals, if needed, or join the 'Mainderettes as a backup singer. Either is fine, but I get to play 'cause it's my ball, OK?

This resulted in:

Of course you should play in the band—someone has to look good and somebody has to know what they're doing and why not you! WE NEED A KILLER HARMONICA PLAYER!

Thought about the ABA concern and talked at length with people at Villard/Random House. Strong feelings that we should be inside the tent in some way and not be seen as a maverick group who went off with a to-hell-with-them-we-do-our-own-thing attitude. So. I want to do two songs on their First Amendment program—early on—acoustic if need be or specially prepared for the equipment circumstances available there—and use that as a come-on for the rest of our event evening.

Robert Fulghum

Some of the band members felt that we should come up with an origin-of-the-Remainder myth that was more magical than the real one. What's a band without a myth?

Michael D. and I spoke the other night. We think that the Remainders are possibly all brothers and sisters (though this poses a problem for Michael and Louise) and have been together for a long time, trying to get their music right. This is why none of us has ever met a book deadline, and in fact, may be an inherent encouragement for editors and agents to arrive bearing well-aged fruit, vegetables, eggs, etc. I do not know who founded the group, probably one of the musicians, but it was merged at some point with Michael's old Alaskan band, Native Soul, and of course, the Masked Marauders, whose chief songwriter was Greil Marcus, who then subverted the whole enterprise by recruiting into it a number of rock critics, who as everyone especially Frank Zappa knows are hopeless re: music per se. We are making our debut now in part because we figure it might be the last chance, the kind of music we perform (I suggest adding "Kick Out the Jams Motherfucker" to the set list; I know the lyrics) being on the verge of illegality anyway—and in any true civilization, the WAY we play would very likely be illegal too.

I think that you have always been in the band, but sort of in the fashion of Wendy in Peter Pan; you're far too musical to be a true Remainder, of course, but it is well established that none of us can function without you, since that is how we all came to know you in the first place.

My equipment needs: A mask or hood would be good. Or just a gag.

Dave Marsh

I got a note from Louise about very important matters. We have in mind to wear one gold and one silver lamé glove, biceps length. As to the rest, anything that's black, tight, and sleazy. I am using this band as my excuse to finally do some exercise. At age forty (minus one month), I've discovered the law of gravity applies to my body. That and the fact that one's triceps begin to look like those of one's third grade teacher—the one who wrote homework assignments vigorously on the blackboard while we all watched the Jell-O wiggle underneath.

By the way, a friend of mine who has heard me humming tunes to the radio asks, "Are you sure they know what you mean when you say you can't sing?"

Amy Tan

The next ominous omnibus fax from Kathi arrived on February 6. From the morass of detail, including the fact that the charities benefiting from gate proceeds and T-shirt sales would be the Literacy Volunteers of America and the Right to Rock Network, emerges:

Dress Code: black, gold, and silver in any combination. Backup singers: slinky short black dresses, one silver and one gold lamé elbow-length glove, perhaps one silver and one gold lamé high-heeled pump? Critics Chorus: you guys decide. I like Hawaiian shirts and baseball caps. Or Dead Elvis T-shirts.

Kathi also asked for "an adorable 'all-purpose' quote" to give to members of the press at her discretion. These eventually included:

"The Remainders are a group of people who have played in bands at some point in our lives, but had to turn to *writing* for a living. This should tell you how we were doing as musicians." (Barbara Kingsolver)

"If this helps one bookseller learn to read then my work will not have—*wop-bopaloobop*—been in vain. (No, don't use that, I don't want to offend booksellers for God's sake, you didn't hear Elvis making deejay jokes. And let me say this: I would a whole lot rather be in a business where you can't afford to offend booksellers than in a business where you can't afford to offend disc jockeys. It's classier.)" (Roy Blount, Jr.)

"This band plays music as well as Metallica writes novels." (Dave Barry)

Barry's motto became our byword—that is, we put it on the back of the T-shirts we flogged to fans and concertgoers. These crucial issues settled, the Designated Worrier checked in:

The size of the new roster scares the shit out of me. We both know how impossible it is to get a quartet up and running in two or three rehearsals, even on the simplest of materials. This present list seems to me to be unmanageable. If Jeff Baxter or someone equally "heavy" is involved as musical director, he or she MAY be able to bring some sense to it, but it terrifies me. (And I'm a thriller writer!) Too many vocalists, too many guitarists (I worked in a band for five years with three guitars and it's a nightmare of sound), too many PEOPLE for a stage, short of Carnegie Hall. If managed correctly—and you are a GREAT manager—I'm sure it can work, but boy, how it is going to need careful management. . . .

This negativity is not meant to bum you out, or to imply that I know it all, because I don't. But this is an army, not a band, and with everyone running all over the ABA doing their "thing" getting even three or four songs up and running will be a challenge. . . . If the rehearsals get out of hand, we'll never even learn the changes.

If we do learn the changes, though, I think we should shoot for Jay Leno's "Tonight Show," Tuesday night. He's right there in Horrorwood, and with Stephen King and Fulghum on board we have some name attraction. Just a thought. . . .

Ridley Pearson

For the record, Kathi agreed that the thought of our stooges playing for Jay Leno during the first week of his NBC run was a great one. Stephen disagreed, prompting Kathi to explain to him *her* rock 'n' roll fantasy: "Seems like it might not happen anyway, but my thought was: 1 gig + 1 'Tonight Show' = perfect rock 'n' roll career." We never did play any talk shows. But others had more important business to conduct:

For purposes of the press kit I'm willing to admit that I am, and always have been, a member of the Remainder family. (I mean, jeez, who could miss the family resemblance? Practically all of us wear glasses, except in our publicity photos.) Our parents, Ricky and Imelda Remainder, forced us to listen to Chuck Berry and practice our rock 'n' roll moves endlessly in our tender years, when all my brothers and sisters and I wanted to do was read Herman Melville.

Barbara Kingsolver

Occasionally, reality intruded even on this project. On February 24, Michael Dorris faxed to say that he and Louise Erdrich, still in mourning over the death of Michael's son Abel just a few months earlier, could not appear with the band. Ridley, our bassist, proposed using as a replacement drummer a "ringer" (i.e., nonauthor)—his old bandmate Josh Kelly, who lived in Los Angeles, where he'd been playing with neopunk hero Paul Westerberg. Kathi left the door open for Michael's return. Michael responded by volunteering to write the band bio, and as it turned out, he was able to turn up in Anaheim to add some percussion to the proceedings.

About the same time, Al Kooper signed on as musical director. Kooper was no ringer; he'd published a memoir, *Backstage Passes,* in the mid-seventies. Kooper did insist on adding a ringer, though, in the person of saxophonist Jerry Peterson, a refugee from session work and *Buckaroo Banzai.*

The list of charities that would receive the money generated by the show was settled: The Literacy Volunteers of America, the Los Angeles–based Homeless Writers Coalition, and the anticensorship Right to Rock Network. Amy Tan drafted a letter offering publishers the chance to sponsor various levels of activity by and around the band: a thousand bucks made you a Fan, twenty-five hundred earned you status as a Groupie, and five grand took you all the way to Remainderhead.

Stephen King wrote to comment on this arrangement, and while he was at it, added a new song to the set list that proved to be a key Remainders icon:

> *I'm really wary of squeezing too much of the juice out of this here grapefruit. I mean, when you get right down to it, we're just a bunch of bangers with only three days to rehearse (and during much of that we're apt to be distracted by press, autograph seekers, psychotic celebrity serial killers, etc.). If we charge too much up front, people are apt to expect a little too much. I'd rather have them come expecting to see a bunch of refugees from the Major Bowes Amateur Talent Hour and get an agreeable surprise when two or three numbers actually* work . . . *get me?*
>
> *Now, you'll notice that I have actually had the temerity to make a suggested addition to the playlist: "Teen Angel," the Mark Dinning weeper from 1959. I've always been deeply moved by the verse that goes* [he quoted the lyrics, but we aren't doing that here, on account of the publisher being Acuff-Rose, whom Dave Barry once did not call a bad name in public, thereby making it unlikely we'd receive permission to quote 'em even if we did ask pretty please]. *It would be a treat to share such a fine sentiment with a group of sensitive, caring book-people, I think. Positively Keats-ian. And how did we miss "Hang On Sloopy" by the McCoys and "Brown Eyed Girl" by Van Morrison?*
>
> *Okay, you can stop tearing your hair now. What I've suggested isn't my* favorite *songs (I could do without ever hearing "Runaround Sue" again, let alone singing and playing it) but the ones on the list that seem to be guaranteed rip-up-your-seat-and-stomp rock and roll tunes. Actually, "Smells Like Teen Spirit" fits, but let's face the stone ugly truth: most of our audience are going to be stodgy old poops who vaguely remember having a good time (listening to Bobby Vinton warble "Blue Velvet," most likely), and I think we'll refresh their memory best if we keep it simple. But there are lots of great tunes on our list. Even the ones I marked as "least favorite" are mostly okay with me, although I'm never really gonna feel good about a girl who sings,*

"And when he walked me home . . . da-doo-ron-ron-ron, da-doo-ron-ron!" I guess we all know what that kind of girl will do, don't we?
                                                                Stephen

The Critics Chorus, however, shared none of King's qualms:

Well, it looks like this thing has really become colossal, which is a shame because that is the one word I am never sure I've spelled right.
    All I have to do is holler "Give it up for (for instance) Amy Tan" a number of times, right?
                                                    Roy Blount, Jr.

We shoulda charged to be in the band.
                                        Dave Marsh

By the end of March, the idea that we'd do an acoustic set at the ABA Freedom of Speech event, then head over to Cowboy Boogie for our two sets, was settled, Kathi nailing down the details in another blizzard of faxes as band members attended to fine points.

You said Al Kooper wants to see a bio. Did you mean my official writer bio? If so, here it is. If he wants to know my musical background, this is it: I played in a blues band in the early seventies, was trained as a classical pianist at DePauw University, and played on and off with a local rock band in the early eighties. My total earnings as a musician would, maybe, take us all out to dinner once. At the same kind of cheap joint I played in.
                                            Barbara Kingsolver

Ridley now found something to *really* worry about: what if nobody could figure out how to play together? So he created the now semilegendary "practice tapes," so that the band members could begin to share a common idea of chords, tempos, and arrangements.

Ridley, you may not think of yourself as a ringer, but you play one wide fuck of a lot better than I do. Sing better, too. Probably turn out to be better lookin as well—ain't life a bitch? Still, the tape was a really good idea. I tuned my guitar to yours, then called up a friend with some recording equipment and asked him if I could try to put a rhythm track and vocal with your bass and drum machine. He said to come over and we'll see. He's going to make up cassettes of the result, and I'll send them to Kathi. If she doesn't kill herself immediately, or book passage to some obscure island in Micronesia, beyond the reach of irate booksellers, you will also get one, as will Dave Barry. . . .
                                                    Steve

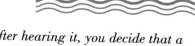

P.S. The tape I'm sending is very short. If, after hearing it, you decide that a new rhythm guitarist would be in order, I'll understand.
P.P.S. Actually, I'm just joking. I wouldn't understand at all.

On May 1, things got even stranger:

Just about all of you have suggested that we make sure there are video and audio recordings of our show, so that we can each have a souvenir of the event. The trick is doing this affordably. [Bob Daitz's friend the video director] and I decided that it would be interesting just to see if we could get anyone in the music industry to put up some development money to foot the bill for audio and video production. This way we'd get the best quality, retain control of the product, and have the freedom to decide later, after the show, what to do with it. We met with Jayne Simon and George Gerrity, my friends at Zoo Entertainment. (Zoo is a subsidiary of BMG, which also owns RCA Records and the BDD—Bantam-Doubleday-Dell—group.) Well, guess what? They passed our proposal on to David Steffen, head of BMG music video, and he said

—big drumroll—
YES!!

Kathi

Everyone signed on for the video project. This would later be known colloquially as Our First Big Fuck-up. The show could have been the second, but it wasn't. It was great. Ask anybody who was there. Not even Don Henley failed to have a good time (see Appendix). And the Remainders—well, the Remainders were head over heels in love with themselves and each other, and most of all with Kathi Kamen Goldmark, who'd thought it all up. (Much of the most over-the-top gush about her has been trimmed out of these letters, believe it or not.)

I lost my voice; I made some friends; I got to play lead while doing the butt dance with Al Kooper. My life can end now, if it wants to. Thanks for including me.

Dave Barry

When I was a kid attending my first birthday parties, my mother instructed me to always seek out the hostess before I left and say, "Thank you for a very nice time." I didn't get a chance to say that to you before Tabby and I headed back to Maine yesterday, so let me say it now: thank you for a very nice time. Also, thank you for giving me a chance to kick ass and take down names in an all-out way for the first time since I was sixteen or so.

Steve
P.S. Please send cassettes, videos, clippings, and lace underwear as soon as

possible. And speaking of lace underwear, one more story. While Dave was introducing Al's song the second time, I picked up a pair of pink panties off the stage and hung them over the end of my guitar. During the sax break, Al came over and asked me what my wife would think of that. "I don't know," I said, "but I think they're hers."

Thank you for letting me realize fantasies I didn't even know I had. I had no idea how much fun it would be to scream "G-L-O-R-I-A" or produce bizarre strangling noises in the middle of "Double Shot"—in public, not just driving in the car—and even more than that, to do it and not care what anyone thought.

Greil

This ends the Anaheim chapter of our adventures. Then, on the very ides of June, Steve King began the beguine that led to . . . well, *this*, among other things:

There have been so many faxes flying about that I haven't known exactly who to reply to first . . . and also, I have been writing. So many people have told me not to quit my day job yet that I went right back to work. Hell, I had to write; for three days following our debut performance, I couldn't fookin' talk, so what else was there? Before moving on to more substantive matters, let me "share" with all of you how much I have come to hate that nasty little piece of advice. I think the next time someone offers it to me, I will snatch up a handful of the person's shirt and scream into his or her face, "If YOU had my day job, would YOU quit it, birdbrain?"

Okay, now that I've got that *off my chest*, let me offer a thought or two on some of the issues that have come up in the wake of our rhythm-and-blues frenzy in Southern California (last month? is it already last month? does it have *to be last month so goddamn soon?*).

Central issue: Should the Remainders rock again?

As Stevie Sees It: *Yes. I think it's about as high as you can get legally.* Speaking just for myself, I have decided—after quite a bit of considera-tion—that it was actually better *than that first wet dream. Not much, as the wet dream involved (as I remember) a hammock and a lot of tropical fruit, but yes, a little better. Seriously (well, I was being serious, but you know), it was a blast, and I actually improved my guitar skills—and my enjoyment of my instrument—quite a bit during rehearsals. Now I'm sure there are people who would say I had nowhere to go but up, anyway, but that seems beside the point. Music aside, I love the immediate response to the act of perfor-mance. Maybe I wouldn't love it so much if the immediate response was peo-ple throwing grapefruits, but realistically speaking, I don't think that's going to happen. Samuel Johnson once said that women preachers had this in common with dancing dogs: people were not delighted to see it done well but to see it done at all. To dancing dogs and women preachers, I think you can add rock bands composed mostly of writers.*

Stephen concludes:

Do you guys want to play in Miami [site of the 1993 ABA]? Will Kathi set it up? Will Al Kooper once again play the part of the Remainders' Rock n Roll Yoda?

This fax comes to you from the Rev. Dr. Fulghum, who this last weekend received his first and only honorary Doctor of Letters degree from Wittenberg University in Springfield, Ohio, in a setting only Norman Rockwell could have portrayed. Along with the hood comes a red velvet medieval-style hat like Martin Luther wore. It's a sign of progress in human affairs in that there was a time when Lutherans burned Unitarians at the stake—and now I'm invited to a barbecue and given a great hat. The gentle green hills of Ohio seemed a long way from Anaheim. But not for long. At a seminar meeting with students I opened with, "What would you like to know?" Did they ask me for the existential implications of my writing or could they touch the hem of my garment? No.

"What was it like to play with Stephen King?"

So we talked Rock Bottom Remainders for an hour. Two young men asked me to autograph their guitar picks. And a coed asked me for Dave Barry's telephone number.

Putting away souvenirs yesterday I stood in front of a mirror dressed in my everyday overalls, Birkenstock sandals, and wearing my black satin Cowboy Boogie Club jacket and my Martin Luther hat, and thought about Walt Whitman's comment: "Do I contradict myself? Very well, I contradict myself. I am large, I contain multitudes."

This evening I am to play the role of grandfather who goes to his oldest grandchild's first ballet recital. Sarah is five. I am fifty-five. She and I already conspire to be keepers of each other's history. The business of making memories goes on for us both. Someday she will ask me to take out my treasures for her. And I've no doubt that one of the best to be drawn from that skin box between my ears is about once upon a time in Anaheim when I made my debut and two weeks later when she made hers and how singing and dancing should last as long as life.

From Anaheim I went to the quiet of southeastern Utah. But what was stuck in my mind was the RBR experience—the music, the rehearsals, the laughs, and most of all the people. Part of my reason for writing is to say thanks again for being in my life and for including me in yours. If we never play again, the Remainders live. And the promise of what yet may come through the connections we made with one another is wood for the fire of imagination. I know I don't have a strong voice, and an electric mandocello doesn't add much to a rock and roll band, but if yearning qualified one for the Remainders, I'd have no peer. Your patience and generosity was noted. I owe you.

While we may be the guerrilla garage band of the nineties, there's a larger concept to consider and use. Here's my thinking and some proposals.

Let the RBRs be a free-floating, one-of-a-kind enterprise that serves as a coordinating center for whatever we want to do that's both fun and serves worthy ends for ourselves and the human community. A kind of unstated revival of Ken Kesey's Merry Pranksters on an invisible, invincible bus ride. Let it never be predictable. Let there be the possibility of a rock and roll concert, but also an acoustic concert, or a gathering to read stuff that doesn't fit what people usually expect of us as official authors, or a theater piece, comedy, or whatever we agree upon that stirs our creative juices and gets us out on the wire. Let the possibilities be infinite. Let us still be doing stuff a long, long time from now. Let us be legends in our own time—right up there with the Romantics and the Bloomsbury Group, the Algonquin Round Table, the Age of Enlightenment, and Dada. A category we own and "they" will have to contend with. Imagine the scar tissue we could leave on the body of literary history.

Well, we didn't quite live up to Fulghum's effulgence, but we did soon thereafter lay plans to meet again in September in New York City, to attend a party celebrating the release of our video (excruciating as it is, it was never more so than that night, when the monitors literally blacked out), and play two sets under the name Al Kooper at the Bottom Line. And a select complement hooked up with Dave Barry for an appearance at the Miami Book Fair in November under the nom de guerre Raymond Burr's Legs.

But energy soon centered on another idea:

Suppose we were to start planning now for a five-city tour next year? I am talking about the total rock and roll experience, starting with a week's worth of rehearsals, followed by that big old tour bus of which Jackson Browne has sung so often, so yearningly, and so stupidly.

This tour would be tied to the ABA in Miami, of course. We would meet in Boston, rehearse for five days or so, learn a few new songs to mix with our Greatest Hits, and then do a two-set gig in Boston. This would be followed by a gig or gigs in New York, Washington, Atlanta, and, of course, the Grand Finale in Miami, home of the blues. Oh shit, that's New Orleans, I guess, but if we were really cookin', maybe we could do New Orleans as an encore. You know, pick guitar, fill fruit jars, and be gay-o.

Well, that's my idea. The best part would be getting to play rock and roll again, but it would also be a riot, just kicking back, talking about books, old operation scars, exotic foot-fungi, baseball, contracts and royalties, and the pros and cons of the putative afterlife. Someone might fall in love, someone might get an idea for a book, someone might get a bad case of the dribbling shits from a bad cheese-burger gobbled at a roadside Shoney's outside of Tired Rectum, Alabama.* The possibilities are endless. I suppose we'd get a certain amount of publicity, too, and while that prospect doesn't exactly fill me with joy, we could probably pay for the bus, hotel rooms, and have a little left over for someone's favorite charity. Preserving Walden Woods, perhaps.

Ha-ha.

Well, that's my current brainstorm. Please write back, youse guys, and tell me what you think. Let's dialogue. Let's network. Let's go out on the road next year and kick out some serious jams.

Stephen King

Did we buy it? All the way. We even let him talk us into financing what Tad named the Three Chords and an Attitude Tour by writing this book. If what's past is pro-logue, the main event is now ready to begin.

---

*As attentive readers will later note, the guy's absolutely prescient. Or at least deeply attuned to the future of his own bodily functions.

Stephen King

THE NEIGHBORHOOD OF THE BEAST

In the summer of 1971, when I was twenty-three and had been married less than a year, something unpleasant happened to me in Sebec Lake. I won't say I almost drowned, because I don't know that I did. (I'm not sure I *want* to know.) What I do know is that I gave myself a hell of a scare, one I can still remember vividly half a lifetime later.

My wife and I had gone to Peaks-Kenny State Park on a beautiful hot day in late June, and while she was putting blankets and picnic things back in the car, I decided I wanted to take one last swim. The water was fine, I had a lot to think about, and I kind of lost track of where I was going, and how far out into the lake I'd gotten. When I rolled over on my back prior to starting back in, I was astonished and a little frightened to see how far away the beach looked—farther away, certainly, than any had ever been before in my extremely occasional career as a swimmer. What scared me (and what I still remember most clearly) was seeing how small the people back on the beach looked, and realizing how small I must look to them . . . if, indeed, any of them could see me at all. Just a black dot of a head in the glare of the afternoon sun on the water, no more than that.

I started back in and hadn't gotten fifty yards before realizing I was really tired. I was barely out of my teens, but I'd been smoking two packs of Pall Malls a day for years, and that'll take it out of your wind after awhile, no matter how old you are. And the beach was still very far away. I swapped my overhand stroke for a less jazzy but more energy-efficient (in my case, at least) dogpaddle and started in again. I decided I wasn't going to look at the shore for a few minutes, because I didn't like the panicky way looking at it made me feel.

I chugged gamely along for awhile—it's hard to tell how long, because time really doesn't mean a lot in situations like that—and finally decided that the cries of the little kids in the shallow roped-off area were closer and I could risk a look at the beach. When I did, it looked almost as far away as before, the bathers nothing but doll-sized men and women with pin heads and stick arms.

Panic almost swallowed me then, and I can remember vividly how that felt, like a hand that was squeezing not my heart but my head. It was suddenly all too possible to imagine trying to call for help and getting nothing but a mouthful of cold Sebec Lake water for my pains . . . and finally sliding under, while the people on the beach went unconcernedly about their affairs: shaking out blankets, drinking cans of soda and beer, playing volleyball, playing slap-and-tickle, floating around on air-mattresses or inner tubes with cool sunglasses on.

The clear thought that came to me then, as I paused there, treading deep water two hundred yards out in the lake, was that I could die right where I was, while people were putting Coppertone and Super Tanfastic on their arms and legs. The thought of drowning in full view of people too preoccupied with their sunburned hides to notice gave the idea such credibility that it took all the will I possessed to start swimming for shore again instead of screaming for help. Now, all these years later, one idea remains clear and persuasive about that incident: If I'd screamed for help I would have panicked. And if I'd panicked, I really might have drowned.

This memory came back to me at around eight o'clock on the evening of May 28th, 1993, while I was holed up in one of two incredibly grotty backstage bathrooms at a honkytonk Nashville nightspot called 328 Performance Hall. I was at that moment having no aesthetic problems with the bathroom decor, which could best be described as Early American Graffiti, because beggars can't be choosers. I had a case of raving dysentery (what my Mom, who had a poetic phrase for most of life's little problems, liked to call "the Hershey squirts"), and I was at a point where even an ugly bathroom looked like the Doge's Palace. My problem was probably caused by the heavy-duty antibiotic I was taking to stay on top of a throat infection, but at times like that, causes don't seem terribly important; the problem swallows everything.

My bowels had been purging themselves for the last twelve hours or so, and at eight o'clock, an hour before showtime, they had gone into overdrive. And there I sat, with my pants around my ankles and my guts somewhere up around my Adam's apple, listening to the warm-up band thunder through the cheap plywood walls (which had been painted Pepto-Bismol Pink, a color I could strongly identify with) and thinking that in fifty minutes or so I might possibly become the first best-

selling novelist ever to have an accident of the shit variety while on stage in Nashville. This thought was good for a grin, but not much more; it was the kind of situation that is amusing only months or years later, when you can tell funny stories about it (as I suppose I am doing, or trying to do, now). At the time it's happening, it's embarrassing, debilitating, and just downright grim. The sum total is a feeling very similar to the one a person gets when he realizes he has swum out beyond his depth, and so it wasn't surprising, I guess, that that was when I happened to remember what happened that day at Peaks-Kenny. I was scared of dying in June of 1971, and I was also scared on that night in Nashville in late May of 1993 . . . although of dying in a different and far less final way.

Performance Hall seats twelve hundred, and the Rock Bottom Remainders had been told to expect most of those seats to be filled by showtime. Most of them were filled by eight o'clock, judging by the sound . . . except no one actually sounded seated, if you know what I mean. From my own seat in the little pink room, it sounded as if the audience were on their feet and boogeying, letting off a week's worth of steam and giving out with those big old mid-south yeehaws. Since slipping in at seven-fifteen or so, we'd heard the crowd accelerate past happy, past tipsy, past drunk, past loaded. Total euphoria seemed in reach for most of them, and you didn't have to see them to know they were reaching. They did not sound like people who had come to see a bunch of authors pretending to play music, they sounded like people who had come expecting to see real musicians kicking out real jams; and all at once I really was scared to death . . . and not of having a little accident on stage, either. I was afraid of having a *big* accident on stage, the kind you can't blame on megadoses of Amoxicillin.

Nashville is primarily a country town, and the warm-up group that night was a country act. I can't remember the name now, and don't think it matters; they were a duo with a couple of backing musicians. Not exactly Flatt & Scruggs, and we didn't exactly mind. Dave Barry wandered up to me shortly before I repaired to the little pink room, an optimistic smile on his face (Dave *always* has an optimistic smile on his face), and said, "Tell you what, Big Steve—these guys ain't hurtin' us. These guys ain't hurtin' us *ay*-tall."

He was right, too, but I had no illusions that that was going to get us off the hook. If anything, it put us *on* the hook. In spite of its country reputation, there's a lot of rock and roll in Nashville (and in these latter days, the differences between urban country music and the sort of rockabilly the Remainders played on tour have gotten harder and harder to find), and the people out front had come to by-God hear them some. They sounded *hungry* for it in a way none of our audiences up to that night had. They're hungry, all right, I remember thinking, and if they don't get fed, we may get a little more rock-and-roll ambience than we bargained for.

That thought led me directly back to Sebec Lake—to the moment when I looked up and saw that, even after some unknown period of hard and earnest dog-paddling, the people on the beach looked as far away as ever. What I remember most clearly about that moment is treading water and thinking that if I was going to get back safely, I was probably going to have to see to it myself. And then it occurred to me that this time my situation had improved quite a lot, because this time I wasn't on my own; I had close to a dozen friends out there with me, also in deep water doing the dogpaddle.

To take my mind off the memory of my scary swim in Sebec Lake—it was not the sort of thing I really wanted to be considering forty-five minutes before going on stage to do what God never really equipped me to do in the first place—I began looking at the pink walls of the modest little shithouse where I was currently enthroned. Performance Hall is one of the few places where Nashville cats can reliably get a dose of rock and roll when they simply cannot take one more song by Alan Jackson or "Picky" Ricky Scaggs, and it seemed to me that every group that had ever passed through had left a few words of wisdom behind on the pink walls of this little room.

None were as good as Al Kooper's favorite, seen on the ceiling of a Los Angeles dressing room—DOGS FUCK THE POPE (NO FAULT OF MINE)—and none quite lived up to the Zen charm of one I once saw in the men's room of The Hungry Bear in Portland, Maine (SAVE RUSSIAN JEWS, COLLECT VALUABLE PRIZES), but there were some damned fine ones, just the same. One was a caricature of a fat little boy wearing nothing but a porkpie hat and eating an ice cream cone. PIEBOY WAS HERE had been Magic Markered under it . . . Pieboy being the name of a group, I assumed. Another one read TEX RITTER IS PLAYING PEDAL STEEL DOWN IN HELL. That was double news to me, because I didn't know Tex Ritter was dead in the first place (although the more I thought about it, the more it stood to reason). Close by the news about Tex was a rather poetic lament (ONLY A FART, ONLY A FART, AFTER ALL THAT, IT WAS ONLY A FART), and below that, a comment as morose as it was existential: I *HATE* THIS PART OF TEXAS. My favorite, however, was dead ahead, written on the back of the bathroom door, and exactly on a level with my eyes as I sat there fifteen hundred miles from home, sick as a yellow dog, and wondering how I ever could have been mad enough to let myself in for this in the first place. This graffiti, as ominous as it was clever, said:

664/668:
THE NEIGHBORHOOD OF THE BEAST

Beyond my current place of refuge—and separated from me by just one curtain and two or three thin walls—the crowd let out a big drunken hooraw as the country duo finished a song which seemed to go, in part, "I got tears in my ears from lyin' on my back in bed while I cried over you." The sound of the crowd made me wince a little; it was hungrier than ever. I mean, we're talking feeding time in the lion house. My eyes drifted back to that graffiti written on the bathroom door. The Neighborhood of the Beast. I had an idea that was just where I was, and that I was once more going to have to get out on my own hook . . . with a little help from my friends, of course. Cry for help? Don't be silly, darling. In Deep Nashville, There's Nobody to Hear You Scream.

Forty minutes to showtime. And then, sick stomach or no sick stomach, I'd have to start swimming again. All of us would.

About five months after the tour was over, our musical director, Al Kooper, sent me a tape of his new album, *Rekooperation*, along with a request that I consider doing liner notes for it if I liked it. I *did* like it—loved it, in fact. *Rekooperation*—a collection of instrumental tracks with a New York state of mind and a throbbing Memphis (as in Stax/Volt) heart—is Al's first album in twelve years, and maybe his best ever. When I talked to him on the phone after my first listen-through, I mentioned that my favorite cut was a soulful blues tune called "How'm I Ever Gonna Get Over You," written by Al and featuring Hank Crawford on alto sax.

Al laughed. "Yeah," he said. "We played like men on that one."

Although that was all in the yet-to-be when we arrived for our Nashville sound-check at 5:00 p.m. on the 28th, I think I understood even then that we might have to play like men—and women—just to get out of 328 Performance Hall alive. My first look at the place certainly suggested it was no yuppie playground, like the Roxy in Atlanta, where we had played the night before.

Three-Two-Eight, as the locals call it, is on Fourth Avenue South, where the fast-food restaurants specialize in catfish and the most common items in the pawnshop windows seem to be straight-razors with pearl-inlaid handles. The wail of police cars was constant, and on our way over for soundcheck and then on our way back to the hotel for supper (which, for the RBRs' antibiotic-stunned rhythm guitarist, consisted of bread for the main course and a generous serving of Kaopectate for dessert), we saw all sorts of people pulled over by the fuzz. At one point I noticed a cop writing a beefy young black guy a ticket. The black guy, who was standing beside a gorgeous gold-flake lowrider Camaro, was protesting the ticket vigorously, the muscles beneath his Gold's Gym tee-shirt rolling as he waved his arms, while his girlfriend looked on silently from the passenger seat, smoking a cigarette in a jade holder. The cop ignored all the black guy's protests, just kept writing. Half a block down the street, on the corner, ignored by both the speeder and the cop writing him a little Friday-night Get Happy note, two young fellows with their hats turned around backward—one white guy, one black guy, is this the greatest country in the world or what—were negotiating a drug deal. As the band van rolled past, I clearly saw dollars being traded for little white packets.

This is it, I remember thinking. *Tonight's the night. This is not a candyass town, and this is not a candyass neighborhood. This is the gig where it either happens or it doesn't. It's come late, later than I thought it would . . . but it's here.*

At the start we were just the Remainders, not the Rock Bottom Remainders. That was back in 1992, when George Bush was still President and I had played guitar in front of an actual audience only once in over twenty years (with John Cafferty and the Beaver Brown Band—there's a photo from that gig on the dustjacket of *It*). I think the name modification came because of a trademark problem, but all I'm sure of is that at some point between the time when Kathi Kamen Goldmark first asked me if I'd like to play in a rock band, strictly as a one-off kind of thing, and the time when Roy Blount actually introduced us at the ABA in Anaheim, we had gone from the Rs to the RBRs. We weren't very good that night at Cowboy Boogie—I have hidden my copy of the videotape of the show and refuse to tell anyone where it is—but we were loud, and the audience was enthusiastic. Some of this enthusiasm was probably a species of diplomatic politeness toward writers who did well for the different publishing companies represented in the audience, and a great deal of it was certainly the gleeful suspension of taste that comes when one passes a certain stage of drunkenness (and that night most of the audience was *well* past it, believe me) . . . but there were also two other things: an element of happy surprise that we could play even as well as we did, and an element of something I suppose you'd have to call *potentiality*. There was among all of us, I think, a feeling that we could sing and play quite a lot better than we had that night if we were given a chance to practice and prepare a little more, and I suppose that feeling had more to do with my presence, almost a year to the day later, in that little Pepto-Bismol-colored bathroom backstage at Three-Two-Eight than anything else.

Playing music again—playing for an actual audience—after all those years was fun. Well, actually it was a little more than fun; it *had* to have been, or the Three Chords and an Attitude Tour never would have gotten off the ground. It was, in fact, exhilarating. I never heard that part of it expressed better than Dave Barry did it an hour or so after our last encore at Cowboy Boogie. I remember him leaning against the wall of a hotel corridor outside the room where the band reception was being held, a bottle of beer in one hand and his cased guitar by his feet, obviously exhausted, both his shirt and his retro-Beatles haircut matted with sweat, too hoarse to talk much above a whisper, but one happy camper just the same. "This was the best time I ever had in my adult life," he said flatly. "I don't know what that says about me and I don't think I *want* to know, but it's the truth. It's the best damn time I ever had in my life."

He didn't go on from there and say he wanted to do it again; he didn't have to.

Neither did I, and I don't think any of us was a bit surprised to discover that discussions on the same subject had begun among the other band members even before the last bagel had been eaten and the last glass of pre-breakfast champagne drunk at the wee-hours reception. I think it's fair to say that everyone who did it that first time wanted to do it again, although a few people who should have been there when the tour commenced were not. The rest of us regarded them with the genuine but transitory sympathy schoolkids might feel for a pal who has had perfect attendance all year long, then comes down with the mumps just in time to miss the class picnic. (Matt Groening, clearly the most bummed of the bunch, sent flowers to every gig.)

But because we're writers, men and women used to the idea that good work means editing, revision, and rewrite, we didn't *just* want to do it again; we wanted to do it *better*. We knew we could do that (*potentiality*, remember); the question was *how much* better, and beyond that, an even more interesting one: Could we do it for real? That question was not answered in our Boston rehearsals, and hardly even addressed at any of our first half a dozen stops. Those were gigs, you understand, where half the audiences appeared to have come with books in their hands. I love reading as much as anyone—and more than most, I have an idea—but I know perfectly well that you just can't fulfill your potential as a dancer with a copy of *Hard Fall* or *Dave Barry Does Japan* in your hand.

I thought things might change in Atlanta, but they didn't. The audience was great and we put on a great show, but the venue was wrong, somehow. The Roxy is a beautiful old movie-house that has been converted into a nightclub, and perhaps its obvious silver screen past was part of the problem. I don't know for sure. I do know that I never had as much pure fun playing, before or after, as I did at the Roxy—I could have sung "Susie-Q" half the night and "Who Do You Love" the other half—but it wasn't what I'd come looking for, just the same.

I just read that last paragraph over, and I hate the pretentious way it sounds (in my head I hear Bono bellowing *"And I stillll . . . haven't founnnd . . . what I'm lookin' for"*), but I've decided to let it stand just the same. The thing is, I can't seem to find a hipper way of expressing it that still rings true. If that means I'm pretentious, I guess I'm pretentious. I *did* come looking for something, maybe for a future book, maybe for fun and excitement, maybe to increase the old self-understanding level a bit, maybe all of the above. I think what I mostly wanted to find was the job of rock—the sweaty, hard-working truth hiding behind the glitzy myth. Or maybe that's bullshit. Maybe all I really wanted to do was to swim out to the middle of the lake again and see if I could still swim back in without yelling for help.

Ah, shit, now it's *worse* than Bono—a *lot* worse. Now I sound like Ernest Q. Hemingway, slogging back from the Big Two-Hearted River with a bull moose slung over his shoulders, a fishing-rod in one hand, and a big shit-eating grin on his face as he cries *Bully! Everything is abso-lutely . . . BULLY!*

I would *really* like to get away from that one, but then I remember how strongly I related to what Al said on the phone that day: "Yeah, we played like men on that one." I knew what he was talking about at once. Not all the Remainders played like men on the '93 tour, of course—Kathi didn't, Amy didn't, Tad didn't, and Barbara didn't—but I have an idea they'd have related to what he said as well as I did. The equation, it seems to me, was the same for the girls as it was for the boys: Could we really play, or were we just dressing up in Mommy's and Daddy's clothes, playing a tour-bus version of Let's Pretend? And was there any way to find that out for sure?

Whatever you want to call it and however you want to phrase the questions, I'd pretty well decided I wasn't going to find answers that satisfied me. There were only two shows left after Atlanta, and the tour-ender in Miami Beach didn't really count. Writers playing for publishers, after all, is a little bit like Brother and Sister putting on a show after Christmas dinner—you expect a lot of applause (and maybe a little carefully concealed boredom) but nothing in the way of trenchant criticism.

Then, as I sat in the little pink bathroom, feeling like a glove that has been turned inside-out and listening to the hungry roar of the crowd, I decided I had been premature. They sounded like the sort of folks who expect you to put up or shut up, and that was fairly intimidating to a man who wasn't even sure he was going to be able to get out of the shithouse, let alone play a bar E or remember the words to "Last Kiss."

Catfish dinners, huge B-B-Q sandwiches, and a generous selection of straight-razors in every pawnshop window—a put-up-or-shut-up neighborhood, all right, and Three-Two-Eight was a put-up-or-shut-up kind of place, no question about it. Do you remember the cover of Creedence Clearwater's *Willy and the Poorboys* record? Well, Performance Hall bears an uncanny resemblance to the Duck Kee Market on the cover of that CCR album, only without the windows. When we pulled up in the alley between it and the next building (also brick, also windowless) for soundcheck, I remember thinking that if I had never before seen a place where booze was an absolute priority—with loud music running a close second—I was seeing one now. Cases of empty beer bottles were stacked along one whole side of the building, to waist height. Beyond them a couple of little kids with bare feet and big eyes stood on the corner, watching us. If they had been black instead of white, they really could have been those two little kids on the Creedence album cover, standing outside the Duck Kee and watching John Fogerty scratching out "The Poorboy Shuffle" on a washboard.

Inside, the place smelled like a brewery . . . one that had been cranking suds since around the time of the Civil War. I remember being surprised at how big it was, how barnlike. I was a little shocked at how *empty* its various rooms seemed. It was like being in the neighborhood haunted house. Most of the other places we'd played had been at least this big, but without the peculiar atmosphere I felt here. There could have been no sharper contrast than the one between Performance Hall and the Roxy, where we had played the previous evening. The Roxy was clean, yuppified, funky art deco; Performance Hall was dark and somehow peculiar. Atmosphere? I'm not entirely sure it *had* one. Although the word *sinister* is the first one to come to mind now, I don't think it's the right one. There was actually a disquieting feeling of *blankness* about the place. For most of the time I was there, I felt like an errant thought in the mind of a cataclysmically retarded person.

And it was hot on stage, man, was it. Even with the overhead bank of colored show-spots off and the dance-floor empty, it was sweltering. I couldn't imagine what it was going to be like by ten that night, with a thousand or so people crammed inside this brick hulk, the booze flowing, the bouncers bouncing, and the guitars cranking. Considering how I felt as I slid under the strap of my own guitar—weak-kneed, nauseated, headachey, and slip-knotted in the bowels—I decided I didn't *want* to know. Sometimes it's best just to take things a step at a time.

The purposes of the soundcheck have never been formally explained to me, but observation suggests that there are at least four: to go over any tunes that may still be a little rough around the edges; to help the sound-mixer (Hoover, in this case) set the levels on his board; to make sure each member of the band has got a good balance coming out of his or her monitor; and to familiarize the members of the band with the stage that they'll be performing on. This last is especially important, since no one really wants to break a leg in spite of what they may say to each other just before going on. Also, if you fall *off* the stage once you've gone on it, it doesn't matter if you play like a man or a woman; you still look like a dope.

Al was rewriting Ridley Pearson's bass part on "Midnight Hour" for the ninth or tenth time on the tour when my lower intestine rang the alarm bell. I put my guitar on its stand—no one really seemed to notice, which didn't surprise me much; Eric Clapton I'm not—and hurried off in search of the men's room (I would not discover the little pink room backstage for another two hours or so). One of the bouncers, a guy wearing a sail-sized tee-shirt with the word COURTESY printed on it in large block letters above a closed, militant fist, pointed past the bar in response to my question, and I hurried on my way.

The bathroom was about what I expected by then, a long room that looked like a brick-walled milking-barn for humans. There had once been two windows in there, but they had been blocked off by tough accordions of dirty yellow plastic. There were no single urinals but rather a wall-length trough—the kind that, shortly before opening-time, is either lined with ice or spotted with circular chlorine tablets (reminding me of the old joke where one drunk says to the other, "Whatever you do when you're in there, don't eat those big Canada mints"). All the doors had been torn off the toilet stalls, a fact that meant very little to me at such a moment. I hooked a right into one, feeling like the victor in an extremely close race.

As I sat there, the bouncer came in and began combing his hair at one of the mirrors (not glass, of course; the mirrors in clubs like Performance Hall, like the mirrors in nuthouses and high-security prison wards, are polished steel bolted to the wall).

"Say, are you the one who wrote *The Shining*?" he asked me.

"Yes," I said.

"Also *Dead Zone*?"

"That's me," I agreed.

"Man, I love all your movies," he said.

"Thanks." For a moment I debated mentioning the fact that *The Shining* and *The Dead Zone* had actually been books *before* they were movies, but this did not seem like the place or the time. Instead, I asked him why there were no doors on the toilet stalls.

In the mirror his face registered surprise that I should even ask. "Keeps em from shootin up," he said. "You can't stop em snortin or droppin pills, but you can pretty much keep em from shootin up if you pull the crapper doors off."

"Oh."

"Yeah, that's it," he said, then turned around to look at me. The fist on his red tee-shirt was very big. *He* was very big—I'd guess about six-five, three hundred pounds. I saw some huge bouncers while on tour, but I really think he was the biggest . . . or maybe that was just because I was sitting down. "Tell me something," he said.

"If I can."

"Can you guys really play?"

I thought this question over carefully. Al Kooper, at forty-nine, is a brilliant rock-and-roll keyboardist/guitarist/arranger who has fronted, played on, or produced well over five hundred albums. (He's also written thousands of songs, including "I Can't Quit Her," "This Diamond Ring," and a charming little ditty called "I Bought the Shoes She's Walkin' Away In"). Ridley Pearson has played bass for a number of pro groups out west, in Idaho, Washington, and California. Dave Barry was the lead guitarist of a pretty good college cover-band called The Federal Duck (one of their staple numbers, I found out later, was Al Kooper's "I Can't Keep from Cryin'"). Kathi Goldmark, when she's not performing author-escort duties in the city where Tony Bennett left his heart, is a talented country/rockabilly singer. She also plays guitar, and a lot better than I do (not actually a compliment; when I think of my own instrumental skills, the phrase "maintenance-level" usually comes to mind). I don't know Barbara Kingsolver's musical background, but I do know she plays keyboards like someone who is used to looking at audiences from between the shoulders of the rhythm player and the bass player. Not everyone in the Rock Bottom Remainders was a pro, or even a pro-am, but enough of us were—and the rest of us were sufficiently improved—for me to answer the bouncer's question with a fair degree of confidence.

"Yes, we can really play," I told him.

He thought it over, then nodded. "That's good," he said. "Because when people come here, they expect to hear music. You know?"

"And they probably get pissed if they don't get it," I said. Just a wild guess.

"You got *that* right," my new friend agreed.

Outside the little pink room, there was a sustained burst of applause and a lot more of those testosterone-fraught mid-south yeehaws. Just as the noise level started to fall off a little, there came a little knock at the door of my refuge. It was Al Kooper. Exhibiting his usual charm, tact, and compassion, he enquired if I had fallen in.

"No," I said.

"You okay?"

"Yes. On my way out."

"Good, 'cause we go on in ten minutes." A pause. "Steve?"

"Yeah?"

"That warm-up act didn't hurt us any."

That made me think of Dave and grin. "Good to know," I said.

I got up, washed my hands (you don't have to spend twenty years on the road to know washing your hands after using the toilet in a place like Three-Two-Eight is a good idea; you'd shower, if you could), and generally set myself to rights. Then I went out.

Backstage was dim and hot and choked with people. The two most identifiable odors were cigarette smoke and Bud Lite (with perhaps the faintest undertone of pot). Al was standing nearby with a very large gentleman in a western shirt, a guy who must have had at least two inches on my six-foot-three. I recognized him at once; the previous winter I'd played his *Doo Dad* CD almost constantly. Meeting people whose work you enjoy (in Washington, D.C., it was Nils Lofgren who showed up) was one of the greatest unanticipated pleasures of the tour.

"Steve," Al said, "I'd like you to meet Webb Wilder. Webb, this is Steve King."

"It's a pleasure," I said, and I meant it. "I loved your *Doo Dad* album."

"Thanks," he said in his deep voice. He cocked his head toward the stage, his spectacles glinting in the dim lights (Webb Wilder's stated creed is *Live fast, love hard, and wear corrective lenses if you need them*). "I hope you're ready for those folks, because they sure sound ready for you. What do you think?"

When I realize that I'm actually going to go on in front of some audience, no backing out, I always get a buzz in my stomach that feels like a hot electrical wire. It's not an entirely bad feeling—it's the sort of feeling you could get addicted to, in fact—and I got a jolt of it right about then.

"I don't know," I told Webb Wilder, just before Al took me over to meet the lieutenant governor of Tennessee or the Nashville Kleagle or the Wizard of Oz or some-damn-body. "I don't know *what* I think."

That little nerve down there went hot again for a second or two, and my thoughts returned briefly to that long, long swim back to the beach at Peaks-Kenny in June of 1971. Here we go again, I thought, and realized the weirdest thing: sick stomach or not, hungry crowd or not, scared or not, I was really happy.

When I go places and talk about my craft (writing, I mean, not playing guitar and singing "Teen Angel"), I emphasize one point over and over again: You don't have to be great to do a thing, you just have to not get tired of trying to be good at it. It's possible to go a long distance on a small smidgen of talent, I like to say, and use myself as an example. There's a *caveat* to this, however, and I always try to point it out, so people won't whine later that they didn't know what they were getting into. The *caveat* is this: Big talent, the kind of ability you can't learn or earn but only get as a gift, is the only thing that ever allows one to be both lazy and successful in any field of creative endeavor. The rest of us have to work like dogs to make the pretty things, and the less talent we have, the harder we have to work. There was a time, I might add, when I actually believed you could succeed creatively with *no* talent if you were willing to work your ass off morning, noon, and night, but that was years ago; I now realize that without at least some spark, you're just plain sunk. It's probably not fair, but there it is; in the words of Coach "Gypsy" Joe Woodhead, from my old high school, some people are born to be athletes and some are born to be athletic supporters. It's a tough old world, and if there's a God in charge of handing out the free gifties, He apparently never heard of the quota system.

But the years had not changed the essentially optimistic bottom line of my creative philosophy, which I have passed on to writing classes and seminars since 1975 or so: The things you really want to do are usually things you *can* do. Accomplishing some of them may be painful, like the strolls Hans Christian Andersen's little mermaid took after she had exchanged her tail for human legs and feet, but if you want to badly enough, mostly you can. You may have to lower your expectations a little to get to where you want to be, but for most of us shmoes, that ain't a problem (usually it's keeping expectations up to a decent level that's the problem). You may have to exhibit extraordinary patience and determination, but those things are within most people's range of abilities. Above all, this gospel of mine went, you have to be clearheaded (and clear-minded) enough to accept three evaluative facts about yourself all at the same time: The things you *know* you can do, the things you *think* you can do, and the things you know in your heart you will *never* be able to do.

I had been talking this talk for a long time; in the Rock Bottom Remainders I saw a chance to find out if I could walk the walk, as well. Because the RBRs weren't about writing, where I *do* have some talent, but about playing and singing music, where I have almost none. Put very simply, I saw a chance to find out how much better I could get simply by trying to *be* better. You know that old one-liner, don't you? Tourist in New York comes up to this sharpie hanging out on the corner of Fifth Avenue and Forty-second Street and asks him, "How do you get to Carnegie Hall?" The sharpie tips him a wink and says, "Practice, man, practice." Sure, you've heard that one, it's an oldie.

But it's also a goodie.

There were two dressing rooms backstage at Three-Two-Eight, both full of band-members and circling folks with backstage passes. I spotted Kathi, Barbara, Amy, and Tad—they were always easy to spot in their glitter-gorgeous Remainderette evening dresses—in one of them. In the other I saw Dave Barry and Roy Blount talking to a cadre of fellows who looked both smart and pretty well squiffed. I decided they were probably college classmates of Roy's. He went to Vanderbilt, this was reunion weekend, and it looked to me like every mother's son of them had decided to drop over to Fourth Avenue to watch Ole Roy (that's what most of them called him—Ole Roy) do his thing.

Beyond Ole Dave and Ole Roy, I spotted Ole Jerry—which is to say, Jerry Peterson, the RBRs' sax-player. He was sitting by himself, sucking on a beer, and looking dreamily into the ozone. Jerry is a big man with a moon face and a natural Zen attitude. He is a man it is almost impossible not to love. Whenever I saw him, a line from Bob Dylan's song about Hurricane Carter popped into my head: "Reuben sits like Buddha in a ten-foot cell." Beyond Ole Dave and Ole Roy, Ole Jerry was sitting like Buddha in a sixteen-foot dressing room, and I sat down beside him.

Playing their way out.

"How you doing, Steve?" Jerry asked. "Heard you were having some problems."

"Everything came out all right," I replied, straight-faced.

Jerry pondered this for a few seconds, then laughed. "Good one, man, that's a good one. Came out all right, huh? I can dig it."

"Yeah."

He looked around. "Lotta people, man."

"Yeah."

"You ready for this?" he asked. It suddenly occurred to me that people had been asking me variations of that question ever since we arrived for soundcheck.

"Yeah," I said. "I think I am." In fact, I *was* starting to feel ready. At some point on evenings like that, a species of benign craziness settles into my heart, and I start being glad I am where I am, even if it looks like what I have is going to be a tough sell. *Especially* if it looks like it's going to be a tough sell.

"Great," Jerry said. "Because this one ain't a book-party. Tonight we're going to have to play our way out."

I thought that over, then nodded. "Good."

As if on cue, Bob Daitz poked his curly head in through the door. "Ladies-zungennlemen!" he announced brightly. "Showtime in five little minutes! Guests should be leaving!"

Five minutes later—those last five minutes always passed so slowly, I remember that vividly—the lights in front went down and Ole Roy strolled out to do his band introductions. When the spotlight hit him, a big cheer went up from his Vanderbilt rooting section. The rest of us were more or less lined up in the order of Roy's announcement, which put me behind Dave Barry. In the dim light washing back here through the breaks in the side curtain, I saw Dave finish the beer he was drinking and set the empty carefully down on top of an amp case. At the same time, my stomach gave another little warning twinge. I suppressed it, made believe I'd never felt it. It was too late for another visit to the little pink room. We had reached that point where whatever happens, happens, and that's always sort of a relief.

There was a tap on my shoulder. I turned and saw my bouncer buddy—the one roughly the size of Godzilla.

"Break a leg," he said solemnly. The time for conventional good-luck wishes was now past, a fact that even the bouncers knew. Beyond the curtain, Ole Roy was asking the crowd how they were doing, eliciting war-whoops and footstomping.

"My friend," I said, "I'm going to try and break both of them."

I grew up fairly deep in the williwags, seven miles from the nearest town large enough to have a blinker-light and fifteen miles from Lewiston-Auburn, which was in the sixties a big city by Maine standards and a small one by almost any other. My mother and my brother and I lived on a dirt road in Methodist Corners, as a matter of fact, beside the church that gave that particular section of Durham its name. I know that sounds like a Joe South song, but it's true.

My best friend, Chris Chesley, lived a mile or so farther down that same road. In 1962 and '63, we discovered folk music together, and fell under the spell of such white "urban blues" singers as Dave Van Ronk, Geoff Muldaur, "Spider" John Koerner, and Tom Rush. We were equally crazy for young balladeers like Bob

Dylan, Tom Paxton, Eric Andersen, and especially Phil Ochs. We were crazy about Ochs because he sounded the way we felt most of the time—pissed off and confused—but *all* of them were playing and singing stuff that had nothing to do with the crap we were hearing on the radio, sweet little Sheila, you'll know her if you see her, blue eyes and a ponytail. And the music had an urgent, homemade feel that spoke to our hearts. When I started smoking Pall Malls a year or two later, I did so because I was morally sure that my hero, Dave Van Ronk, smoked them. What other brand could the elucidator of "Bed Bug Blues" possibly smoke?

Chris got a beautiful Gibson guitar during one of those years—which year I can't remember, only that Lyndon Johnson was President—and I managed to scratch up enough bread (that's what we called it back then, bread) to ransom my own guitar from a Lewiston hockshop. It was a tinny-sounding dog of a guitar, but it was *my* dog, and I loved it. I loved just walking up the road to Chris's house with it over my shoulder. I wouldn't have it in a case, because I couldn't have felt quite so much like Woody Guthrie with my tinny-sounding made-in-Taiwan ax in a case.

The first song I learned to play on it was "Rock My Soul (In the Bosom of Abraham)." It consisted of just two chords, D and A7. The second was "Bed Bug Blues," a three-chord blues that went in part "I got myself a wishbone/ These bugs has got my goat/I wish every one of 'em/ Would cut their own goddam/throat." Anyone who could put *goddam* in a song and then get the song on a record was all right in my book, and that same blues form served as the basis for a good many Remainder party-raves, from "Susie-Q" to "You Can't Sit Down."

I never played with a pick until I was in college, and even then I wasn't very enthusiastic about it. Chris and I started with simple finger-strumming, then went on to fingerpicking (by then I'd realized my friend was quite a lot better than me on the guitar—that troublesome talent thing, you know—but I plugged along gamely, dividing my senior summer equally between trying to get laid and trying to learn how to make a F-chord that would ring true). For awhile I played with a plastic milk-bottle cap, which had an interesting ricky-tick sound, but in the end I gave it up. I broke too many strings that way, and I hated changing strings more than anything. Even in high school, I could have used a guitar roadie.

I played briefly in a band during my senior year—organ, not guitar—but I didn't last much past the original rehearsals. My rock-and-roll aspirations (such as they were) foundered, as almost all my other extra-curricular activities did, on the fact that I lived seven miles from town and had no car even after I had managed to get my driver's license. (My mother, the parent in our single-parent household, never learned to drive.) But of all the things I missed, the only one I seriously regret is having to drop out of the Mune-Spinners (and was there ever a more gloriously sixties name for a band?). If I'd stayed in, I might actually have learned how to play a bar chord before I turned forty-four, and that would have considerably eased my path as a Remainder.

I *knew* about bar chords, of course, but in the way most Baptist ministers know about whores: by reputation rather than actual experience. The easiest one is bar E, where you make the chord with your last three fingers instead of your first three, thereby saving your index finger to press down all the strings as you slide your movable E up the guitar-neck to whatever position you want. Bar E on the third fret makes G; on the fifth it makes A; on the seventh, B. Like most simple concepts, the execution is just a wee bit more difficult than the explanation.

I was introduced to bar chords not by my buddy Chris, but by his youngest brother, Jamie, who had all of Chris's musical talent but little or no use for our beloved folk music. (He *did* like John Hammond, which was a mark in his favor.) Jamie was strapped to the big beat from go, that's all, a hip-from-the-stroller kid who was into grunge groups like the Barbarians and the Standells before Kurt Cobain was ever born, let alone whizzing lemonade into his didies. Jamie didn't like "Bed Bug Blues," but he loved "Susie-Q" and "I've Had It" and "I Put a Spell on You." He also loved "Gloria," a song on which I would find myself singing backing vocals years later. Back then it was the Shadows of Knight version, not the Van Morrison one, that we thought the cooler of the two.

Anyway, Jamie and I were in the Chesley basement one day while Chris was in his room finishing his homework. I picked up Jamie's electric guitar and started playing "Gloria" in E. I played it the way I'd learned to play "Bed Bug Blues" and all the other three-chord blues numbers I knew—which is to say, open, at the top of the neck:

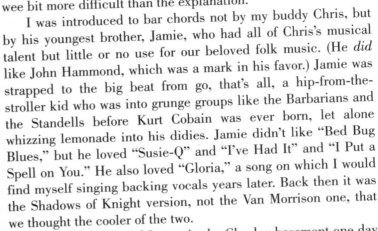

E   A   D

Jamie put up with this awhile, even playing drums behind me, then took the guitar himself and showed me the corresponding bar chords, which I have described above. "It's a hell of a lot quicker this way," he said, echoing almost exactly words Dave Barry would say to me in a Miami Beach hotel room twenty-eight years later. The difference is, by 1992 I was ready to listen. When Jamie showed me bar E, bar A, and bar D, I saw no point to them. You couldn't play them at hootenannies, that was for sure; when Bob Dylan had strapped on an electric guitar at a Forest Hills concert, the audience had damned near jeered him off the stage. That wasn't my only problem with Jamie's chords, however. The biggest one was that they sounded bad when I tried to play them—it was as if someone had stuffed the body of his electrified acoustic full of cotton.

So bar chords and I parted company for a long, long time. I played a lot of coffeehouse guitar in college, and before I graduated in 1970, I must have played "Bed Bug Blues" a thousand times . . . not to mention such other staples of the day as "Blowin' in the Wind," "500 Miles," and everything Donovan Leitch ever recorded. But don't judge me too harshly; unlike many of my contemporaries, I never sang "Elusive Butterfly of Love." (I *did* perform Leonard Cohen's "Suzanne" on a regular basis, however, so I guess everything balances out.)

Time passes. King marries the wonderful Tabitha Spruce (the smartest thing he ever did in his life), King works in a laundry and teaches high-school English, King almost drowns (or maybe just thinks he does) in Sebec Lake. King publishes his first story in 1968 and by 1978 has become America's Best-Loved Boogeyman, a kind of Norman Rockwell version of Freddy Krueger, how goshdang lucky can a guy get. Finally, in 1991, King writes Kathi Kamen Goldmark a letter saying he would be glad to play guitar at the ABA with a bunch of other writers, as long as it's okay for him to play like Steve King and not Steve Vai.

So the wheel of karma turns, I guess, always coming back around to where it started, and that's the Reader's Digest Condensed Books version of how I ended up on stage in Nashville in the late spring of 1993, with Chris Chesley's basement in Durham fifteen hundred miles and twenty-eight years behind me . . . but once more screaming Gee-Ell-Oh-Ar-Eye-Ay at the top of my lungs.

When we came on stage the night before, in Atlanta, we came on in a euphoric rush. The first tune at every show was the old Barrett Strong classic "Money," and when Al counted it off at the Roxy, he did it fast, driving us into an accelerated performance that never really let down. We stumbled off stage at the end of the show exhausted and sweat-soaked, but still feeling as high as a handful of kites. The group consensus was that we had put on the best show of the tour.

Euphoria can be misleading, however, a fact that every junkie knows, and how the people on stage feel about the music isn't always the way the audience feels. I'm not saying the people who came to our show in Atlanta thought we sucked; I'm just saying that maybe on that particular night we were a better audience for our stuff than they were.

In Nashville, Al counted off "Money" slower, and I thought the number dragged a little. In fact, I thought they *all* dragged, until we got past "Susie-Q" and I noticed that the *audience* wasn't having any problem. That was when I realized that, instead of dragging, we were punching the hell out of the material, really killing it.

Even the vocals sounded good. At some point on the tour, maybe in D.C., Al Kooper remarked that the biggest problem with the Remainders was that no one could really sing. He had something there, but I think *would* rather than *could* might have been closer to the truth. Until the gig at Three-Two-Eight, there was a tentative quality to a lot of vocals, an *I-can't-believe-I'm-doing-this-outside-the-shower* quality. Until Nashville, the vocals never got near the band's improved instrumental capability, but that night at Performance Hall they did. The audience knew; as Tad Bartimus finished up a potent version of "Chain of Fools," they were clearly knocked out. Wherever my bouncer buddy was, if he was listening, he must have been pleased.

Maybe he was even dancing—a lot of people were that night. Nashville was the only gig where Kathi Goldmark was really successful in getting people on their feet and moving to the old Dovells' tune "You Can't Sit Down," and once they got up, most of them really *couldn't* seem to sit back down. They were loud, they were boisterous, and they were getting off on what we were doing. When Al dropped to his knees, took someone's empty longneck beer bottle, and started using it to play slide guitar on "Who Do You Love," the whole place went up.

I never once during the Nashville show felt the euphoria I felt in Atlanta—not even pogoing up and down to "You Can't Sit Down" with Kathi—but that was okay by me. Because, dig: Performance, whether as a writer or as a rocker, is not about getting *yourself* off; that's called masturbation. Performance is about getting the *audience* off. It's about making people glad they hired a babysitter and came out to see the show. As to how *you* feel about being there, that's maybe for your diary or letters you write back home. It's got nothing to do with the job you're getting paid to do.

Nashville was a slower-paced show than any of the ones before it (or the Miami Beach gig that followed it and ended the tour), but it was also sharper and more confident. Some of the most potent numbers in our repertoire, it turned out, were numbers that played broadly, for comedy—Amy Tan wearing her s & m rig and doing "These Boots Are Made for Walkin'," Amy and the Remainderettes doing "Leader of the Pack," "Last Kiss," and the crazed "Teen Angel" duet Barry and I developed more during performances than at rehearsal (I don't remember Al ever calling for "Teen Angel" at a soundcheck—I think he was afraid it might get stale). At the Nashville show I got the feeling that none of us were really very amused any longer by these bits, but the audience seemed to be getting a *big* kick out of them.

Nashville was the night it all worked, in other words. Nashville was the place where all of us, ladies included, played like men.

During rehearsals for our first show in Anaheim, Dave Barry was clearly amazed at the way I was top-necking "Gloria." It was the attitude of a man visiting someone who has never bothered to have his house wired for electricity.

"It's easier with bar chords," he said. "Look." And then he showed me exactly the same basic riff Jamie Chesley had showed me in the basement all those years before.

"I know," I said, "but it sounds just as good this way, I think." I played the chords open, top-necking them again just as I had all those years ago. "Also, I can keep up with the chord changes. Don't worry about that."

"Try keeping up with these," Dave said, and played the hook that leads into the instrumental break of "Gloria" and then ends the tune. Instead of the D-A-E progression of the actual song, which is fairly fast but nowhere near the speed of light, that little lead-in hook goes E-D-A-D/E-D-A-D/E-D-A-D, before kicking back into the basic riff. Dave could do it easily with bars, and I could do it playing open chords . . . but I couldn't do at Dave's speed no matter how hard I tried. I think it was at that moment, sitting on a hotel room bed and watching how little he was moving his fingers and how much he was still doing, that I understood how much I had to learn, and how much of it was going to begin by unlearning the techniques I had been practicing ever since the days of "Rock My Soul" and "Bed Bug Blues."

Al knew it, too. I was on stage in Anaheim, I remembered most of the changes, but I didn't play very well. I'm low in the mix, almost non-existent, in fact, and that's probably a good thing. Then, during our brief rehearsals for a gig we played in November of 1992, Ridley Pearson (known as "Bo" Ridley to the boys in the band) showed me something interesting . . . except to me it wasn't just interesting, it was downright *fascinating*. It had to do with a lovely rock song called "634-5789." The song is in the key of G, but the chorus—the digits of that phone number—switches rapidly back and forth between G and C, each number eliciting a different chord. Written out, it looks like this:

G   C   G   C   G   C   G
"Six-three-four-five-seven-eight-nine."

I was able to keep up with these changes—barely—by top-necking, but by then I had been working on bar-E variations for about five months, practicing until my fingers ached (except when you're first starting to bar, I found, what *really* ache are your left wrist and left thumb . . . and it's the thumb that takes most of the punishment, at least until you're able to get your hand up off the fretboard a little bit). Casually, feeling a bit like an imposter, I made a G-chord on the third fret and then asked Rid to show me bar C, thinking it would probably be some impossible stretch of the fingers

that I wouldn't be able to manage. Instead, I was astonished to find it was a simple change, from

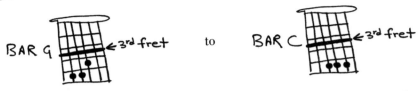

The fact is, to switch from bar G to bar C (or from bar A to bar D, for that matter), all you really have to do is rock your fingers back and forth to the beat of the song you're playing. It takes some practice, but so does learning to rotate your thumbs in opposite directions when you twiddle them (and if you don't believe that takes practice, just try it).

It was at that moment, understanding that I was probably going to be able to do a lot more than just keep up with "634-5789," that I decided my idea about being able to go a pretty long way on a small amount of talent—if one was willing to work, that was—had been correct . . . plenty correct enough for my purposes as a Remainder, anyway. When I began practicing for the Three Chords and an Attitude Tour, I did so with more confidence in and hope for my abilities than I had had previously. Hope is a great and uplifting thing, but I believe that when you've got a hard job to do, confidence is an even better thing—a magic elixir, in fact.

As things turned out, I was still barely audible as an instrumentalist in the floor-mix, but that's okay; I could hear what I was doing in my monitor, and I know it was quite a lot more, and quite a lot better, than what I had been doing in Anaheim. That's a cheerful thing to report, but I know something even more cheerful: I'm still getting better. Not a lot—when your talent in a given field is small, there are few quantum leaps—but a little. And although I don't think I'll ever be able to do much more than the dogpaddle when it comes to my Farrington guitar, most times I can still make it to shore. That makes me happy, and it makes me grateful that Kathi asked me in the first place, and that I had guts enough to say yes. I've had a wonderful real-life experience (what Al Kooper once called "rock camp") that has brightened my life, taken me out of my middle-aged rut, and changed me in ways I would not have expected. I also made some new friends along the way. They are marvelous friends for all sorts of reasons, but the best thing about them is that they don't think the way I make my living is strange and peculiar, because it's also the way they make *their* living.

My best moment on the tour? Easy. It didn't come at Nashville, or at any of the gigs. It came during our first rehearsal at Musician's Wharf in Boston. Al Kooper came up to me and asked if I'd been practicing my bar chords. And I, with the insane nonchalance one can muster only after finally learning (or partially learning, in my case) a skill that has eluded him over many long years, ripped off the rapid bar G's and bar C's that constitute the chorus of "634." Al's eyes widened in an entirely unaffected expression of surprise, a look I will be able to remember—and treasure—even if I live to be as old as George Burns.

"Holy shit, that's not bad," he said, and that was really all I wanted for my six months' worth of sore fingers.

I can remember times—lots of them—when I wrote something that seemed so right I just kind of blew myself away. I imagine Al Kooper and Ridley Pearson and Barbara Kingsolver and Dave Barry can remember instrumental

breaks like that, or songs, or maybe even whole gigs. But it's different when you get that feeling doing what you were made to do—it's great, but it's also like a free ride. When you're doing something that doesn't come naturally, moments like that are sometimes even better; they're like stealing little embers from the fire of the gods. That probably sounds a bit presumptuous to some people, or arrogant, but they're the same folks who go around muttering killjoy stuff like "If God meant us to fly, He would have given us wings." That's bullshit, folks. If God had meant us to fly, He would have given us the brains to think up airplanes and hands clever enough to build them.

There is a distressing trend in American life right now, a movement so strong it's almost tidal, to turn talented people into famous people and famous people into celebrities—or just "celebs."

Once you become a celeb, two things happen to you. The first is that you find you have forfeited your right to be a proper stranger; celebs discover they apparently have a duty to be everyone's friend. Michael Jackson becomes simply Michael. Elizabeth Taylor becomes Liz. Arnold Schwarzenegger becomes Arnie. The second thing to happen is that you find you are forbidden to transcend the public's perception of you; once a hamburger, always a hamburger, the unspoken creed goes, and if you dare pretend you're broccoli, we'll beat you half to death for being pretentious and egocentric. If you are a rock singer, you're not supposed to write novels (tell that to Kinky Friedman or Jimmy Buffett). And if you're a novelist, you're not really supposed to play the guitar and sing. In this world, where the Princess of Wales has become simply Di and Edward R. Murrow has been replaced by Maury Povich, the perfect celeb would be someone like Charo, who seems to do nothing but appear on game-shows like *Hollywood Squares*, or those vaguely familiar "Hollywood personalities" who can be glimpsed from time to time on cable TV, huckstering continence pants, no-physical insurance, and hair-growth products. But then without them what would *Spy* magazine do for its "Party Poop" column?

If talented people really *were* just celebs, there would be no excuse at all for a bunch of writers to tear off on a tour-bus and become Rock Bottom Remainders—the whole thing would have been an exercise in late-twentieth-century *hubris*. The truth is, however (just let me remind you in case you happen to be one of the millions who seem to have forgotten), that talented people are really just people—they eat, they sleep, and sometimes they have stomach and bowel problems when the antibiotics get to them. For me, the Remainders weren't about being famous, getting seen, or promoting the new book (I didn't *have* a new book, which was why I was able to go out and play in the first place). The Remainders were about going back to the beginning, doing things the hard way, taking some risks and trying to make them pay off.

It was about finding out if I could manage to learn some bar chords at the advanced age of forty-four . . . and finding out that I could.

"Teen Angel" had been our show-closer all the way back to the first gig in Anaheim, and it also served as the closer at two gigs the Remainders played between "official" appearances—one at the Bottom Line in New York (October 1992) and one at The Cameo in Miami Beach (November 1992). What really made this old tear-jerker funny on the Three Chords and an Attitude Tour was Dave Barry's introduction to it, and we had music publishers Acuff-Rose to thank for that.

Dave's intro was always a fine moment, but he outdid himself that night at Three-Two-Eight. Acuff-Rose's problems with our version of the tune started when they saw the video of our Anaheim gig, and realized—with the humorless outrage only Grand Ole Opry veterans can manage—that I had substituted the phrase "vial of crack" for "high school ring." This change, I should add, was not calculated but completely spontaneous.

They were allowing us to do the song on the Three Chords tour, but only with the understanding that they would sue our asses off if we diverged so much as a syllable from "Teen Angel"'s inane lyrics. Dave's introduction thus became a masterful example of how one goes about turning a sow's ear into a silk purse. At every stop he solemnly warned audiences not to think of the word "assholes" whenever he mentioned Acuff-Rose. The result was a hilariously vulgar responsive reading between Dave and the audience late in the show. And just when you felt that standards of taste could not be lowered any further, Dave Marsh wandered out, wearing a saintly look and a prom dress. It was, in short, American entertainment at its finest . . . but never finer than in Nashville on the night of May 28th.

Dave was advised—*strongly* advised—to keep the word "assholes" out of his Acuff-Rose patter during the Nashville show; it would be too much like bearding the lion in his den, we were told (it turned out, in fact, that one member of the warm-up duo was related to Roy Acuff). Dave's response was to tell the audience not to think of the phrase "no sense of humor" when he said the words "Acuff-Rose." It was clean, and it somehow worked even better, producing an amusing iambic beat from the beered-up audience.

"Now I just want to assure you we'd never do anything to offend Acuff-Rose," Dave began with carefully calculated sincerity.

"NO-sensa-YUMA!" the audience roared back gleefully.

I think that by the time we brought that show to a close, the people I'd been rather afraid of when I heard them from my seat in the little pink room would have cheerfully gone out and burned the offices of Mssrs. Acuff and Rose to the ground, if Dave had asked them to. He didn't, of course . . . but I'd be lying if I didn't add that the gleam in his eye made me suspect he was tempted.

"Teen Angel" was our final encore number, and as we left the stage at midnight (with a five o'clock wake-up call scheduled to catch a 7:00 a.m. plane to Miami), I realized a number of things. One was that the band was the calmest it had ever been at the end of the show. Another was that it probably *had* been the best show, not for us but for the audience, which was still out there, footstomping and yeehawing and calling for more. A third thing was that my stomach felt fine again. My throat infection got quite a lot worse after that night, but I made the Miami gig and didn't have another bit of stomach trouble on the tour. And one other thing. I felt tired, but I also felt good, the way I do after I've had a good day on whatever I happen to be writing. I felt for the first time as if I had really done my job, that I had worked hard, and that I had a perfect right to be where I was. I didn't feel like a celeb; I felt like somebody who's just come off-shift at work. The last part was and is terribly important to me; I was raised to work, and working makes me as happy as the idea of playing at the work of others makes me uneasy.

As we went out to the bus, Dave Barry asked me if I would be willing to do this again next year. I thought it over, then nodded. Sure. It's the neighborhood of the beast, all right, but that is not necessarily the worst place in the world to be.

And besides, like I said—I'm still practicing my bar chords, and still getting better.

Kathi Kamen Goldmark

I'LL TAKE THE BLAME

Blount rehearses with his siren helmet. (Inflatable sheep cropped out.)

*T*he first actual Remainder moment involved Roy Blount, a few shots of bourbon, and the song that made Rockin' Sydney famous. In January 1990, Roy jumped on stage with my band, the Sweethearts of the Bancroft Lounge, and performed a sterling rendition of "Don't Mess with My Toot Toot." He was a natural performer, and it seemed odd to think of him sitting alone at a word processor. "Aha!" I thought, then packed up my gear, argued with the bartender, paid the band, loaded out, went home, and forgot all about it.

Roy's fabulous "Toot Toot" success reinforced some illusions I'd held about the nature of performing, the true purpose of music in the lives of creative individuals, and human nature in general. Every one of these illusions bit the dust in the process of creating and maintaining the Remainders.

KATHI'S LIST OF NAIVE ILLUSIONS

1. *Everyone in the world can sing.* I always believed that every person has at least one song that he or she can sing great. (My friend Beverley Wilshire, for example, can sing "Cry Me a

Left: Everyone in the world *can't* sing (left to right: Marsh, Selvin, Blount).

Who knew that just taking a nap on the bus required repealing the law of gravity? (Top to bottom, Daitz; Pearson and Blount; and Marsh's legs vs. Barry's head)

River" if she's draped on a piano.) I still think there's a song out there for Dave Marsh, despite the increasingly mountainous evidence to the contrary.

2. *People will always tell you the truth*, even if they're desperate to get in your band or make your video.

3. *If someone tells you that he or she doesn't need special "star" treatment, he or she means it.*

4. *A big gig is just like a little gig, only bigger.* I thought it would be like multiplying a recipe for more people. Wrong.

5. *Everyone over the age of twelve has learned enough manners to say "please" and "thank you."*

6. *You can tell a person's true nature by how he treats the waiter.* Wrong again. It's how he treats the roadies.

7. *I can charm anyone, if I try.*

8. *People on rock & roll tours don't care about sleeping.* Sorry, guys.

I've spent the last ten years knocking around San Francisco as a freelance media escort for touring authors and moonlighting as a free-lance honky-tonk sweetheart in several local country-rock bar bands. My day job as a paid professional codependent involves providing transportation, briefing for interviews, and general assistance—anything from changing an airline ticket to providing a condom (this really happened when Cynthia Heimel fell in love on a morning radio show). I often end up being an exhausted author's best pal for a day, sharing desserts, listening to love problems, brushing dandruff off a shoulder. It's an artificial intimacy, but every once in a while some spark cuts through the book tour routine, and "my" author and I do become friends. An invitation to join the Remainders was partly a thank-you to some of these people.

EVENTS THAT INSPIRED THE REMAINDERS, BESIDES ROY'S SINGING

1. *Bob Greene.* "You play in a band? You're so lucky! I always wanted to play in a band. What do you wear?" I told him that if he was ever in town when I had a gig, he could be in my band on the condition that I be allowed to dress him up.

2. *Many conversations with Dave Marsh about the elitist nature of popular music vs. its tribal and participatory history.* Dave was invited to put his money where his mouth is and sit in. Same condition, although I never could have predicted the ultimate consequences of my offer to dress him up. (He gave a new meaning to the term "getting in her underwear.")

3. *Former folk singer and contemporary folk hero Robert Fulghum sharing my fas-*

cination with roadhouses and honky-tonks. I made the same offer, vaguely wondering what would happen if everyone showed up on the same night.

4. *Gita Mehta, elegant and gracious, digging through my blues tapes—even singing along to the Bo Carter classic "Let Me Roll Yo' Lemon"—all the way back from San Jose.*

5. *Michael Dorris regaling me with tales of life as the drummer of Native Soul, Alaska's most forgettable bar band, while Louise Erdrich hummed along to country music tapes in the backseat.*

6. *Dave Barry coming through town right after a Tupperware convention at which he'd sung his original "Tupperware Song."* The experience of playing for two thousand screaming fans was, he said, the best thing that ever happened to him. (At that point, I didn't know Dave well enough to realize that he says that about everything.)

7. *Driving Ridley Pearson from Carmel back to the city and learning all about his band the Sensational Toastpoints.* We stopped in at my husband's gig, and Ridley made the proper appreciative and musicianly comments about Joe's pedal steel playing.

8. *Steely Dan.* Twenty years ago, I good-naturedly embraced the role of "drummer's girlfriend," always secretly wishing I could be in the band, too. Even from the sidelines, it was my biggest rock & roll adventure—until the Remainders.

In early 1991, when I wrote the letter to Dorris, Erdrich, Barry, Marsh, Blount, Greene, Fulghum, Mehta, and Pearson asking if they'd like to form a rock band to perform at the upcoming American Booksellers convention in Anaheim, I included a few other authors I believed to be musical: Amy Tan, Oscar Hijuelos, Barbara Kingsolver, Maya Angelou, Anna Quindlen, Matt Groening, Doreen Virtue, Toni Morrison, and Tomie dePaola. I had no idea what to expect.

What I got was faxes. Amy's came first: she suggested wearing wet suits and flippers on stage. She played classical piano, so I ordered an instructional rock video and put her on keyboards. Ridley said, "Yeah!" to bass. Dave Barry would play guitar as long as he could wear spandex (a promise he has yet to keep). Michael, enlisting as drummer, signed his fax "Ringo." Louise would overcome her stage fright and sing backup vocals. Oscar, Gita, Toni, and Anna politely declined, and Bob Greene ignored my letter completely, but it didn't matter. We had a band.

Dave Marsh, Roy, and Matt also said yes. Doing this gig without the three best friends I'd made on book tours seemed impossible, but there

It's how you treat the roadies, not how the roadies treat you. (Hoover, Goldmark)

was the small problem of what to do with them, musically. Then I remembered our tenth anniversary party, at which Joe and I showcased our new band, the Ray Price Club, and where I'd decided to indulge a ridiculous lifelong fantasy, leading everyone I know and love in a sing-along. We printed three hundred copies of the lyrics to "Double Shot (of My Baby's Love)" complete with a photo of the Swingin' Medallions in all their madras-slacked glory. Two of the guests were Joel Selvin and Greil Marcus, friends who work as music critics.

I didn't know about Joel, but I was pretty sure the quickest way to send Greil into the next room, if not county, was a sing-along. Yet when "Double Shot" began, no one sang with more passion than Greil—was he really standing on a chair?—and Joel. Afterwards, Greil confided that it's his favorite song; he claims he once even heard a great version in an elevator.

Five "musically challenged" band members seemed better than three, the conceptual hook being that all of them were, or had once been, music critics. I liked the idea of making some of our most opinionated rock critics perform rock & roll. Maybe they'd develop some humility and compassion (and maybe they wouldn't). They'd already demonstrated that they could get through "Double Shot," we could add Tomie on kazoo for extra zaniness, and it would be a shame to let all those lovely song sheets go to waste. Thus, the Critics Chorus was born.

Fulghum's letter sat on my desk, his address a closely guarded Random House secret. I finally coaxed all-star publicist Suzanne Wickham into divulging a fax number.

Five minutes later my phone rang. "Goldmark, it's Fulghum. Thanks for doing this. I'll play mandocello."

"Um, does it rock?"

He assured me that a mandocello was capable of behaving like a rock & roll instrument, and we hung up.

The phone rang again. "Goldmark, it's Fulghum. I've found an anonymous donor, who's offered up to ten thousand dollars to help finance the show. Let me know when you need some money."

The only appropriate response to a call like that is:

"WA-HOO!"

Dave Marsh's wife, Barbara Carr, convinced me to contact Stephen King. I had misgivings. I'd recruited band members intuitively, feeling that my special connection with each one would mean they'd get along with each other. Stephen had never experienced the hostage bonding with me that happens between authors and escorts, but Barbara told me that Steve was a great guy who played some guitar. I wrote him a letter, and he joined by return mail.

When Barbara Kingsolver checked in from the Canary Islands, volunteering to play keyboards, I panicked. How would Amy react to the idea of a second keyboard player? When I finally worked up the nerve to call her, she was thrilled to move over to background vocals. I think her exact words were "Thank God! Now all I have to worry about is what to wear!"

Meanwhile, back at the fax machine, Ridley had assumed the role of Designated Worrier. My favorite Ridley fax went on and on about how terrible we would be, how impossible to get this together in so little time with so many band members, how stupid to have all those singers. In the next paragraph, he suggested I book the band on "The Tonight Show" the day after Anaheim. I decided to let Ridley do all my worrying for me.

There was no obvious lead singer, so I decided to rotate lead vocals in order to give everyone a moment in the spotlight. Fax machines started buzzing with ideas for a song list, the band's name, and worthy charities to benefit from the proceeds of what had become an outlaw event. We were making up our own rules, paying no attention to standard protocol at the ABA convention, the most high-impact date on the publishing industry calendar.

Tad Bartimus, on tour for *Trinity's Children*, overheard me talking on a green-room phone and asked about the band. She wasn't a famous writer with the kind of clout the others had, and she didn't seem like a rock & roller, but something behind her eyes needed to be included. Maybe it was the story she told me about giving up a singing career to attend journalism school, or the funny little rhinestone pins on her standard-issue touring-author outfit. Hoping Ridley wouldn't kill me, I asked Tad to join the Remainderettes. Our band was complete.

"There was no obvious lead singer . . ."

REMAINDER SURPRISES

1. *Getting to know the "bad daughter."* I'd worked with Amy, and since we lived in the same city, we talked occasionally, but she maintained a reserved distance—a combination of shyness and self-protection. It all changed the first time we went shopping for stage clothes. The oldest customers to set foot in Betsey Johnson in six centuries, we actually found a dress that worked for both of us—very different body types—on the sale rack, no less! As Amy emerged from the fitting room in skintight black sequins, so did the gutsy, bad-ass pool-playing rock & roller I now call my friend.

2. *Turning the tables at ABA.* Since we're regarded as just above the earthworm on the evolutionary scale of publishing, media escorts don't get a lot of attention at

ABA. I invited every escort I knew to join our volunteer crew. What a thrill: the chauffeurs of the publishing industry throwing a party that *everyone* wanted to attend!

3. *Tapes rolling.* My son, Tony, with some help from Joe, used his vast knowledge of rock oldies to prepare a tape of the original versions of all our songs, as well as a "book tape" to use as break music. Stephen made a cassette of himself singing and strumming his guitar. And Ridley locked himself in his home recording studio with a song list and everyone's keys and made the band a practice tape. I had provided lyrics and chord charts, but Ridley's tape was the single most helpful thing that anyone did.

4. *Just call me Mom.* Consistent with my caretaking role on book tours, the band seemed comfortable labeling me Band Mom. In accordance with the title, I was often used as a go-between in intraband communications. For instance, Dave Barry called to tell me he'd found the perfect gift for Roy—an MC helmet that he could wear on stage. Roy loved his helmet but couldn't figure out where to put the batteries. "Tell Roy the batteries go inside the siren," said Dave.

   A couple of weeks later, I heard from Dave again. He said Roy had sent him an inflatable rubber sheep and asked me to thank Roy for him. "But you know, I'm embarrassed, because that helmet only cost four ninety-five, and I happen to know those sheep go for around thirty dollars." I dutifully passed this information on to Roy. "I never heard of anyone being embarrassed by an inflatable sheep before—on account of the cost," Roy said.

5. *The car audition.* As word got out that there was going to be an all-author band at ABA, I started hearing from what seemed like All Authors. People started getting into my car with demo tapes, harmonicas, small (and not so small) percussion instruments, even a banjo. They started singing lustily without warning, dropping hints about old concertinas and D-18s in their attics. Publicists tried to book their authors into the band as though it were a TV talk show, and I began feeling like the band leader in *The Commitments* who advertises for musicians and then can't take a walk, or even a bath, without someone auditioning. I developed Kathi's Secret Rule: Anyone Who Volunteers Is Automatically Disqualified. Our only hope was to form a group of people whose response was "I'm not sure I'm good enough, but I'd love to!" Volunteers guaranteed ego problems.

In Anaheim, we rehearsed in an airless basement that smelled like sewage. No one cared. Al Kooper was the right combination of funny and terrifying to get the best performance out of the band, though he fostered a boys'-club atmosphere that Barbara and I found daunting. Amy and Barbara were so busy with ABA commitments that it was impossible to get all four women together to work on backup harmonies, and rehearsals were conducted at such ear-splitting volume that it was impossible to hear our own vocals anyway. When I asked if the band could turn down so we could hear ourselves, Al's reply was that we wouldn't be able to hear on stage either, so we should just get used to it. I was frustrated that no one seemed to care about vocal arrangements, my favorite band thing. People sang loud and off-key whenever they felt like it, and I was too overwhelmed, busy, and intimidated to insist.

But we were actually making almost mediocre garage band music. It looked like we were going to pull this sucker off.

Carole Eitingon, one of my media escort associates, had the phenomenal job of supervising the volunteer crew, making sure there was food at rehearsal, providing rides to and from the convention center for band members who had to do things at ABA, and handling all the logistics of staging the show. Lorraine Battle, another of my colleagues, helped out with costumes, makeup, last-minute errands; together with Joel Selvin's wife, Keta Bill, she also worked on remedial choreography.

At night, back at the hotel, Amy and I changed into our trashiest rock & roll outfits (why were the hotel detectives watching so closely?), sat around the bar, and got excited about the gig together. Al hosted weird video screenings in his room, while downstairs in the Hilton bar Dave Barry and I tried to impress each other with how many verses of "Violets of Dawn" we each knew, and Roy demonstrated by example why Wild Turkey on the rocks is the coolest drink in the universe.

The night of the show, an honest-to-god rock & roll tour bus picked us up at the hotel. The toilet didn't work (we seemed to have a hard time escaping that ever-popular aroma), but it had fake velvet upholstery, real bunks with curtains, a back bedroom, and a card table. We only got to ride about ten blocks to the gig, but I think the real reason we ended up going on tour the next year was that everyone wanted to spend more time on that bus.

We waited in the wings as Roy, the designated master of ceremonies, launched into his hilarious introductions, then took the stage one by one, NBA style. I came out last, and the roar of appreciation from the crowd made me want to giggle, cry, and pee all at the same time. Instead I felt that ear-to-ear grin starting and didn't try to stop it and marched out on stage, slapping Dave Barry's hand in a high five on the way to my microphone. I smelled sweat and hot electrical wiring and some-one's lavender perfume and my song was strong and clear and the band was actu-ally *there*, and it was a dream come true.

We did our second show and got on the bus to go to our after party, sweaty, gig-gly, and exhausted. Only no one could find the bus driver. We sat there congratulat-ing each other until someone finally found the driver asleep in the luggage compartment under the bus. *This* was rock & roll!

It was Steve's idea to do a rock & roll tour. After the usual flurry of faxes, he wrote a book proposal, since we needed to finance the project, and we somehow talked Viking into buying it.

Around Remainders World Headquarters (a.k.a. my house), it was becoming clear we'd need a little help. My friend, music-industry lifer George Gerrity, led us to Stephen Pillster, who became our booking agent. After one false start, we went back to Bob Daitz as tour manager, with help from Carole and Lorraine, who handled merchandising and wardrobe, respectively. Audrey deChadenèdes had been my best friend in the Steely Dan days. She used to live with Walter Becker, and left L.A. in 1974 in the final chapter of a soap opera that involved the band's last live show, several altered states of consciousness, everyone's boyfriend, and a little slut from England. Audrey showed up in San Francisco just as things started going crazy, and she became my office manager, the Remainders' answer to Krazy Glue.

Meanwhile, Al was insisting that he was the only person in the world who knew how to organize a rock tour, Dave Marsh was urging me not to listen to Al about business matters, Steve wanted to hire his buddy Jim England as guitar tech, Tad wanted to sing a couple of *really* hard songs, Amy suddenly realized that guys would see her on the bus without makeup, and Barbara informed us that she wouldn't be able to make a couple of the tour dates. Joel had a problem with the set list that indicated he might be taking it seriously. Ridley and I whipped up practice tape number two, this time with vocals, and Dave Barry actually practiced. So did Stephen, and rumor had it that he could just about play a barred D chord by Christmas.

A TYPICAL DAY AT REMAINDERS WORLD HEADQUARTERS

5:40 A.M.:	Fax from Dave Barry, with updated keys for his songs.
6:30 A.M.:	Phone call from Oren Teicher at ABA, to discuss several issues, one of which is that the Miami nightclub seems to have removed its stage.
7:10 A.M.:	Call from client in N.Y., who has a *perfect addition to the Remainders*—a diet doctor who plays the accordion! Coincidentally, he has a book coming out next fall.
7:30 A.M.:	Call from Ridley's publicist, wanting to know about band commitments in Miami, so Delacorte can book every other waking moment with book publicity stuff.
7:32 A.M.:	Emergency message from tour bus company.
7:35 A.M.:	Call from college newspaper in Northampton, Mass. (our second stop), wanting interview with Stephen King.
7:42 A.M.:	Call from Judi Smith, Dave Barry's assistant, to discuss Dave's schedule.
8:01 A.M.:	Call from Al, worried about tour bus overcrowding. Also worried about security for Steve.

9:10 A.M.: Call from L.A. talk show wanting to book the Remainders.

9:15 A.M.: Call from Patti Kelly, Viking publicist, to discuss ABA and tour publicity strategy. Also to tell me she has given my number to some guy who wants to be our tour manager.

9:30 A.M.: Call from wannabe tour manager.

9:35 A.M.: Call from T-shirt guy to discuss placement of logo.

9:40 A.M.: Call from printer; halo stickers are ready.

9:53 A.M.: Call from Chicago newspaper requesting interviews with Stephen King and Dave Barry.

10:02 A.M.: Message from hairdresser, who wants Amy's address, because another client of his wants to invite her to a play.

10:15 A.M.: Pick up stickers at printer.

10:45 A.M.: Return to office to find six messages: five requests for interviews with Dave and Steve, one call from Amy saying there are great leopard shorts at Macy's.

10:50 A.M.: Call Macy's.

11:00 A.M.: Call from Al, with solution to tour bus problem: segregating men and women on two separate buses, with the women riding with the roadies. Among other things, this would mean keeping an entirely different schedule from the rest of the band. I explain why this will not be a popular solution.

11 A.M.–NOON:
- Return other calls; pack up press kits to send to media people.
- Call from potential Philadelphia guest critic who doesn't appreciate our invitation to join the Critics Chorus for a night but would really like to play sax, because his "musicianship is too highly developed to yell 'Louie Louie' with a bunch of critics." I say no, he gets rude, and I figure we'll get mooned in Philly. (We don't.)

12:10 P.M.: Fax from Ridley's office asking how to get some VIPs into the VIP reception in D.C. We've already told them we have no idea.

12:15 P.M.: Fax from Al, with request that we fax all Remainders.

12:15–1 P.M.:
- Send everyone Al's fax.
- Call from Hoover, our sound technician and stage manager, about backline budget for New England shows.
- Four calls from promoters and journalists, wanting photos for show advertising, and interviews with Steve and Dave.
- Call from Stephen Pillster, our booking agent, who complains about Al's attitude.
- Call from Al, who complains about Pillster's attitude.

1:06 P.M.: Call from Steve's office, about Miami schedule.

1:08 P.M.: Call from publicist who *must have* extra passes to ABA show.

1:10 P.M.: Call from Esther Levine, Atlanta media escort and our point person there, to ask if band will appear on 6:00 A.M. TV show. Also wants to know about T-shirts and book signings.

1:30 P.M.: Call from bookstore in Nashville whose owner claims Al promised the Remainders for an in-store appearance.

1:42 P.M.: Call from Ken Follett, who wants to talk about the opening ABA set he's rehearsing with Douglas Adams.

1:50 P.M.: Call from Amy, wondering if bus has a sound system for her karaoke CDs.

1:55 P.M.: Call from Douglas Adams, describing in detail the harmony lines of the last chorus of "The Boxer," on which he asks for assistance.

2:00–3:00 P.M.: Two calls from publishing big shots needing passes to Miami show; three calls from volunteer crew members needing acknowledgment and appreciation; four calls from various journalists seeking interviews with Steve, Dave, and Amy.

3:06 P.M.: Call from Atlanta journalist to check time of Hard Rock Cafe press conference.

3:08 P.M.: Call from bookstore owner in Atlanta, very upset that we are not willing to organize an in-store appearance.

3:18 P.M.: Call from Audrey Eisman at ABA to check spelling of names for program and to read us the little blurbs she's written about everyone.

3:45 P.M.: Call from Neal Edelson and David Steffen at BMG, to discuss possible lawsuit over our video's version of "Teen Angel."

3:50 P.M.: Call from journalist asking for interview with—yay!—Greil Marcus and Dave Marsh.

4:00–5:00 P.M.: • Call from Philadelphia venue's publicity guy, wondering if Matt is coming on tour.
• Call from promoter in Worcester, Mass., to find out if we can play at his club.
• Fax from backstage-pass printer with design for approval. Make changes and fax back, Fed Ex deposit.
• Call from Barbara, who cannot tune Ridley's rehearsal tape to her piano. Pack up and send my son Tony's tape recorder, which has speed and pitch control; hope he won't miss it.
• Call Dave Marsh to check in. Get stern lecture about tour managers.
• Call from friend in D.C., wondering if we can have dinner there and if I can help her get her book published.

5:02 P.M.: Call from Bob Daitz, on the road with Van Halen—just checking in, wondering if we've worked out our tour bus problem.

5:09 P.M.: Call from travel agent, about Nashville hotel.

5:18 P.M.: Call from Optek guitar company, wondering if I ever sent their

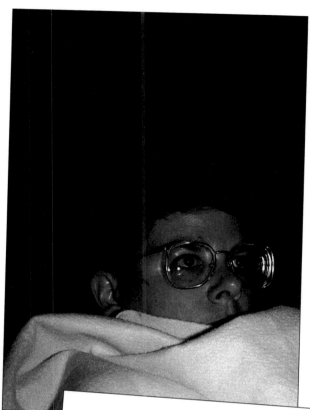

These two pages:
What really happened at
those legendary Remainders
editorial conferences.

press packet to Dave Barry and Steve, and if they want to invest in their company.

5:30 P.M.:   Call from Tad—long discussion about body image as it relates to gold lamé.

6:00 P.M.:   Roy returns my call from a couple of days ago, but neither of us can remember what it was about.

6:10 P.M.:   Call from journalist friend who wants to join the Remainders, wondering if everyone is still on for the tour.

7:02 P.M.:   Call from bass player of opening act in Northampton to discuss equipment needs.

8:30 P.M.:   Call to George Gerrity to discuss radio station tie-in possibilities for the tour.

9:00 P.M.:   Put Tony to bed, clean up kitchen.

10:00 P.M.:   Catch up on paperwork, collate and pack up press kits, update tour schedule, list of people to receive VIP passes.

10:36 P.M.:   Call from Carole, to check in and ask some questions about tour logistics and volunteer crew. Has list of local contacts to receive T-shirt shipments.

11:02 P.M.:   Leave voice mail messages for Patti Kelly and Oren Teicher, updating them on publicity requests and ABA rooming list.

1:00 A.M.:   Finish paperwork, pass out on office couch.

4:03 A.M.:   Awakened by fax from Ken Follett's office, describing his itinerary in amazing detail.

4:22 A.M.:   Fully awake, place call to England to discuss with Ken Follett's publicist why we cannot close the Paragon an hour before show time so that British *Esquire* can get a photo of Ken onstage with the Remainders.

5:00 A.M.:   Read yesterday's mail. Really nice letter from Ridley, and a bunch of bills.

Once we got to Boston, where we'd be rehearsing a few days before the tour started, it took about four minutes for everyone to feel like we were in high school again. Amy looked so cool smoking in the band room that I wished I smoked, too. It had been about thirty years since I'd coordinated outfits with my girlfriends, but Amy, Tad, Barbara, and I had long discussions about which gowns to wear for each show. At night, we wandered the Cambridge streets in a big middle-aged

gang, Amy and I wearing our leopard bathrobes as jackets, Ridley and Dave Barry looking like Ivy League college boys, and Roy ambling along saying things like "You gotta put down some kibble where the slow dogs can get it" and other words of wisdom.

I don't remember how the guy thing came up. I know it was during dinner on the second or third night of rehearsal. I boasted to Dave Barry that due to long years as a woman in mostly male bands, I was really good at being one of the guys. He didn't believe me. I made a bet with Dave that by the end of the tour I would be an official band guy. He said it was impossible. I tried very hard to win that bet:

- When we stopped the van by the side of the road so people could pee in the woods, I peed in the woods.
- I drank beer and said "fuck" a lot.
- I ate lots of saturated fats and no vegetables.
- I was a *really good sport* about tit jokes.
- I even stuck my finger in the hole of the rubber sheep, which Roy or maybe Dave brought backstage in Miami.

Dave said that if an actual guy moment occurred and I was part of it, he'd let me know. I definitely lost the bet after the tour ended, because I tried to work out feelings with Al Kooper.

Just like a girl.

TRANSCENDENT MOMENTS AND WHOLESOME ROCK TOUR FUN

1. *Mouse's little flashlight.* Twenty years ago, when Steely Dan played, there was a thrilling moment right after the house lights died: in the darkness on stage, you could see tiny spots of light as the crew led the band to their places. Those tiny lights and the anticipation in the air felt like the essence of big-time rock & roll to me. In all the hundreds of gigs I've played with little bar bands, I'd never been led to the stage with a flashlight. When Mouse led us out with his, it became my absolutely favorite tour thing.

2. *Sex, drugs, and rock & roll.* The three alleged staples of rock tours were not much in evidence. There didn't seem to be enough privacy for anyone to have sex. The "Code of the Road"—that is, the tacit agreement not to blab stuff you see other people doing on tour, especially to those people's spouses—was called on mostly for cigarette- and lemon-meringue-pie-related incidents. We did a little better with rock & roll. As the doorman in Atlanta said the morning after we slipped him show tickets, "You guys get *down* . . . but not that far!" At least Amy brought her beta-blockers.

3. *Will the real Amy Tan please stand up?* I don't know what got into us, two perfectly nice adult women at a reception in D.C. Just 'cause I was wearing a black wig, shades, and Amy's pass, and she was done up like a blond bombshell looking like a young Etta James, wearing *my* pass, was no reason to fool that poor aspiring writer, who probably pawned her heirloom jewelry to pay $100 for a VIP ticket to meet her favorite author and get advice on publishing her manuscript, which was in the car. And it was *certainly* no excuse for Amy to abandon me because she felt a little ignored. All I can say is, it must have been the drugs (the beta blockers, I mean). And if that woman is reading this, we're very sorry.

4. *Butt Ridley.* I actually saw Ridley moon a *radio phone interviewer.* I don't know why, but Dave Barry said it absolutely did not count as a guy moment.

5. *Medical school.* I watched closely as Tabby King, our tour photographer, demonstrated how to do transverse colon massage and perform a tracheotomy with a pen.

6. *You two cut it out or we'll have to separate you.* Lorraine and Tabby repeatedly demonstrated their black-belt shopping status. A partial list: rubber boobs, six different wigs, the Dave Marsh trousseau (which ultimately rivaled Barbie's), polka-dot boxer shorts, an Elvis jigsaw puzzle, and a couple of lethal bustiers. They were also the two best dancers on the tour.

7. *The Bob Daitz Show:* At night, after group activities, Amy and I often found ourselves in Daitz's room, where we were thoroughly entertained by his end of conversations with the next city's promoters. We never really understood about all those sneakers, though . . .

8. *The breast is yet to come.* OK, OK, when Roy did that thing where he introduced me—in Northampton, lesbian feminist stronghold of the Northeast, no less—as having the "best tits in the band," I admit that the sputtering, outraged feminist part of me was, well, sputtering and outraged. But under the circumstances, the only course of action was to stick 'em right out there and take my place on the bandstand. After the show, Roy explained, "Well, I just spotted 'em out of the corner of my eye, and there she was right behind 'em." But I wasn't in the mood to get mad at Roy, and that other part of me that obsesses over five pounds and likes to go shopping was actually sort of flattered. Hearing him say *"worst* tits in the band" probably would've been worse. (Anyway, the "worst tits" honor would certainly go to Dave Marsh, who try as he might will never fill out his white bustier.) And I admit for the next week I had excellent posture.

9. *The hootenannies.* Racing through the night from Cambridge to D.C., Al pulled out his acoustic guitar and started playing old folk songs, rock songs, and Perry Como songs. I started singing three-part harmony with Al and Dave Barry, marveling that I was on my very own rock & roll tour bus, having a hootenanny

The lion lies down with the lamb (Kooper as Jim Morrison, Goldmark as Janis Joplin).

with Al Kooper, and who could have imagined this when I was a Blues Project fan in college? I looked over at Dave, who seemed to be having similar thoughts. Suddenly, I felt a tap on my shoulder. It was Amy, sitting just in front of us. "Kathi, what song is that?" she whispered. "'Long Black Veil.' Why?" "I'm making a list of all the songs we sing on the bus. You know, for the book." Amy was indeed sitting there with her laptop computer, listing all the songs. So if you want to know what else we sang, you'll have to ask her. I'll bet in high school she handed her test papers in early.

10. *The shows.* What luxury, afforded by our crew, to be able to focus all your energy on the night's show! Stephen and Dave's "Teen Angel" setup; making Josh take solos, longer each night, on "You Can't Sit Down"; Amy's quick change to Rhythm Dominatrix; Ridley's grin; Tad's increasing confidence; the critics'—and Hoover's—underwear; the Dave Marsh fashion extravaganza . . . These were the moments I lived for.

11. *Rockin' Ralph*: I sat next to Roy on the plane from Nashville to Miami. In between dodging Marsh's spitballs, we talked about a lot of stuff—wallets, Roy's love life, Tony's school. Roy looked down at his personalized, laminated tour pass. "These'll be worth something someday," he said. "Yeah, Roy, especially yours."

"Just think—what if we had one that said 'Ralph Waldo'?"

Back home, the first couple of "regular" gigs felt weird.

- Where was Hoover, to set up my PA, and Mouse with his little flashlight?
- What about Steve's maniacal grin, Dave Barry's high five as I took my place on stage, his periodic reminders that it was OK to stop organizing things once in a while and let myself be a "total rock & roll bitch goddess"? Amy's whip and rubber tits? Barbara's humor, integrity, and musicianship? And Daitz, phone glued to his ear, advancing the next show?
- Where was sweet Ridley, and where was Tad, who had somehow turned into a wanton siren in two weeks?
- I missed Greil, who actually told me I *stomped*, which I took as a compliment; Dave Marsh and his nightly fashion show; Joel, and his scream solo; Matt, who sent flowers to every show and, when he finally joined us in Miami, took about seven seconds to fit right in; Roy, the only living human

who can make jokes about my anatomy in front of a thousand people and get away with it; Fulghum, who also made a cameo appearance at ABA; Josh, keeping the beat; and Jerry, who thinks he might read another book one day.

- And where was Al, who, despite the fact that he was worried I'd somehow learn the secret handshake, was one hell of an asset at a hootenanny?
- I missed Tabby the most, and secretly hope she'll move to San Francisco and open a Finishing and Charm School for Young Ladies with me. Imagine the uniforms!

Chris Kee, the Ray Price Club's bass player, meant to bring a little flashlight to the Blue Lamp and lead me to the stage, but he left it home. It was all right. I knew the way.

Al Kooper

FROM ACID TO ANTACID
(Al Kooper's Version)

A phone message from Joel Selvin? *This is pretty strange*, I remember thinking. Joel had interviewed me for his Rick Nelson book and I had been less than thrilled with the results—a viewpoint passed on to him through mutual friends. *What could he possibly want?* I returned his call at a time when I suspected a machine would intercept and was rewarded handsomely. "Why are you calling me, Joel?" I inquired, and hung up. Now I could screen my calls until he called back and then I could get to the bottom of this.

The answer came the next day. The trap was sprung and the cheese was gone: "Hi, Al. Selvin here. This woman I know . . . uh, Kathi Goldmark . . . is putting together a band of famous authors who play instruments, and they're interested in you being the musical director. If you're interested, here's her number. It sounds like it'll be a lot of fun. Talk to ya soon." Famous authors? Norman Mailer beating the shit out of the drums? Germaine Greer doing her best Diana Ross? Stephen King pounding Jerry Lee–style on the piano? This was mind-boggling. I had to know who and what. Now *I* was nibbling on the cheese: "Hi, Kathi? Al Kooper here. I got your number from Joel Selvin and I hear you've got a band together. *Who's in it?*" (Significant pause.) "Oh, really? Yeah, it sounds like fun. Count me in."

I impulsively assented for two reasons. One was that I had dropped out of the music business per se and moved to Nashville, vowing exodus from record executives. The other factor was more seductive: a chance to hang with Jerry Lee—er,

Stephen King (actually donning a guitar, so really more of a Link Wray persona), a major presence on my bookshelves, and Dave Barry, who I believed to be the funniest man on earth. And no A&R men to deal with! This sounded better and better. We would preselect the material, rehearse for four days, and play for the annual booksellers' convention in Anaheim. I could whip them into shape, I thought. Hey, could they be any worse than some of the bands I had had to deal with in a thirty-five-year career? I thought not. Shortly thereafter, *It* started.

It—not the odyssey, not the great adventure, not the Stephen King book, but the Kathi Goldmark Incurable Never-Ending Facsimile Diarrhea Attack—began the next day. My God, *I hope she has a forest in her backyard*, I remember thinking on Day Four as I scurried to change yet another fax roll. Suffice to say, this woman needed a crash abbreviation course. *Well, on the other hand, I'm certainly becoming well informed here*, I thought. *I now know the full lineup of the band, their birthdates and underwear sizes, what songs they'll be attempting three months from now, and the astrological signs of all the songwriters.* I faxed casually with my new charges and prepared for the Anaheim rehearsals.

The Anaheim Hilton is primarily a convention hotel, but many families on the Disneyland trail will take up the slack when a circus is not in town. When the Remainders arrived, the circus was definitely in town. The American Booksellers Association had mounted a frightening invasion of Anaheim: bookstore owners, publishers, authors on leashes, reps all running around frantically while I'm trying to put a band together. *The nerve of these people!* I arrived in the hotel lobby to meet for the drive to the first rehearsal at a semiabandoned cafe just off Broadway in downtown Anaheim Kathi had secured, and was startled by a frenetic "Hey, Al!" It was *him*—*the* Stephen King. The horrormeister himself sat unnoticed on a fluffy couch with a guitar case at his feet. He was out of context. No one noticed him because of the guitar case! A book convention's worth of nuisance held off by a hard-shell shield. I liked that. They were all here: my literary rockers, ready for tutoring. We drove to the rehearsal exchanging pleasantries and goofing on our common predicament.

Then came the mitigating factors. Kathi had hired an overseer / road manager to navigate the troops through all the maneuvers, and he had to cancel at the last minute to go on the road with *Van Halen*, of all things. He replaced himself with a pal named Rick Kelly, road manager for REO Speedwagon, a band not as busy as Van Halen at that time. On top of this, Kathi had negotiated a video deal with BMG, and somehow it had become Rick Kelly's job to direct the video as well as keep track of twenty neophyte rock stars. *Don't ask me!* Add a 95-degree daily heat wave to the cauldron and mix with a schedule that didn't allow the entire band to unite till the last rehearsal. My work was cut out for me.

The Nadir of Western Civilization, even with their pants on.

My style is to approach these sorts of encounters with a sense of humor, and this was certainly tailor-made for that. There were some beacons: Dave Barry was a decent guitarist, Barbara Kingsolver could rock on keyboards, and Ridley Pearson played bass in bars every chance he got. Kathi had rehearsed the Remainderettes, our female backup troupe, and they had a nice headstart that way.

There was no hope for the Critics Chorus, however. I liked that. These frustrated English majors who had been the bane of my existence when I cared about the record business were nakedly exposed as devoid of any musical leanings whatsoever throughout the show. *This is my revenge*, I smiled to myself. (Dave Marsh, one of these devos, is smiling now as he edits this book. I don't stand a fucking chance.)* Selvin, Marsh, Roy Blount, Jr., Greil Marcus, and Matt Groening kind of bellowed on cue over in the corner, and their unbridled uninhibitedness made them quite palatable. *Heh-heh. Can't wait for the reviews on* these *guys.*

Amy Tan, inscrutably in character, was the standout in the Remainderettes. She'd bitten off more than she could sing, but her bravado was intense. The vulnerability was there (and quite charming), but her sheer will to do this showed fortitude above and beyond blah-blah-blah. Tad Bartimus, an Associated Press war correspondent(!), was quite nervous, which balanced out Amy. Kathi Goldmark was the doyenne of the Remainderettes; she had played many beer-soaked evenings in her band, the Ray Price Club, at the *café noir* Blue Lamp in San Francisco. She instilled the fear of Kathi in her charges, and they earnestly approached each selection.

Stephen King was unduly nervous. Clutching his Gibson SG (a gift from AC/DC in gratitude for *Maximum Overdrive*), sweating profusely with eyes wide, he would get mini guitar lessons from Dave Barry at every lull in the proceedings.

*Smiling?—Ed.

When we began, it was very much like my first band in the seventh grade. *Do they really want to play like this in front of their friends and business associates?* Oh, c'mon, Al—you can make this better with a little work. Work? Who said anything about work? This had to be *fun*! We struggled along that first day, and at the end of rehearsal I felt a little reassurance was in order, so I gathered everyone around. The exact content of my speech has disappeared from my memory, but the gist of it was: "Gang, when we started off playing five hours ago we sucked really bad. But now, we actually suck pretty good. . . . Good work—see ya tomorrow." During those five hours, however, I began noticing that the crew Rick Kelly had assembled was concentrating on video production and not on being roadies. *This is not good*, I thought.

Barry scratches his head over a lesson with King.

Over the next four days it came together okay. Well, qualifiedly okay—okay for a book convention, anyway. Kathi had booked a cavernous C&W bar called Cowboy Boogie. The night of the show it was filled with thousands of book people and Don Henley. Marsh had invited him to review the show for the local rag the *L.A. Weekly*. I knew Henley, but he wisely avoided me. After all, I was in the enemy camp with the rock critics. No matter that I was exposing them to the bone for all to see; I was also accompanying them on guitar and organ. It was worth it. We played our little hearts out. I was real proud of my charges—they done good. There was a party back at the hotel, but a band was playing, and that was the last thing I wanted to hear at that point in the evening. I sadly bade farewell to all, and that was that, I thought.

The reason it wasn't, at least initially, was Don Henley's fault. His review was, of course, scathing. His main targets were the Remainderettes and Dave Barry's coiffure. We empathized with each other over fax lines, and even Amy's Uncle Chun got involved. Henley's pan catalyzed us. In faxland we came together again, but we had no concert to play. This became obvious to everyone, and the animals began clamoring for food.

Rick Kelly's video had become a soap opera, and eventually Kathi kind of took it over. Due to a lack of funds, focus, and hardly any usable footage, it was a sort of homemade version of How I Spent My Memorial Day Weekend. BMG kept its commitment to release it, though, and a New York City press party was formulated to celebrate the date. Plans were afoot for the band to play at the press party. I was dead set against this. After all, we weren't that good, and here were all these professional killers (reviewers), not pretenders like Don Henley, and look what *he* did to us! But the animals were gaining momentum, and it looked bleak. I had to get out of this one fast.

So here's what I did: I booked a gig for *myself* at the Bottom Line, the night after the press party. I then suggested that the Remainders open the show as surprise guests. It worked. We would *not* be playing at the press party, and the press wouldn't know about the gig until the last minute and there was no guest list for them. How do you keep a rock critic away from your show? Leave him off the guest list. It works every time.

Fulghum and Kingsolver couldn't make it. It was also financially impossible to bring Josh and Jerry in from L.A., so *my* band members filled in for them and Kingsolver. (No sub mandocellists hanging around the Musicians Union, however.)

The thing I remember most about that gig was how we filled the stage. There are fifteen or twenty of us at some points in our show, and that made the Bottom Line's very small stage feel like a subway car at rush hour, with musical instruments added. Each soloist had to push to the front when their moment came, then slink back two or three people when they were done. It was hilarious. I played four shows that night (two of mine, two with the Remainders) and was totally wiped, but the band was saying goodbye to each other at a bar crosstown and I had to attend. Fortunately, by the time I got there it was basically ending. I lay on a couch upstairs at the party and smiled. Again, sad goodbyes, but this time I knew better. These people were bound together now for a reason, not for a season. I knew the Remainders would rise again. As our good friend Don Henley once said: "You can check out but you can never leave."

So it was that one rainy afternoon in Bangor, Maine, Stephen King came upon the germ of an idea so ludicrous that he was actually able to bring it to fruition. What if, he reasoned, the Remainders did a proper tour and played in front of the real people, as opposed to the book people. You know—a tour bus, a road manager, T-shirt sales, folk songs on the bus, the works. What if, he continued, we presold a book that we gang-wrote about the tour? Only it wouldn't be about the tour, it would be about these grownups gone berserk in a steel tube with ten wheels that took them to the masses where they behaved like children. We could call it, uh, *Mid-Life Confidential, or From Acid to Antacid.* Yeah, that's it—and we use the book advance to fund the tour.

As Judy Tenuta is fond of saying, "It could happen." The mere fact that you're reading this right now is a testimony to the selfishness of twenty-three bored people. Once again, under Kathi Goldmark's steam, the Remainders machine began to roll. Before you could say "book deal," Viking was seduced by Stephen's nine-page book proposal. A booking agent was engaged and eight cities were firmed up.

In the meantime, a major contingent of the band, led by the intrepid Dave

Barry and including Steve, Kathi, Ridley, and a few friends of Dave's, booked a gig at the Miami Book Fair under the fetching moniker Raymond Burr's Legs. I was invited to attend, but I think my parents were coming to visit that weekend, or I had to pick up Madonna's clothes from the cleaners. I know one thing, though: it fired up those who did attend. The faxes flew furiously on Monday morning.

Queen Fax sent out a list of seventy-five or so songs, and we were supposed to put them in order of preference and send them back—that's how the set list got picked! Before any of us could come up with a good title for our trip, we were in possession of an official "Teen Angel" halo for our upcoming sojourn!

I looked this item over. It had a chin strap. Who is going to buy something like this? (Kathi had ordered hundreds of them.) Adults usually don't gravitate toward anything with a chin strap on it, I recalled. Oh well, there's always the T-shirts. We had our own T-shirts at the Anaheim show, with a wonderful caricature on the front and, emblazoned on the back, Dave Barry's quote: "This band plays music as well as Metallica writes novels." We signed many of them en masse, and they were sold for fifty dollars each, with the profits going to the various charities that particular gig supported. I now personally have enough Remainders shirts to go a week in costume (three shirts), unless the air conditioning fails.

For the tour we had new shirts, with new caricatures and a new slogan, courtesy of Roy: "Suspend Your Credibility!" This was a slogan I had to adhere to. These god-damn upstart authors had put together the real McCoy: a genuine rock tour with fucked-up routing, a tour bus, road manager, roadies, a sound technician, and a slightly embarrassed musical director. It's one thing to play at a book convention for store owners and agents. What do they know about music or Al Kooper? But to go out into the real world and play for real people with this amateur band might have a crippling effect on my already suspended credibility. *Well, what the hell*, I thought. *If I can play some of these Blues Project reunions and survive them, I can make it through this.* Dave Barry is actually as good a guitar player as Steve Katz from the Blues Project. I don't mean that as an attack on Steve or a compliment to Dave. It's just a fact, boys. So I decided to hold my head up like Pat Riley and put a bitchin' team on the court, damn it. That's how I felt as I boarded the plane to Boston for rehearsals.

Right off the bat, it was different from the year before. Everyone had judiciously done their homework. Kathi had the girls tuned up quite well, and the song choices were much more ambitious. I had been worried about Tad singing "My Guy" and "Chain of Fools"—well, not as much worried about her singing them as about our band *playing* them. But these writers had been doing something else at home besides churning out verbiage. They were actually almost good! We played Tad's tunes; Amy sang "Leader of the Pack" and "These Boots Are Made for Walkin'"; Stephen sang "Who Do You Love" and "Susie-Q" (the Dale Hawkins version); Dave

Barry sang the Stones' "The Last Time" and Jerry Butler's "He Will Break Your Heart"; the Critics sang "Wooly Bully" and a song from my past, "Short Shorts"; Kathi sang the Dovells' "You Can't Sit Down"; Ridley sang "634-5789" and "Midnight Hour"; Barbara even sang "Dock of the Bay" fearlessly.

This was much more ambitious and professional than Anaheim. As we rehearsed, we grew more and more confident. Breaks were spent sitting around tour manager Bob Daitz as he detailed our grueling itinerary. I was amazed at the amount of things we had to do (press conferences, radio interviews, photo shoots) besides just playing. As the end of rehearsals neared, some sales figures began to come in. We had sold out the first three shows, and in Cambridge, a fourth show was being added in the late afternoon. I was impressed, but not flattered. It had become apparent that we were in a band with the literary Beatle—not John but Stephen. Everyone knows and recognizes Stephen King, and they're usually carrying a copy of *The Stand* in their back pocket that it would be great if Steve could sign for them, 'cause they're *his biggest fan.*

Providence was our first stop. We were booked into Shooters, a converted warehouse on the waterfront. I have relatives all over Providence, and my cousins Melba and Sue came to visit with me right before the show. I had been holed up in a dayroom at some hotel and got to the gig about twenty minutes before we went on. My cousins and their broods were there and we sat down to chat. I was all dolled up in my Nashville finery (custom-made longcoat with rhinestones all over it), and here were my *mishpocheh* that I hadn't seen in fifteen years sitting and shooting the family shit with me while twelve hundred people stood out there waiting like Roman lions. It was kinda lysergic, actually. Daitz came and rushed me off as I bade my fond farewells. Reunited with my troops, we put our hands all together, gave a resounding "ARGGHHH!" and took the stage.

This was much better than I thought it would be. The set list that I'd struggled with at the hotel came together magnificently. Our tradition (after only two shows) was that Roy Blount came out and introduced the band individually. This would take four to twenty-seven minutes depending upon whether our dressing room beer stash requests had been looked after or not. In Providence, Roy was in rare form. We were in hysterics backstage, which put everyone in the right frame of mind as we walked on. We played a great show musically, and with the addition of Dave Barry's comedic improvisations, a well-rounded, *entertaining* one as well.

Of special note this first night was the debut of the "sleeper" selection of the tour, Amy Tan singing "These Boots Are Made for Walkin'." I dreamed this up one night back in Nashville when we were selecting songs for the tour. I faxed Amy with the idea and she was appalled. Her reply included a picture of Nancy Sinatra and alluded to the fact that Amy has "always hated the song."

Admittedly, I hated the song too, but the thought of Amy dressed in bondage gear and brandishing a whip, Joel Selvin trailing on a leash, tantalized me. I faxed Amy as much and she kinda acted amused by it, but remained reticent, claiming that her children's books audience would be horrified. They won't be at these shows, I assured her; no one that reads those books will venture into the upholstered sewers we're booked into. Her sense of humor was being reached and I felt there was a glimmer of hope. Anyway, as I mentioned, our touring repertoire was selected by popular vote. Once "Boots" was placed on the ballot, I knew my fellow Remainders would rise to the occasion and vote bondage—as they did.

As the tour progressed, "Boots" metamorphosed into the show-stopper it deserved to be. Amy had her whip, bondage outfit, dog leash, and thigh-high patent leather boots. But perhaps the best addition to the number was the spontaneous appearance of Roy Blount at any given moment in the song to light her prop cigarette.

Now, his actual moment to do this was right before the end, when she says, "Are ya ready, boots? Start walkin'," at which point Roy was supposed to whip out a Zippo and, cringing, light her cigarette, while all the males in the band would lie down and Amy would, in fact, *walk on them.* But the funniest part of the whole bit was that Roy would come out—every night, for two weeks—what seemed like hours before he was actually due. Finding himself onstage prematurely, Roy would begin to do what Dave Barry and I referred to as the Zippo Dance.

Conjure, if you will, first of all, the vision of Roy Blount, Jr., himself. Then imagine consumption of mass quantities of various mixed drinks that were usually in the crimson or red color spectrum, occasionally with parasols in them. Then allow for the fact that this is almost the end of a two-hour stint onstage and Mr. Blount, Jr., has nightly by this time already convulsed the entire band with his introductions, dropped trou, screamed himself hoarse, and downed much crimson liquid with and without parasols.

Ah, the Zippo Dance. Remember those little wooden men with springs in their necks that people were fond of putting in the rear windows of their Buicks? As they navigated the rougher terrain, their little heads would sway from side to side. Well, imagine one of those little men on a premium fifties Christmas-morning bongo board (if you're too young, a bongo board was a barrel in the rolling position with grooves on each end and a board over the top locked into the grooves—a sort of seesaw) in extremely slow motion. So you've got the side-to-side movement and the head bobbing of the Buick man and the added inebriation from two hours on- and offstage

King works up his nerve to adjust Tan's crooked strap. Barry drools in background.

with little to do but ingest beverages in the crimson color spectrum. Phew! That's as close as I can get to the mechanics of the Zippo Dance within the narrow confines of the English language and my comparatively short stay here on the planet Earth.

When we played Anaheim, we closed the show with Stephen's rendition of the death-rock classic "Teen Angel." Now Stephen changed some of the words to, well, sort of update the song for the nineties. His updates were met with appreciative chuckles by the audience, and it should have been so much for that. But the BMG video included the updated "Teen Angel," and the song's publisher, Acuff-Rose (a venerable and litigious Nashville firm), on behalf of the songwriter, took exception to Stephen's updates and threatened to sue if we persisted in performing them.

Ever fearful of attached incomes, we decided to perform the song in its original version, but with a spoken intro explaining our plight. I must now revert to Hollywood script style to fully convey this trialogue among Dave Barry, Stephen King, and the audience in Atlanta (where we did our best show, I thought):

Dave Barry (bottom) is not making this up. But Zippo Dancer Blount (top) definitely is.

DAVE BARRY: Ladies and gentlemen, we cannot do this next song without a semilegal explanation.

STEPHEN KING (*remorsefully*): I did something wrong.

BARRY: Stephen did a bad thing. (AUDIENCE *begins hooting*.) What I'm about to tell you is true. I'm not makin' this up. This is an old song—a lot of bands have done this song. We are the only band in the history of the world ever to get threatened with a lawsuit about the way we do the following song. (*More* AUDIENCE *hooting*.) Now, I'm gonna need your help as an audience to get us through this song in a legal, safe manner, because we could end up in big trouble. This is the truth. Now what happened is this: This is a song that is published by a very reputable Nashville publishing company called Acuff-Rose, which, as it turned out, was not real happy with what we did, and so we got in a little legal trouble. That's why it's very important tonight when you think "Acuff-Rose," you do not think the term "assholes." *(Laughter and applause from the* AUDI-ENCE.*)* All right! I wanna just ask you this as a favor to us, a legal favor. When we say "Acuff-Rose," please do not think *(points to* AUDIENCE*)*—

AUDIENCE *(screaming)*: ASSHOLES!

BARRY *(two-beat pause)*: Thank you so much for your cooperation in this matter. Thank you. Because what happened was we gave this song to Stephen to sing and, by gosh, he went and took a few liberties with the lyrics, if you can believe that. (AUDIENCE *cheers.)* Boy, you could've knocked us down with a feather!

KING: It was just a few words . . . just a few little words.

BARRY: As a result of that, Acuff-Rose—

AUDIENCE: ASSHOLES!

BARRY: —had a problem with it, and Acuff-Rose—

AUDIENCE: ASSHOLES!

BARRY: —came to us and said Stephen had to do it the right way or no way. So we do it the right way at the request of Acuff-Rose—

AUDIENCE: ASSHOLES!

BARRY: —and that's why tonight when Stephen sings this song you will at no time hear him use the phrase "vial of crack." (AUDIENCE *cheers.)* Okay? So when we get to the key point of the song, *please do not think the term (cups hand to ear)*—

AUDIENCE *(screaming)*: VIAL OF CRACK!

BARRY: Thank you for getting that out of your minds for us tonight. We really do appreciate it. *(More cheering.)* 'Cause we wanna do the right thing by Acuff-Rose!

AUDIENCE: ASSHOLES!

KING *(suddenly very concerned)*: Dave, wait! Now if I screw this up, we get sued, right? This song tears my heart out to sing to begin with. . . . *(Waving:)* Thank you, ladies and gentlemen—good night! *(He begins to exit.)*

BARRY: NO! NO! NO! *(Grabbing Stephen's T-shirt, preventing him from exiting:)* This is a hard song for Stephen to sing because it tears him up. He has to be strong. Be strong, Stephen, be strong! *(Releases Stephen's shirt and, patting him on the back à la Danny Ray with James Brown, leads him back to center stage.)*

AUDIENCE *(chanting à la Springsteen fans' "Broooce")*: STEE-VIN! STEE-VIN! STEE-VIN!

KING: *(waits for the audience to quiet, then with a synthesized choir rising behind him)*: Ladies and gentlemen, this is a song about love, death, and the senior prom. *(Beat.)* My favorite subjects.

AUDIENCE: *(His other favorite subjects begin to cheer.)*

BARRY: Be strong, Stephen, be strong. . . .

Stephen then sings "Teen Angel." For the uninitiated, the lyric concerns the singer and his high school sweetheart; their car gets stalled on the railroad tracks. He pulls her out in time, but she goes running back to retrieve what may be his

high school ring or a vial of crack, we're not sure at press time. Meanwhile, the Remainderettes and Dave Barry have donned the aforementioned halos-with-chin-straps and thrown them out in mass quantities to the nearest audience members, many of whom actually wear them. (After the first few shows, we realized these chin-strap items were not selling compared to the T-shirts and autographed pics—zero sales, in fact—so we decided to sacrifice them in a Woodstockian manner. This was a good choice, because now certain audience members got to look as stupid as we did *and* receive a free memento of their harrowing evening.)

Meanwhile, back in constitutional rights land, a small debate brewed about how to approach performing "Teen Angel" when we played Nashville, home of Acuff-Rose. We decided to do the same shtick, but we changed the "asshole" part to "no sense of humor." Now the ironic part is that Acuff-Rose came to the show not in Nashville but in *Miami*, by which time we were back in "asshole" mode. So there we were, playing to a packed gay discoful of two thousand booksellers suffering from heat exhaustion and being in a gay disco at the same time. And there the Acuff-Rose guys were, too. But because we did perform the song as written and only editorialized our humor, there was nothing Acuff-Rose could do about it. The injunction they'd obtained against further distribution of our video was lifted the day after seeing our show. I guess they didn't like two thousand drunken booksellers shouting "ASSHOLES!" after each mention of their corporate name. It was just us and justice.

For me, the truly wonderful thing about the tour was the emergence of the butterflies. Much like the pods in *Invasion of the Body Snatchers*, they looked like the same band, but inside they'd changed. Amy's self-confidence was certainly the most improved from Anaheim, where she could barely muster "Bye Bye Love." Now, whip in hand, she "punished" only the Critics Chorus, not the audience. Tad, who was very uncomfortable singing "Da Doo Ron Ron" in '92, had miraculously pulled off "My Guy" and "Chain of Fools," perhaps our two most difficult songs. And the band was handily able to play those songs, which it could never have done the year before. Stephen, who is truly the spirit of the Remainders, rocked hard on tour. I especially enjoyed his numbers because they incorporated the kind of guitar playing that is the most fun for me—fingerpicking blues in a Roy Buchanan / Robbie Robertson fashion.

The Critics Chorus used "Short Shorts" as a platform to collectively drop trou and show the sort of boxer shorts men like these prefer. Each show, I would stand slack-jawed, incredulous at what I was seeing. As a matter of fact, the first time they did it, I turned to Stephen and Dave and said: "This is the nadir of western civilization. Right here, in our show."

But perhaps the biggest surprise was Barbara singing "Dock of the Bay." It was the most vulnerable part of the show, a rare serious moment in the Peepee-Caca Revue. Barbara came center stage, the other singers exited, the band came way down in volume, and with a rare abandon and vulnerability, she would pull off this

basically untouchable song. Stephen iced the cake when he appeared, virtually out of nowhere, to whistle the chorus at the end. Between the two of them, they brought the house down nightly.

You get the picture. We had metamorphosed from a mediocre garage band to an average bar band. In our crowd, that was a big accomplishment. Dumbo's feather was relegated to the junk pile, and the Rock Bottom Remainders became a true band. And that, my friends, was no mean feat.

Ridley Pearson

CUJO MEETS THE BOOGER MAN: THE REHEARSALS

The question was this: How does a wannabe band made up of over a dozen strangers from all over the country, all with absurdly busy and conflicting schedules, practice? With only three days of rehearsal scheduled ahead of our first and only performance in Anaheim, California, how could we hope to sound any good? Answer: we couldn't.

About two months after Kathi Goldmark's call inviting me to play bass in the band, I was sent a song list and a tape of the original performances of the songs. This officially marked the first day of rehearsal for all Remainders.

Just because the Temptations performed a song in the key of E minor does not mean that an author can sing it in E minor. In some cases, not without surgery. Choosing keys depends on the vocal range and abilities of the lead singer, and occasionally on the instrumentation involved. Therefore, this tape we all received was not something we could practice to—in Bangor, San Francisco, Miami, New York, and Sun Valley—because the originals were not recorded in the keys in which we had chosen to perform the songs. Writing out the chord changes and transposing the songs to the proper keys seemed the logical way to get this act of self-rehearsal back on track. A problem arose: not everyone in the band could transpose, or as Dave Barry put it, "Not everyone can *spell* transpose."

Kathi hired a *real* musician to transpose the songs. The routine was: read and study the transposed chord changes, listen to the tape of the original (in another key), and then stop the tape and attempt the song in the new key. Trouble was, "reading" the music was a bit like sampling perfumes in a department store: written out, thirty oldies, all composed with three or four of the same chords in different combinations, start to smell the same. Things became a little atonal.

An alternative to practicing to written chord changes was to make a tape. I made just such a rehearsal tape for myself, playing the bass lines in the new key along with a drum machine that kept the proper time and even sounded a little like rock and roll. When I forgot a song, I would go back and listen to my tape and remind myself of how it went. I could sing to the new tape in the proper key. Talking one day to Kathi, who was experiencing similar rehearsal frustrations, I offered my tape. "A practice tape?" she exclaimed. The next day it went out Fed Ex to the whole band.

Rehearsal had officially begun—for the second time.

Within a week I heard from several of the gang: combined with the new charts, this tape was just the ticket. Strangely enough, we would never know if it would make us sound any better.

ANAHEIM

Because we were a band of overeager, nervous, but willing strangers, our first rehearsal in Anaheim was an odd, clumsy one, destined for a display of high volume and low abilities. We faced the terror of the proverbial ticking clock: in three days we were to be passed off as a band. Us? This was more Keystone Kops than Brill Building.

Picture if you can: a forty-five-year-old adult male, known for his humor and outrageous behavior and practiced in the art of booger jokes, turning on his amplifier, as wide-eyed as a ten-year-old with a new bike, and jumping on all the buttons attached to the amplifier via a foot pedal, instantly creating raw feedback capable of breaking glass (or coffee mugs) and sending sixteen other adults running for cover as they desperately, and defensively, clasp their palms to their freshly injured ears. Now picture Al Kooper, who cannot be described as the gymnastics type, *diving* across the rehearsal room, wearing an apoplectic expression of pure horror, and reaching the amplifier just prior to the moment when the speaker cones self-destruct. Now picture the humor-type adult male regarding

Who walks around in all these autographed sneakers? wonder the Toastpoint and the Booger Man.

his fellow band members, who are all quivering with palms still pressed to their ears. A Fender Stratocaster dangling from his shoulders, he is blushing a violent scarlet. He swallows deeply and says, "The foot pedal works."

This kind of occurrence was not uncommon. As it turned out, the equipment seemed to fascinate those of us who were (mistakenly) allowed access to it. A certain writer known for listening to *loud* rock music while he writes best-selling horror novels commonly played his guitar so loudly in the early days of rehearsal that the rest of us would casually sneak in behind him and turn it down, hoping to avoid insulting him. As it turned out, he never even *knew* we were doing it.

But volume tolerance, like musical talent, is relative. Al Kooper, who preferred his guitar to be at least *twice* as loud as any other (and louder than some aircraft), proved he has tremendous ears. He could pick out missed notes and chords in this deafening Wall of Sound, while the rest of us couldn't hear *anything*—not even our own instruments or voices. After one of us was chastised for playing too loudly or out of tune, or for missing notes, the most common reply was, "Was that *me*?" This must have proved extremely perplexing for Al, whose job it was to make us musically coherent—within three days.

Although in hindsight a lot of fun, that first day of rehearsal in Anaheim was an unqualified disaster—like turning a bunch of kids loose, unsupervised, in Toys "R" Us. Worse, at the end of rehearsal, the clock was still ticking.

On the way back to the hotel that first day, the core instrumentalists were all in the same van. Al, riding shotgun, leaned around the edge of his seat looking absolutely exhausted—trashed is more like it. He allowed a sheepish grin, commanded everyone's attention, and said, "Well, people, this may be the beginning of your musical careers, but it's the *end* of mine."

We took that as a challenge: we went drinking in the Hilton bar. (One of the Remainderettes, deciding to come to the bar in band costume, was stopped by the house detectives on suspicion of being a hooker.)

The next two days of rehearsal in Anaheim confirmed Al Kooper's genius. Song by song, he impatiently restructured everything. The weeeks many of us had spent memorizing parts, using the rehearsal tape, proved for naught—Al gave us new bass lines, new arrangements, new drumbeats. Piece by piece he rebuilt the tunes to our abilities, rather than trying to fit us into the demands of the song. We weren't going to sound like the record; we were going to sound like the song—and there's a big difference. Much of what we had committed to memory had to be unlearned—instantly. Dave and Stephen, working with chord changes, seemed to negotiate these new arrangements more easily than Barbara and I, who had worked out specific, note-for-note parts. But Al rode us with a whip, and the music began to take shape. And so did our friendships.

FIRST IMPRESSIONS

Bass players and writers have something in common, which is refreshing since I'm both: we are observers. Practiced in the art of supporting door jambs and watching a room of activity unfold, I also enjoy supporting a three-chord rock anthem with a bass line. Observation is the fodder that feeds my fiction. What would it be like, I had to wonder, to watch a room full of Dave Barry, Amy Tan, Stephen King, and Al Kooper all trying to put together a viable version of "Teen Angel"? This I had to see.

I came to the Remainders having spent the seventies traveling to gigs in a silver, custom-fitted, sixty-six-passenger Bluebird school bus complete with five bunks, a kitchenette, and an active wood stove (which more than once got us pulled over by state troopers, who pointed out that it was illegal to drive down the highway with a fire burning inside your vehicle). I accepted Kathi's offer to be the bass player more from rampant curiosity than from a desire to attempt to relive those halcyon days of bar-hopping between beach and ski resorts in alternate seasons. To this day I play music locally in the Sun Valley area with a band called the Sensational Toastpoints; when I received Kathi's music-for-literacy invitation, I answered the call.

When she called I found myself wrestling with my writing success. If you're lucky as a writer, you are developed into a commodity by your publisher. You become "a name." They move that name to the top of the book. They are selling *you*, and the reader's trust in you to deliver. As a police procedural/crime thriller writer who'd become "a name," my publishers wanted "bigger and better" books from me, "just like the last one, but different." I felt a bit confused by all of this. Instead of things getting easier with increased sales, they were becoming more involved, and I wondered if this was really what I wanted. A born-again workaholic, I had not taken a legitimate break from writing (more than two days without) for over seven years. Kathi's offer promised two things: a *four*-day break—an *eon* to me—and the opportunity to meet and work with other, more successful writers, who might both understand and be able to shed some light on this quagmire of best-sellerdom in which I found myself. Nonstop writing is a lonely existence, and more than anything else the Rock Bottom Remainders offered me a chance to meet other writers—living, breathing people who actually did what I did. Writing isn't done for a living; it's done for life. I needed a break.

One year and a ten-day tour later: forget the music, forget the shows (although it's hard to), especially forget the press conferences and the hype of being a Rock Bottom Remainder. These friendships are now hard and fast. When any fifteen adults are thrown together to form a team—artistic, athletic, doesn't matter—they bring the excess baggage of the human condition right along with them. *Everyone.* It's unavoidable. Personal tragedy, illness, divorce, emotional bankruptcy—all arrived along with the various members, and all continue to evolve. The role of band members on stage is to support each other musically, with harmony, bass lines, rhythm lines, clapping, dancing, and even cross-dressing. But the beauty of this band is the support away from the stage. We came together briefly, but we *remained* together—The Rock Bottom Remainders—supporting each other through unavoidable hardships, inevitable change, and the joys of well-deserved publishing successes. As an observer—as a participant—it is this sense of family, this warmth, that I treasure, that endears this ragtag bunch of eclectic, unpredictable personalities to me. It isn't smile for the cameras and head back home. It is hugs backstage and late-night phone calls months later. There are collisions, of course. Fifteen objects cannot move randomly without colliding occasionally. Problems—interior and exterior—surface and must be handled. This is a collection of interesting, caring, professionally successful, extremely human people. And suddenly, one day, I wake up to realize that I'm a part of it.

Go figure.

The most commonly asked question I receive about being a Rock Bottom Remainder is what my fellow band members are really like. What follows are my first impressions of the various band members, in order—as I recall—of meeting them.

ROBERT FULGHUM. Wise. Immediately comfortable to be around. No pretensions. Nice overalls—custom-made. A public personality who wears khakis, bow ties, and plays big brother daddy guru, all in one; a private man who has seen many miles and remembers most of them. Generous, of spirit and with material goods. (Left a twenty-dollar tip on a thirty-dollar dinner and said, "It's one of the only ways our society makes it easy for us to share our riches.") Folksy in appearance, but by nature city-wise and street smart. Bright-eyed. Likes to laugh and loves to sing. Tells you the weather when you call, because that shapes his moods.

Sometimes goofy, sometimes intense.

STEPHEN KING. Tall. Sometimes goofy-looking, sometimes intense. Always thinking. Very fast mind at work. Quick, witty one-liners. Side-splittingly funny, which surprised me. Sweet, gentle, and warm. Slightly impatient—he has another book to write, after all! A walking rock and roll encyclopedia—knows every rock lyric ever written. A ham. Not afraid to risk it all if it'll make the performance work. Extremely likable. He calls you on the Fourth of July, finds you at the office, and laughs because you're both type-A workaholics—so who's manning the holiday barbecue?

DAVE BARRY. Brotherly, right from the start. Funny, yes, but not that kind of loudmouthed, can't-get-away-from-it humor that makes you want to leave the party. A leader—musically, spiritually. Light on his feet. Wickedly quick mind. A nego- tiator—always able to mend the other person's broken fence. Has probably mended a good many lives in his time. Good guitarist. A walking rock and roll encyclope- dia—knows every lyric ever written. A ham. Extremely likable. Anxious—always moving. Jumpy at work. Mellow at play. Likes to share a beer and laugh at auto- matic toilets. Can get on a roll and have an entire room crawling on the floor beg- ging him to stop. But he seems to not even know how it happened. Can listen to your trou- bles and actually hear them.

"No, those other two guys are not with me."

AMY TAN. At first: quiet. Hard to get to know. Timid about her musicality—until she hears the *rest* of us. Then: articulate and intel- ligent . . . scary intelligent. Speaks up; speaks her mind. Very fast learner and completely dedicated to becoming a viable part of the band. An accomplished pianist, she passes on playing and devotes herself to singing. In Anaheim she can't project her voice, and she's terrified. One year later, she's wearing boots well up her *thighs*, walking over all the males and stealing the show. Thoughtful. Considerate. Sleek and pretty. Funny and self-deprecating.

AL KOOPER. Not so nice—at first. Gruff. Tired. Ulcerous. He has a job to do and he's the only one who understands how big a job it is. Musically famous and aware of it. A legend. But not recently. We *all* grew up with this man's music. We are in awe. But then, later: More bark than bite. He's a puppy underneath the shouting and the gesticulating. He *cares*—about us, about the need to sound the best we can, about all those things no one but he and Kathi is paying attention to. About how easy it is to look stupid up there. He's here to save us from ourselves. He's the coach. He's the boss. He takes immediate control—or tries to. With this group, it's not easy: there are too many jokes flying around. He favors Dave Barry and Stephen because—surprise!—*he* is in awe. He's human. He's a *fan*—of *some* of us. No fan of mine: he crushes me in the first two rehearsals, changing bass lines away from the originals, throwing fits, contradicting himself—actually taking the bass right off my back at one point. But he's Uncle Al—twenty years ago I wore *Super Session* down to nothing!—what are you going to do? You do what he says— and surprise: it works. Stage time: he's brilliant. Even the critics—with whom he has had many protracted battles over the years—respect him. No small feat. Walking rock and roll encyclopedia—knows every lyric ever written. (Even *wrote* some of them! Wrap your mind around that!) Does the impossible: tunes Stephen's guitar.

BARBARA KINGSOLVER. Pushed by her publisher to be six places at once. Intellectual. Studied. Like me, she's thrown off when Al abruptly changes the parts she has studied and learned so diligently. Uncomfortable with this whole *idea*, but reluctantly accepts her commitment and therefore tears into it. Speaks softly and with a slight southern accent. Private. Reserved. Nothing to prove. Nice smile, and uses it freely. Says a lot with her eyes across stage, like: "What's the next chord?"

ROY BLOUNT, JR. A natural. Likes the stage. Likes everybody. Funny. Southern drawl it takes a while to hear correctly. Nosey, in an emcee kind of way (he has to tell stories about each of us in the introduction). Humor, at his own expense. At *anybody's* expense. A very good storyteller—maybe a great one. A good traveler—the kind of guy who, after knowing him one day, you would invite to join you on a six-week tour of Zimbabwe. Or home for dinner. Women *like* Roy—quickly. Men too, but *definitely* not in the same way. He knows the single-digit hours well. He knows the best barbecue for sixty miles—in *every* city. (This begins to amaze me.) He probably sleeps in that blue blazer. Don't know *when* he gets it cleaned—or even *if*! Makes a point of rearranging his schedule to meet you in the hotel lobby on the one and only night you're in Manhattan, just because. When in the company of Dave Barry, dangerous. A real gentleman; aren't many left.

MATT GROENING. Extremely quiet and private. Humble. A giant sponge: he seems to be absorbing everything and having a hell of a good time. Quietly funny. Neat laugh. Instantly comfortable around Dave B. and Stephen. And Kathi. And a bunch of the critics. One of the three busiest persons in the band— and in *this* company, that's saying something! Maybe has the best attitude toward the band of any member. When he can't make a gig, he sends telegrams or flowers or notes, or faxes. I get the feeling he honestly misses it. He'd make an excellent neighbor—but I think his window shades would be pulled.

TAD BARTIMUS. Sister. Compatriot. Humble to a fault: doesn't know how she got here. (As if any of us do. We have Kathi to blame for that.) Timid singer, but willing to work. Squints when she laughs. Pats you on the back when she knows you're frustrated. Wishes you good luck before "Entertainment Tonight" snares you for an interview (which they later omit). Happy to be here. Happy to let the type A's run the show. She's had a bad year, but doesn't complain, doesn't let on. She hugs you if you've been quiet too long.

DAVE MARSH. Sincere. Cautious about lots of this. Understands Al's job almost as well as Al does. Maybe better. Strong, as a rule, but gentle, like all those perfect friends in the old black-and-whites. A leader, and one willing to listen. *The* walking rock and roll encyclopedia—knows every lyric (but can't sing a one). He'd give you his last five bucks—if he could find his wallet. Disheveled. Ready to voice an opinion, even an unpopular one. Talks street slang—intentionally, one gets the feeling. Likes the sneakers-and-jeans image. In fact, this band could do some endorsements for sneakers and jeans.

JOEL SELVIN. Talkative. Knows rock and roll, and is right in his element with the aforementioned encyclopedias. You can't judge a book by its cover, and you can't judge a rock critic by his hairy chest. He and the other critics form a pack. Lots of in-jokes dealing with defunct rock groups with names I'm thinking they made up just to test me. Al refers to them en masse as "the kennel"—and there's a reason for that, *besides* the way they sing (or pretend to). Joel surprises everyone by stepping to the microphone and letting it rip; he shouts, but we prefer to call it "singing with gusto." He howls a solo—"This may be a first in rock and roll," says Dave Barry. At peace with most of this. Tolerant. Wouldn't miss this for anything, and lets you know it.

GREIL MARCUS. Unflappable. Instantly friendly. A true band member despite a schedule that doesn't allow very much time. Willing, like so many of us, to make a complete fool of himself, just for the chance to be there.

TABBY KING. The generous cheerleader: shows up with presents for people, like wild ties and prom dresses for the Critics Chorus. Demonstrates medical procedures in hotel lobbies. (Performed a tracheotomy on me.) Bouncy. Bright. Quick humor, quick tongue. Calls a good song good and a bad one bad—even if her husband sang it. Friendly. Sticks a lens in your face at four in the morning and says "Surprise!" She is a surprise. Unexpected. Fits right in.

KATHI GOLDMARK. Met her first but saved her for last. She's complicated. A working musician. A walking rock and roll encyclopedia: knows all the lyrics. Knows all the karaoke bars. Knows a *lot* about people. Where to push. Where to pull. If she juggled (and maybe she does; it wouldn't surprise me to find this out: after all, Dave B.'s assistant, Judi, juggles; that Dave, he can really pick 'em), then she could keep six pins in the air at once, no problem. "No problem" might be her motto. She's a problem solver. She's tireless. Maximum overdrive. Her feistiness can and does get her into some jams, but she knows the water. She wants control of something no one can control, and yet is willing to fight most of the right fights and let go at all the right moments. She has the hardest job of all of us—even Al. Can't really know what it's like to be an author despite her job (she tours authors). Hers is a public life. Ours are intensely isolated and private much of the time. This is play for us. She, by design, must work. She works hard to keep it all together: our Remainder Mom. Band members seem to hug her first when we come off stage. Her hotel room becomes the clubhouse at every stop. She keeps us autographing T-shirts (and sneakers!), and she's intensely aware of everyone's problems, though you'd never know it. She is the Wizard of Odds. Only she knows all the real back story of this band—the illnesses, the divorces, the deadlines, the discouragement. We are here to forget real life, but Kathi isn't allowed that luxury.

BOSTON—REHEARSAL, SECOND TIME AROUND

In Boston, a year later, many of us close friends now, we had the benefit of hindsight. We had a new rehearsal tape, sent out *months* in advance. The press was not invited to rehearsal. The Critics Chorus was conspicuously absent on the first day. Al kept the numbers down and the work level up, changing as little as possible. He gave things time to develop. Maybe we lacked the Attitude from the title of our tour, but we had finally learned the Three Chords, and what a difference! When Al asked for a chord change, the instrumentalist could actually execute it! Amazing. "Try this lick." "The bass should go like this!" "More piano on the chorus." Al manipulated his building blocks. Click, click, his musical Legos fell into place. We could stand on these songs. We could even attempt—dare I say it?—*dynamics*. There was a giddy mischievousness that swirled through the room—it sounded better. Us? Was it possible? The band had done its homework, and it showed. The band *wanted* to sound good. Now we even had the Attitude.

Al's response, too, was 180 degrees from Anaheim. Following the first day of rehearsal in Boston, eyes darting nervously, he ventured, "Don't quote me on this, but I think we've made that quantum leap to palatability."

For three days we had *fun* in rehearsal. Songs came together to the point where we could try some theatrics. This was a group of intensely creative people, and we weren't lacking for ideas. We weren't lacking nerve, either. In the Anaheim rehearsals we had been polite and shy to the point of being bashful. In Boston, things began to hang out. We developed some skits to try on stage. Stephen, encouraged by Al, began ad-libbing introductions to his teenage death anthems and stopping songs to add famous quotes. Dave Barry was simmering: waiting like a rodeo bull to be let out of the gate. When performance time came, he let go an arsenal of one-liners and song introductions that floored the crowds. By overcoming some of the musical frustrations, and working off the energy of the Anaheim performance a year earlier, we were open to making it fun. And the rule of music is generally: when it's fun for the band, it's fun for the audience.

In the Anaheim rehearsal we came together as eager strangers; in Boston, as eager friends. In Anaheim, the pervasive vibe was that of a blind date; in Boston, it was more like we were moving in together. This "moving in" required a certain amount of social organization, and threw the Remainders into that rock and roll phenomenon, the group meeting.

Given this particular set of people, group meetings required a democratic format. In the rehearsal room, band members would flop into chairs, sit on dead pizza boxes and instrument cases, and start out discussing "agendas," "logistics," "schedules." Before long, we usually slipped into favorite rock memories, musical stories from the critics, and accounts of Life on the Road with Uncle Al.

But group meetings were also used to try to encourage us. Sometimes these pep talks backfired. During our first Boston group meeting, Al told us how new-and-improved we were and made his palatability speech. A few minutes later, Bob Dietz, our tour manager, having missed Al's talk, settled us down and said in all seriousness, "You have a lot of nerve to do what you're doing."

The camaraderie of group meetings inspired group huddles just prior to performances. Like a college football team, we took to all grabbing hands together and raising our voices simultaneously into a victory shout. And there was the occasional odd rejoinder. Stephen King, in a huddle prior to our first gig, bestowed upon the band these words of wisdom: "Birds always shit before they fly." I climbed up on stage scratching my head.

Rehearsals, which included a liberal amount of impromptu group meetings and many shared meals, became the nesting ground for the performance band to come. The real test, of course, came not in rehearsal, but once we were out on the road.

SOUND CHECKS: REHEARSAL ON THE ROAD

One thing going for us was that, as authors, we all had toured extensively (bookstores, speaking engagements) and were somewhat accustomed to the rigors of the road. But rock and roll is quite a different experience from the standard book-promotion tour. The nights are extremely long. The bus rides are exhausting because of no sleep. The food is God-awful, grease-endowed, formerly frozen roadside fare (although the band seemed to flock to fast food). And a week can, and does, seem like both a month and an hour at the same time. Rehearsal had prepared us musically for the tour—but not for the Road.

Sound checks are road rehearsals. Al was constantly working on songs in sound check, pointing out problems, working out stage logistics—every stage is different in size and shape. Many of us looked forward to sound checks because these road rehearsals were private performances in huge empty bars and halls with giant sound systems and roadies running around at your feet doing things with wires. They were performance foreplay.

Al would change the set lists, bringing in songs that we hadn't touched since Boston, keeping variety in the act so we wouldn't be complacent, keeping us on our toes. Amps would break down. The drum kit would need work. And the monitors would *always* feed back, with Hoover, our sound man, shouting from the back of the hall, "That won't happen tonight!"

It didn't—Al saw to that.

Sound checks are places to get the kinks out, the chance to exercise your musical muscles after seventeen hours in the bus; to try a new harmony, or to figure out how to get out of Amy's way when she comes at you with her whip in hand. There's no audience, so mistakes are free. In one song, "Short Shorts," the critics decided to drop their pants. We worked on this difficult move in sound check. But what came out of that rehearsal, and what stayed with the show for the rest of the tour, was that Hoover stood on his chair and dropped his pants as well, shaking his butt and grinning ear to ear. In several of the upcoming venues we managed to arrange a spotlight on Hoover during this boxer-shorts solo. Unlike what's typical in rock and roll, even the sound crew was part of this band.

SHOW TIME: REHEARSALS FOR REAL

Performances are exciting, seat-of-the-pants moments of group creativity and inspiration. Instead of writing alone in a room with a word processor, we found ourselves on stage, making music with friends, roadies trailing wires, and *thousands* of Stephen King fans waving copies of *The Stand* above their heads. It was an electrifying experience, emotionally, physically—in every way.

The true test of any band is staying power. Can the fifth gig in as many nights sound as good as, or better than, the first? When the fifth gig comes fourteen hundred bus miles later, it is not uncommon for a wet-behind-the-ears rock band to fold from sheer exhaustion. The Remainders somehow avoided this disaster. The Anaheim Amateurs became Road Warriors of the first order, but the transformation had its price. Physical exhaustion was written on every face by week two. People walked slower. They talked less. They smoked more. At one point the bus had been quiet for ten minutes or so—a rarity—and Stephen, reading a novel, called out, "Unclear antecedent!" and went back to the novel. The band was too tired to even hear it, much less come up with a reply. Things had changed.

As the tour progressed, without any discussion, the gig became the band's single focus. Energy built slowly over the course of the day, awakening from slow-motion mornings to the frenetically charged seconds just prior to curtain call. Band members seemed to be storing energy, saving themselves. They dozed when they could find a few extra minutes. They ate. If they felt sick, or something went wrong at home, when curtain time came it was Show Time: the smiles lit up, the volume knobs were set, and the costumes glittered. We were "on." Nobody was going to take a performance away from us. If anything, as we died physically on the road, the performances improved: the music sounded better, the theatrics came together. New jokes. New lines. New acts. Transvestites wearing halos—this act had it *all*.

Ten minutes after the performance: excited exhaustion. We were living rock and roll. This was what we had come here for.

With the reserve lights on our fuel tanks lit, we were, by day, too close to empty. But not at curtain time. We became, in our own small way, professionals. Not rock star professionals, but Remainder professionals. We took it on the road, and it worked. Every show was sold out. Every performance earned an enthusiastic encore.

Three days of insanity in a soundproofed room with padded walls on the Boston waterfront had developed into a hall filled with cheering fans, boogying and bouncing to the rock of yesterday, singing along, chanting, stomping. Wanting more.

We all had our own reasons for joining the Remainders. I didn't find answers to a lot of my questions, but I somehow ended up with fewer questions than I started with. To a person, we came away with more because of this experience. What started in rehearsal ended as rock and roll fantasy. Over a dozen strangers formed a unique family, and audiences down the East Coast learned what earplugs are really for.

Roy Blount, Jr.

I HAD THIS REVELATION IN THE CREW RV

We are probably the only rock and roll band that ever caught itself watching "MacNeil/Lehrer" in the bus before a show. I don't recall any nudity at all, though I suppose I took some showers. As for drugs—although Al would occasionally hark back to an earlier time by saying something cool like "When does this effect take stuff?"—it was predominantly a natural-high tour, except for beer, occasional beta-blockers, and the inevitable natural lows.

Furthermore, the only intellectually honest answer to the question "Did you inhale?" is surely "Oh, *man*, just then, when you said that, you know?, it was like—waitaminute, waitaminute . . . this is so . . . I could actually see . . . your . . . lips . . . *forming the words.* . . ."

Either that or "I don't remember."

But I must have. Inhaled. Some kind of fumes must have seeped into the crew's RV from a passing time machine or something, and in an unguarded moment I must have inhaled them.

Roy Blount, Jr., auditions for the Fabulous Thunderbirds lead singer slot, much to the amazement of Miami guest critic Leonard Pitts, Jr. Imagine how either of their fathers would react.

Mouse and Tan.

Because it is not just my lingering sense of rockgodliness (the after-halo, if you will) from an evening in concert, nor is it just the ongoing effects of the bottle of dark rum that the crew and I scored some hours ago from a friendly D.C. barmaid, that I am feeling at four in the morning hurtling down the interstate between Washington and Philadelphia at increasingly excessive speed in the crew's RV with the side door open—and Mouse's entire body is leaning out over the blur of the pavement, and he is magically (well, it's a natural function, but everything seems more magical than usual) making water, and I am holding him by the belt with one hand, and what am I doing with the other hand? Holding on to the RV, I suppose, or to the rum, or to Hoover. It all has to do with our becoming blood brothers.

Mouse looks like Cheech. Hoover wears plaid Bermuda shorts and wildly patterned shirts whatever the weather. They are the only thing cooler than musicians: roadies.

I am fifty-one years old.

I am doing this because I can't sing.

Now, months later, I am listening to "Land of 1,000 Dances." I stop writing—stop thinking, indeed—to sing along. I still can't get all the *na-na-na-na-na*'s right.

I just can't. I have tried and tried. Along about the eleventh *na*, I am *na*-ing when I shouldn't or else not *na*-ing when I should. Every time. This was also true when I was up there in the thick of the Remainders in front of hundreds of paying customers. Not *na*-ing when others all around you are *na*-ing is not so bad. *Na*-ing when all others are between *na*'s, however, drives a stake into the soul. There is nothing quite so naked as a solitary, trailing, insupportable, resoundingly wobbly *na* hurled all alone through a loop in the rhythm into a mass of wriggling communicants.

I am by no means altogether L-7. (Though to be sure I did not know the meaning of the term until I asked about it during rehearsals of "Wooly Bully.") I have spent the night in the room where Bessie Smith died; I have abused three different substances (four, if you count sausage patties) with country-music immortals; I have shaken hands with Ray Charles (he feels up your forearm if you're male, on up further otherwise); I can hump and write verse that scans; you'd think I would be better than I am at musical things. But I'm not.

I believe I can *listen* to it as well as the next person (assuming the next person is not a musician or a rock critic), especially in a car (ideally, the next person has her bare feet on the dashboard and her skirt hiked up to get the good of the AC, and we're tooling along down a back road eating ribs); and I love to watch

Musical director Kooper is glad he doesn't have to figure out what to do with all those halos.

Girrrrls!

Yes, a true reflection of our multicultural spread.

good dancing as long as there is any pelvic thrust to it or it's Fred and Ginger or somebody who can jump really high (ballet otherwise, I don't know—I *like* swans, but . . .).

As a matter of fact I love to *sing* something I feel secure with, like "The Old Rugged Cross" or "My Baby Loves Western Movies" (if I am alone or among others who are singing-impaired). And if I am drinking and sweaty and the floor is fairly crowded and nobody expects, you know, *steps*—hell, I'll get out there and dance, too. I've danced in France, I've danced in Peru, I've danced at Delta Burke's wedding—I don't believe there is a single major ethnic group (yes, smarty, including Native American—anyway half, she said) that doesn't include at least one woman who has danced with me and seemed to like it all right at the time. I danced with a Peruvian woman to some kind of Inca music I think it was. That's where pisco sours come from.

And yet after I danced on stage in Anaheim—well, let me say that I don't know why I danced on stage in Anaheim. It wasn't premeditated. I felt like dancing, and Lorraine was up there and she was our choreographer and she didn't stop me, and I didn't try any splits or anything, and there were all these *other* book people out there dancing in front of us, and they looked like they were having fun. And I had had seven beers. And when I did start dancing with Lorraine, nobody gasped at my presumption.

And after the show I'm bopping onto our veritable by-golly-miss-molly tour bus, whooping and beaming and drenching wet, and *People* magazine has just taken our picture (they didn't run it, though), and somebody—I forget who, now—says to me, as if it might be something I'd get a kick out of hearing . . . he says to me:

"Dave Barry says you are the world's whitest person."

I am sensitive about my race. Once at a party for a Spike Lee movie, a man looked at me and said, "So this is a real Caucasian," and I decked him. Or I would have, if he had been white and if I hadn't realized that what he'd actually said was, "So, this is a real occasion." Hey, I spent the night in the room where Bessie Smith died! Did I say that already? Okay, here's something: I once posed as Reggie Jackson's parents. Interviewing him in his Cleveland hotel room, I mentioned that I had not been able to get a room there myself. "I'll get you one," he said. "I'll call the manager."

"What will you tell him?" I asked.

"I'll tell him you're my parents."

I was no more than a few years older than Reggie, and I was only one person, to boot. Yet (and I just acted the way I usually do in hotels) no one connected with the hotel questioned my bona fides, not even Housekeeping, who was herself African-American. And then of course—well, I could tell you a lot of other stories of fitting right in with black culture, but you might come back with something to the effect that those are the kind of stories only a white person would tell.

What I came back with on the bus there—when informed that Barry regarded me as a flaming whitey—was "That's the pot calling the kettle . . ." And then I sat down and tried to improve on that in my mind. "That's the sepulchre calling the golfball white" was the best I could come up with on the spot. But *then* it came clear to me that what Dave actually probably said was that I was the world's (Quietest . . . ? No. Lightest? No. Brightest? Oh, well, no, probably not. Tritest? Well, I should certainly . . .) *tightest* person, which is of course good in soul-tinged rock and roll—means, you know, together. I like it tight like that, you know.

Hey, Dave Barry is my man. When we run into each other on the street he says "Home" and I say "Money" and he says "Word." When "60 Minutes" interviewed me about Dave, trying to dig up dirt the way they do, I covered for him. I said I had *heard* he used to run a string of whores out of Lauderdale but I couldn't swear to it, they ought to check it out further—sending them down a blind alley, see. Well, "60 Minutes" wanted to know, isn't somebody as funny as Dave bound to have a whole lot of anger bottled up inside? Here was my response: I asked them why people never ask extremely angry people whether they have a whole lot of humor bottled up inside. (A rhetorical question. Everybody knows that if you ask extremely angry people whether they have a whole lot of humor bottled up inside, they will hit you, at times with a bottle.) Okay, then, isn't anybody as funny as Dave Barry bound to have a dark side? "60 Minutes" wanted to know. To my knowledge, I said, he is so bereft of a dark side that the moment he wakes up in the morning after a night on a band bus, he is already funny. *Cheerful.* Maybe that is his dark side, I said. They didn't use any of my interview.

If *I* had a dark side, I would have been willing to believe that Dave Barry is the kind of person who goes around calling people white, and therefore I would have told "60 Minutes" that Dave Barry is too white to have a dark side. After all he *is,* unless I am greatly mistaken, the son of a Presbyterian minister, and he grew up in the town where *Reader's Digest* is headquartered, and you don't see Ben Vereen playing him on TV, do you? But what I do have, deep down inside, is an honest side. So I have to admit that Dave is one of many Americans who have—*in the musical sense*—more rhythm than I. Therefore he is—*in that limited sense*—more colorful than I. He can play a musical instrument, and he can sing. According to Kathi, he is even an excellent dancer. I venture to say he is no James Brown, nor even any Dionne Warwick. But, okay, when it comes to dancing, when it comes to singing (as opposed to when it comes to eating, say—don't get me started on sweet potato pie), compared to me Dave Barry is a fucking rainbow, I guess, okay?

While we are on the subject of color, let me say a few words about my college reunion. I am a member of the class of '63 of Vanderbilt University, in Nashville, and our thirtieth reunion was on the weekend of the Remainders' Friday-night concert there. The belief arose among the band that we were in fact going to play *at* my reunion. On the face of it, what could be cooler than showing up at your reunion with your rock band?

Any number of things could be, as it turned out. The reason colleges bring their alumni together, of course, is to get money out of them, not to pay their rock bands' expenses. The alumni association tried to get us to pop in at the all-classes Saturday-night affair: "You'd just have to play for twenty minutes," someone told Kathi, "and it would be in front of two thousand people."

"You don't understand," Kathi said. "We'd rather play in front of twenty people for two thousand minutes."

It did seem vaguely feasible for some of us to show up and do a number for my class's Friday-night cocktail party. But it would mean my organizing this appearance, and I don't like organizing more than—in fact as many as—one person. "Oh, hey," I kept saying, "I'll just drop by my reunion by myself."

But various of my band brothers and sisters would answer no, no, they couldn't let me down. It was clear to them that this meant a lot to me. It wasn't clear to me.

What with one thing and another, Amy, Dave B., Tad, Kathi, Lorraine, and I showed up at my reunion, which was at the palatial home of Mrs. J. C. Bradford, *née* Tootie Robertson, a beautiful and greatly hospitable classmate of mine. My bandmates fanned out into the crowd, eating, drinking, and saying God knows what—both Amy and Lorraine, I believe, informed various members of my class that they and I were married.

Amy never saw so many tan pants, but Tad, who'd been to Vietnam, remained unfazed.

Now I would be extremely proud to be Amy's and Lorraine's spouse in any company. It wasn't that. It was that—well, think how strange a college reunion is anyway. You are suddenly surrounded by what appear to be the parents or possibly the grandparents of people you last saw thirty years ago wearing togas. I mean they were wearing togas thirty years ago. Now they are dressed like upper-middle-class Southern white parents or grandparents.

And if you leap into the middle of your classmates' cocktail party trying to look, yourself, sort of like a rock and roll person, and bringing with you several people who actually do look sort of like rock and roll people (let me say this: almost anybody can look sort of like a rock and roll person at *somebody else's* class reunion), your classmates look at you as if to say, "Why is this guy who looks like he must be old Roy's father or grandfather acting like such an asshole?"

I went to the bandstand, stammered apologies to Jimmy Hunt and Tommy Wells (who were a lot cooler than me in college and who always play at our reunions, so that we can dance like white people, but we Remainders had showed up during their break, while they and most of the crowd were going through the buffet line), and my bandmates reassembled with odd looks on their faces and we did a quick rendition of "Leader of the Pack" (my part: *brmmmm . . . brmmmm . . . BRMM-MMM!*) as three or four of my classmates held plates full of ham and looked at us oddly, and then we fled into the night.

Blount to dog: "Look what happened to this band's last pet."

"So this is your crowd," said Amy as we drove away, I sobbing into my folded arms.

"It's not my *crowd*," I snuffled. "It's my *class*."

"I never saw so many people," said the ironically last-named Amy, "in tan pants."

Let me just say that it is wrong to judge people by the color of their pants, and leave it at that.

I have never denied that I often wear tan—khaki—pants myself. They go with anything and are easy on the road. But that is not the nub of the issue.

The nub of the issue is that I can't do the *na-na-na-na*'s. And if you can't do the *na*'s and you're in a rock and roll band, you have to compensate somehow.

It helped, of course, that I was a member of the Critics Chorus. Ordinarily the function of a music critic is to remind people that a show is supposed to be good. The role of the Critics Chorus was roughly the opposite. At about the time when the audience was beginning to think, "Hmm, this band isn't all that bad. So why isn't it good?"—that's when we of the Chorus would come out and drop our trousers or erupt into an even-more-cacophonous-than-might-have-been-expected rendition of "Louie Louie," and the audience would relax and think, "Oh, that's right, these are just authors."

Even amidst the critics, however, I felt insufficiently harmonious. I will never forget the moment right in the middle of our Bottom Line gig—between choruses, in fact, of "Double Shot (of My Baby's Love)"—when Joel Selvin turned to me and said, "There are *notes* in there," and went so far as to hum them to me out of the side of his mouth. I actually did get the timing of "It wasn't wine that I *had* too much of . . ." pretty darn near right, quite often; but *notes*?

I will also never forget Mouse and Hoover testing the sound in Atlanta, Mouse going "Two"—not "Testing, one, two," but rather, in this really cool way, just "Two"—and then saying, "Can you hear me?" and Hoover answering in the affirmative, and Mouse responding, "Well, we better do something about that—this is Roy's mike."

My pipes aren't the worst of it. Well, all right, they are. But my singing wasn't the only thing that made me feel out of place. The other thing was this: not only am I no singer, I am also no rock critic.

Now I daresay that very few people around the world are kept awake at night by the anguish of not being a rock critic. But how would you like to have it on your conscience that you once tried to *pass*, in public, as a rock critic? Years ago I did serve for a while as *Esquire's* country music reviewer, and I have written about Elvis (saw him in the coffin), but my rock tastes run almost exclusively to songs written and performed by people at least as old as I am. Since I am the senior Remainder except for the rarely-in-evidence Fulghum, I was frequently lost even during our *conversations about* music. I wouldn't know Van Halen if I ran into him in the street. Dave M. and Greil would be arguing the fine points of Abba or something and I would be reminded of how at sea I felt in the Army, listening to people talk about asthma, I thought, but then learning that they were in fact talking about ASMER, an acronym for I had no idea what.

Then there was the audacity element. I can imagine being a wild Lester Bangs kind of rock-crit *writer* (I would call my posthumous collection *Horseshoes and Hand Grenades*); but when Dave M. came out in his bustier and wig, with blood all over him, and I looked at him openmouthed, he said, "I can see that we have different ideas of rock and roll."

Do you realize how uncool it is for one rock critic to look at another one—for *anybody* to look at a rock critic—openmouthed?

And surely a rock critic should know a little bit more about the nuts and bolts of kicking out the jams than I do. Once during rehearsals I swung into a quick little air-guitar riff and somebody told me I was holding the pick wrong. It wasn't true, but I had to stop and think.

Frequently, in the Critics Chorus, I was reduced to doing air doo-wahs.

Fortunately, my primary role in the band was not musical. I was the emcee. I introduced us.

Have you ever walked out onto a stage and looked down at several hundred low-groaning, garnet-eyed, transcendence-hungry, brewski-swilling music lovers who are tentatively hunching in place, emitting soft little judgment-reserving yips, wearing *Faster, Pussycat! Kill! Kill!* T-shirts, teetering back and forth on the cusp between flatline and frenzy, and counting on you to make them commence flinging themselves about like cartoon animals and yelling the yells of rebel angels and screaming the screams of Mrs. Bobbitt throwing away her husband's penis—and your job is to *say a few explanatory words*?

I have. So that my work in this connection not be lost forever, let me set down here—as best I can in cold print—a typical introduction.

"HEY! It is true that we are writers. But this is not going to be a literary experience. In a literary experience, you are not even supposed to move your lips. We want you to move *everything you've got*! We are *tired* of being writers! We are here to kick ass! WAAAAAAAA!

"But first [Note: this was a tricky segue] let me *WAAAAAAA* tell you—hey,

WAAAAAA—about this band. We may not look like we can even *read* anymore, but that is because we—hey, *WAAAAA*—okay, we may not look like it, we hope, but we are a bunch of authors. *HOLD ON!* Some time ago an idea was born in the mind of a rockin' little author-escortin' lady named Kathi Goldmark, who *ANYWAY, WAAAAAH*, she decided to form a band, and she needed a musical director.

"*YEAH, RIGHT*, she *WAA* [Note: from here on out I will just let you assume frequent *WAAAA's*]—she, Kathi, went out and found just the right man. Having no

more worlds to conquer in the field of music, he had taken up work in the rice fields, but she bought him some new teeth and persuaded him to inculcate in her ragged band of authors the two essential truths of rock and roll: one, be at one with the Oneness; and two, never do number two on the bus. Here he is—he used to play with Dylan and Hendrix, now he is playing with . . . me: Al (He May Be a Mother-You-Know-What, But We All Call Him Dad) Koooo-per!

"And next, a novelty portion of the band, two actual professional musicians. We thank God for these men, and so we believe will you. On single and double saxophone, fresh from your video store, where he may be rented as a performer in *Buckaroo Banzai*: Jerry (Check It Out) Pee-ter-sonnn! [Incidentally, Jerry told me the entrance he always dreamed of making was to fix two saxes up with butane so they would be belching flame as he glided onstage by means of a cable over the heads of the audience. "That would be cool," he said. "Then what would you do?" I asked him. "Play good," he said.]

Jerry Peterson levitates: "Check it out!"

"And on drums, one of the best drummers in Los Angeles, which ought to make him *mayor* of [whatever town we were in], a man who not only keeps the beat but also sends the band little soft erotic messages on his skins: Josh (It's Talkin' to You Daddy) Kel-ly!

"And now, getting into authors proper, a man who will soon be immortalized in a sitcom, so get a good look at him now before he starts to become Harry Anderson—on lead guitar, Dave (His Mind May Be Full of Boogers and Dog Poop, But His Heart Is Full of Love) Bar-reee!

"And on rhythm guitar (and if he is a little bit off sometimes, remember that *Elvis* died of arrhythmia), a man who we have learned in late-night bus discussions is the only person in America who was *not* subjected to ritual Satanic abuse: Stephen (and Still the) Kingggg! [Note: I did not see this myself, but Mouse told me that once while Steve was singing "Teen Angel," a woman standing at the edge of the stage squirted lighter fluid onto her long fingernail, lit it, and held up her finger like a candle.]

"And on bass guitar, the author of so many spine-tingling thrillers he thinks he's brave enough to stay in tune alongside Stephen King: Ridley (He Do Know Diddley) Pear-sonnnn!

"And on keyboards, the author of *Pigs in Heaven*, and all I can say is that us guys up here have been accused of being pigs and she sure looks like heaven: Barbara (She May Be the Answer to Stephen) Kiiiing-*sol*-ver!

"Let me say that if an element of what may appear to be sexism enters into this show, that is part of our nostalgia thing."

And on occasions when they were with us I would add, "On mandocello, Robert (But Then I Forgot It All in Grade School) Fulghum" and "On tambourine, Michael (Whoever Heard of a Man Named) Dorris" and "On piano, Jimmy (He's So Fi-fino) Vivino."

"And now a portion of the group that is especially dear to my heart, because I am in it: the Critics Chorus. Also known as the Rough Consensus. At the risk of sounding critical myself, let me say that we do not sing all that harmoniously. But that is because we do not feel it appropriate to operate in lockstep. Some of us will be moving to the beat and others not; some of us remembering the words and others not; but always we will be upholding the true spirit of rock and roll—that is to say, we will be pouting, bickering among ourselves, trying not to show how insecure we are: in short, acting like teenagers.

"The man who introduced rock and roll to the Bay Area: Joel (If You Rearrange His Name It Spells Nelvis) Sel-vinnnn!

"And now, author of a book that is sure to render all other book-length studies of 'Louie Louie' obsolete, Dave ('I'll Say Fuck tha Police If I Want To') Marrrrsh!"

"And now, standing before you with his hot-typing fingertips still atingle: Greil (Elvis Is Dead in My Book) Mar-cusss!

"And now—clap loud so he doesn't have a cow—Matt (Happy Families Are All Alike) Groeninnng! [Note: I tended to whip through the individual critic introductions pretty quickly. No one in the audience ever complained.]

"And now as Guest Critic . . . [whatever local music critic joined us for that show—for instance, in Atlanta my friend John Huey, who is not a critic but who had heard every note Al Kooper ever recorded and whom I was able to introduce as the only living author of Sam Walton's autobiography].

"And now, yet another group of the band, and this one is the best because it has the most makeup on—the women, or, as we call them, the Remainderettes.

"The author of *Trinity's Children*, a person who has covered foreign wars for AP but she sure don't moooove like a war correspondent: Tad (Just a Tad *Tooo* Bad) Bar-ti-musss!

"And we are joyously lucky to have with us tonight, as vocalist and also as our Rhythm Dominatrix: Amy (If You Can't Stand the Heat, Get Out of *My* Kitchen) Tannnn!

"And now, the spiritual mother of us all, a woman who—I'd like to make this clear, because last night I didn't enunciate sufficiently and therefore may have caused her some embarrassment—what I meant to say was, the person with the best *breath-control* in the band: Kathi (the Queen of the Book Tour) Gold-marrrk!"

"Now! At last! ["Let's go, come on," the band is muttering behind me.] It's time to give it up! Turn it loose! Suspend your credibility! For the Rock [here I made a fist] Bottom [here I did a bump] Re-mainnn-derrrs!"

And we swung into "Money."

And sometimes I came in at the right time on "That's . . . what I want!" And sometimes I didn't.

Even when I went out to light Amy's cigarette on "These Boots Are Made for Walkin'," I—well, I think I cringed and cowered like a champ, frankly. But I could never quite get down exactly which verse it was that I was supposed to go out and start cringing and cowering on.

So, see, what I had to do was, I had to outflank all the musical people. I announced that I would hang out with the crew.

Hoover and Mouse both live in East L.A. They work with Carole King and Jackson Browne and Los Lobos and Crosby Stills and Nash.

"Hoover is a god" is what Dave Barry said about Hoover. Hoover's real name is Chris Rankin. His *father* is a rocker, Kenny Rankin. Hoover has been on the road since he was thirteen. His mottos include "I'm easy, but I'm not cheap" and "You can't miss wakeup call if you don't go to bed." He was officially the sound-mixer/stage manager. "Hoover's lifting board DATs," someone technically versed would say, and we author/rockers would say, "That is so cool."

Ringers and roadies: Josh Kelly, Jim England, and Mouse.

We knew we were cooking pretty good when we would look over at the board and Hoover would leave off mixing us ("polishing the turd" is how he put it) and start dancing. Or he could mix and dance at the same time.

I guess it was in Boston that Hoover came leaping onto the bus—he tended to *bound*, like Tigger in *Winnie-the-Pooh*, only in a cool way—and cried: "Tonight—the second set— That was the shit, man!" And leapt off.

"Is that good?" said Dave Barry. (Dave Barry the arbiter, you may recall, of non-Caucasianism.)

"Yes," I said. You don't say (this is perhaps one bit of *useful* knowledge that the reader can carry away from this book), "That was some good shit." Not anymore. You say, "That was the shit."

"It's so hard to keep up," said Barry.

Yes. So it is a good thing that *somebody* was bold enough to ride with the crew.

Mouse's real name is Danny Delaluz, but he is said to have a passport in the name of Mouse. He was officially our drum and keyboard tech. Personally I feel that Mouse was—what is maybe even cooler than a god? An oracle, maybe. Mouse would say, "You guys have become the best touring garage band in America," and we'd say, "Oh, gee, thanks, Mouse, really?" And he'd say something affirmative, perhaps in street Spanish, and then a little later we'd start trying to imagine a touring garage, and we'd wonder.

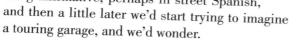

There *must* be a whiter man somewhere.

When we came into Miami a policeman charged with brutality had been acquitted and Mouse said, "Scattered unrest. It'll get worse. They turned the cop loose and now they're letting you guys sing."

Just before we went on stage that night in Miami, Mouse suddenly appeared before my face and blew smoke into my mouth. I had never had an experience like that before. "I didn't want to waste it," he said.

Earlier, while chatting with Matt backstage, I had noticed a great-looking young woman at the stage door and I said to Mouse: "Get that girl for Matt and me."

Kidding, you know. Doing a mock-rocker number.

The next thing I knew, there she was.

"Here she is," Mouse said.

Matt, a firmly married person, ran. There is no other word for it: he *ran*. And yet you did not hear anybody accusing Matt of being white.

"I, uh . . ." I said to this extremely smashing young person of roughly one-third my age. Younger than my daughter, she stirred in me Oedipal feelings: I was afraid that somehow or another I was going to wind up sending her through college.

She looked baffled.

"What did you say to her?" Al asked me later. "Well, I . . . tried to be nice to her." Al burst into satanic laughter.

When he worked with one band, Mouse said, they would divide the dance floor into a grid and a band member would say, "Blonde, B-4," and Mouse would get her for that member.

Well, hey, she was with somebody else. I daresay Mouse would have had him thrown from a speeding RV for me, but I didn't want to impose.

So, but, anyway, I did hang out with the crew some. I interviewed our bus driver, Dave Worters, who drives for Aretha. Actually we had several bus drivers, including Bob Dannic and—in Washington, I think it was—a man who looked exactly like

Muddy Waters and was named Mr. Quick. And Kathi told me of Jerome Anaton, who drove for Steely Dan years ago when she was traveling with them, and who doubled as their emcee. He had the idea that Donald Fagen was a guy called Stevie Dan. They would take Jerome aside and say, "It's *Steely* Dan, and that's the name of the *band*," and Jerome would go out and say, "And now, Mr. Stevie Dan, or whatevah."

Dave Worters—this doesn't have much to do with rock and roll, but I found it interesting—told me about bachelorette parties. A group of young women will hire him and the bus for four hours, during which time they will drive around to their friends' houses to show off the bus, and they will stop by a liquor store, and then the women will go into the back of the bus and Dave will cruise up and down the interstate while they try on lingerie for each other and sing and giggle and flash truck drivers. Bachelorette parties.

Here's something that does have to do, at least tangentially, with rock and roll: in Philadelphia after the show a woman came up to Worters as he guarded the bus, and said, "I'm a language arts teacher and I will do anything I have to do, right here, if you'll get Stephen King to sign this book. I promised my fourth-graders." But Dave, a professional, declined.

Another thing Dave told me was that he took his young son along on a trip with Aretha and her band, from Toronto to Buffalo to Boston, in hopes that the boy would develop an interest in music. The boy came out of it wanting to be a bus driver.

I came out of the Remainders tour wanting to be what I thought I was before: a reporter. A reporter, however, has to take halfway-coherent notes. You don't think I was enough of a paleface to do *that*, do you?

I do remember Hoover telling me, as we hurtled through the night in the crew RV, that it was his job to *make things right* for us, the band, whether we were the shit or not. That's the pride of it, which sustains the crew through the long hours of setting up and indulging whims and tearing down: serving the music *as if* it were the shit. "It all comes from making things right for my father," said Hoover, son of a star. It was almost a religious statement.

I also vaguely remember Mouse telling me, "You're playing for the illiterate? That's *me*. You're playing for me, man! *I* can't read!" But then I *distinctly* remember Mouse reading the entire set list to me in Miami, letter perfect, right after he blew me that smoke.

Was I also supposed to cover our road manager, Bob Daitz? All I can say is that he had a deft way of asking, in passing, how many beers I had had before the introduction the night before (I moderated thereafter), and that he said a really funny thing in Providence: he was talking to a woman on the phone, and he put his hand over the receiver and said, "Her name is Sidmel—sounds like two uncles."

Can it be that I have come this far without mentioning *Tabby*? And her transverse colon massage? Well, plenty of others will mention Tabby. Yo, Tabby. And Carole and her cockpit story. . . .

I am losing the beat, aren't I? *Na . . . na-na-na*—no, *na-na, na. . . .*

I'm winding it down, I'm rag-ending around, I'm putting off the climax, the final *naaang, naaaaaannng, n'naang'nang, ng'ng'ng'eeeng n'nang'eeeeeerang'n'nang 'nggggg . . . b'dum WOMP.* The revelation I had in the crew RV.

Whoot, here it is. The most astonishing thing that happened in the crew RV was this: after I held Mouse out over the highway by the belt, it was my turn to be held out over the highway by Mouse, and hey, maybe I can't sing, but I will usually do something crazy. Maybe I won't do it right, but I will take a shot at it.

But I just said no. I didn't need to pee, I said, which was true, but that wasn't it—I probably *could've* peed, if it had been a doctor's office.

It wasn't that I didn't trust Mouse, either. Mouse's sense of humor was subtler than letting me splat facedown on the interstate at ninety miles an hour.

I could say that I didn't trust my belt. But that wasn't it. It wasn't the whole white thing, either. (I might mention in passing that white bread is served in the best black barbecue places. I might also mention—do you know what Barbara told me as we were saying our goodbyes? "You're okay for a white boy." Maybe she said that to all the boys, I don't know.)

No, the reason I declined to round out the blood-brother rite with Hoover and Mouse was this. Right there in the crew RV, on my once-in-a-lifetime rock and roll tour, only hours after surging around onstage *inside* the music (it's a wonderment, being up there in the middle of the music, like being inside a forest fire that you're helping, however modestly, to spread—and you're actually working with someone who has a soul patch, not to mention the author of *Mystery Train* and a sinewy bewigged little Chinese woman with a whip), I came to this truly weird realization: that I could imagine being—and living with being—fifty-one.

Na.

Joel Selvin

THE CRITICS CHORUS

By the third show, Dave Marsh was wearing women's clothing onstage. The Critics Chorus appeared headed in the right direction.

It wasn't full drag, just Amy Tan's leopard-print robe he wore when he carried away the leftover barbecue ribs from the somewhat incongruous southern restaurant downstairs at the Cambridge lesbian bar where the Remainders were appearing. Marsh slipped quietly, if not unobtrusively, onto the stage while Steve King sang "Teen Angel." Just as King reached the touching, sentimental part about his girlfriend expiring in his arms, Marsh tapped him on the shoulder, handed him the remains of his dinner, and muttered some dire imprecation along the lines of "Here, Steve, this is all we could find of her."

Nobody really understood the bit, but at least we were on the right track.

Having spent virtually all of what could laughingly be called my adult life employed by a major metropolitan daily as a critic, figuring the role of the Critics in this rock and roll burlesque came easy to me.

The night the Remainders snuck into New York's Bottom Line as an unannounced opening act to Al Kooper—the band's second-ever performance; talk about not paying your dues—the only Critics that could make the show were Blount, Groening, and myself. The stage was a postage stamp, and we wound up sitting in the dressing room when we weren't singing our background parts, which, Blount pointed out, amounted to little more than singing the song titles.

Sensing no small bit of confusion mixed with abject fear in my colleagues, I turned philosophic. "The Critics are the heart and soul of the Remainders," I said. Groening and Blount looked puzzled.

"Without us," I continued, pointing toward the stage, "those people out there are merely mediocre.

The Critics Chorus, Unplugged.

Groening only looked more bewildered, but Blount caught my meaning immediately.

"I see," he said. "We drag them down just enough to where they are truly awful."

Critics are no more popular at rock shows than umpires are at baseball games, maybe less. Umpires, at least, serve some obviously purposeful function. Most people seem to think critics are as useful as tits on a priest. Fans hate them. Performers only like them when the reviews are good. The rock critic is often the lonely voice of dissent in a sea of acclaim.

Nobody in the Critics Chorus possessed any discernible musical skills. None could sing, play an instrument, or so much as hum with any approximate melodic content. Kathi Goldmark's perverse notion of including a cadre of critics in the legions of the Remainders was a cruel joke, either on the audience or the critics themselves. Nobody is sure which to this day.

The first day of rehearsals in Anaheim, it was obvious we were in deep poo-poo when I had mustered all my meager skills and managed a passable vocal performance on "Louie Louie." Passable enough, at least, to convince the other poseurs in the band that I knew something I didn't.

But when musical director Kooper sauntered over next to me after a particularly wretched run-through of "Land of 1,000 Dances" and confidentially allowed that he wanted me to contribute a specific harmony part—"What I need here is a fifth" were his actual words—a shudder of panic rippled through me. These people actually expected me to commit music?

Buffoonery was the only acceptable answer.

In Boston, the Critics didn't even show up until the final day of rehearsals, what Critics would be making the whole tour anyway. Greil Marcus wasn't hooking up with us until the final three dates, and Matt Groening couldn't make it until the last show in Miami, although his floral tributes, witticisms attached, would dog our every show.

So, with songs to be practiced, parts to be learned, and taskmaster Kooper running a taut dress rehearsal, Marsh and I went for a walk. Talking about the inconsequential things that friends who haven't seen each other in a year do, not trying to catch up on every event that had transpired in our lives in the interim, we strolled around the vast, ugly industrial area surrounding the warehouse where the band was stationed.

We instinctively understood—and, in fact, explicitly discussed—our role as troublemakers, playing hooky from Kooper, looking to be noticed in our absence. Marsh expressed some apprehension toward the rapidly upcoming enterprise, which was understandable but nevertheless kind of cute coming from someone so surly and cynical.

I suffered no such anxieties, not even fleetingly—no brain, no pain. I had a fatalistic attitude. It was not a question of our being any good. I knew we couldn't be any good. Ray Charles is good. My wife the professional singer is good. We are the Remainders. Even worse, we are the Critics Chorus of the Remainders. We aren't going to be any good. Of course, I was going to embarrass myself. I'm not merely being modest, although I have plenty to be modest about.

That out of the way, there was really nothing to worry about. Marsh and I returned to the studio, slightly disappointed to learn nobody really missed us. Marsh stretched out on the couch and took a nap.

The Critics section had two songs left over from Anaheim, "Double Shot (of My Baby's Love)" and "Louie Louie" (The F.B.I. Version). The rest of our participation was limited to some slight gang vocals—"vocals" may be too strong a term here—on a few numbers like "Money," "Gloria," and "Land of 1,000 Dances." It was not an arduous role; it was entirely expendable. We amounted to little more than some extra window dressing on an already crowded stage.

But Goldmark devised a truly wicked scheme to co-opt the local press along the way. She invited one or two key critics in every city we played to serve as guest members of the Critics Chorus. The pair of locals that turned up at the first show in Providence showed how insidious her plan was. Not only did one of them pimp the show with a big splash in that day's paper—and we needed the help, since the show was running opposite the final episode of "Cheers"—but both made it immediately clear they were puppy-dog-eager to get up onstage and make idiots out of themselves alongside us.

While tactically inspired, the scheme also served to underscore the basic level of competence necessary for the Critics Chorus; after a brief run-through at sound check, *anybody* could do what we did. It also made our end of the stage untenably crowded, especially when we were called on to lie down and have Amy Tan walk over us during the finale of "These Boots Are Made for Walking."

Our level of musical prowess helped ease the burden of the more skilled amateur musicians in the group. If somebody wanted to laugh at the idea of writers playing music, no need to chuckle at Dave Barry as he fumbled his way through a semicredible lead guitar part—not when the Critics were available. Even our own bandmates showed no mercy. Al Kooper was lolling on a bed, holding forth to the book reviewer for the *Washington Post*, when, with playwright's timing, I walked into the room as he said, "Nobody in the band's really musically incompetent." The place busted up.

At the second show on the tour, in Northampton, I started burnishing the out-chorus of "Louie Louie," which was turning into one of the set pieces of the act, with a ragged, unmusical scream, a long, arching blast as loud as possible, attention-getting plain and simple. For me, it fit the mood of the piece as performed by the Remainders, raucous and completely untrained, informed only by the energy behind it. At the first show, I glanced up after the display to see Dave Barry staring at me, agape in utter shock. Perverse pride coursed through my chest.

We were singing a "dirty" version of "Louie Louie"'s lyrics, a rock and roll Rosetta Stone that Marsh discovered in the FBI files while researching his book on the subject. On top of not making very much sense, this version had several prominently placed vulgarities that helped draw distinction to the performance.

Later, when I overheard Barbara Kingsolver complaining about the racket— "They come to the show and all they remember is 'Louie Louie,' " she sniffed—I completely understood her objections. Quietly, she is probably the most gifted musician in the lot, and her careful, scrupulous vocal that tiptoed respectfully through "Dock of the Bay" was one of the most musically accomplished performances the 'Mainders managed. My raw-throated eruption was a clear affront to anyone with genuine musical sensibilities. But it did get noticed. What did it matter that I sounded like Andy Devine the next day?

All along the way, our fellow members of the press evidenced zero interest in the Critics Chorus. Dave Barry, yes. Amy Tan, maybe. But as long as Steve King was available, everybody was happy. "Stephen King, Others Killed in Crash" went the joke on board the tour bus. But our fellow band members accorded the Critics full respect, a kind of fascination born of not really knowing what to make of these mysterious, apparently useless professionals who somehow managed to make a living. The lengthy, droll band introductions with which Roy Blount brought the Remainders, one by one, up to the stage every night were an in-house favorite, the band crowding around the wings in whispered quiet to hear what he would say, especially after the night in Northampton, where, after one beer too many, he introduced Kathi Goldmark as having "the best tits in the band."

Marsh was routinely deferred to by his band colleagues on questions of censorship, which came up frequently since one of the charities the Remainders were supporting in every city was the fight against censorship. "Of course, after you hear this, you might think this is an argument *for* censorship," said Dave Barry, introducing "Louie Louie" one night.

The imp inside Marsh, in fact, was struggling to escape his churlish exterior almost from the start of the trip. Not only was he making wry wisecracks at every opportunity—who wasn't?—he was growing increasingly obsessed with stunts he could pull onstage while the other band members were performing. He stalked Steve King, getting further and further into cross-dressing with virtually each show. He expressed his distaste for Dave Barry's habit of passing out earplugs to the audience when the Critics took the stage for "Double Shot" by ramming two of the rubbery pellets into his nostrils. "Why not?" Marsh countered. "The music *stinks*, too."

Being the least-well-known Remainder never bothered me. It actually kind of amused me. Nobody came up to me with copies of my Ricky Nelson biography to sign. Fans approached Marsh occasionally, but Blount was zip for signed copies on the tour, too. One woman did stop me outside the Bayou, where the band played in Washington, D.C., and asked me to sign a newspaper ad for the group.

"Who the fuck is this?" asked King.

Before I was out of earshot, she puzzled over the signature and turned to her friend. "Who the fuck is this?" she asked. On the other hand, so many people waited outside the clubs for Steve King, we began joking about "those rare *unsigned* copies of *The Stand*." Maybe all these other authors were having a fantasy of being rock and rollers. My fantasy was that I was a best-selling author.

In Philadelphia, Blount, Kathi Goldmark, and I wandered away from the riverfront outdoor nightclub the band was playing on some ostensible errand. We headed in the direction of South Street, wisps of the Orlons song dancing in my head, and found ourselves in some strange and terribly old neighborhood, full of restaurant-supply stores in three-hundred-year-old buildings. "What is it with this city and all these flags?" I wondered aloud, as we walked past a building that proclaimed itself home to a flag company.

"I don't know," said Blount. "Betsy Ross and all that."

"Really, she was from Philadelphia?" I said.

"I think so," said Blount.

We took three more steps and there was another ancient house festooned with flags. Signs outside identified the modest dwelling as the Betsy Ross Home and Flag Museum. Oh.

With Goldmark getting nervous about being away so late (she lacked the Critics' constitution for irresponsibility in the face of a pending performance), we negotiated a cut-rate fare with a horse-drawn carriage that happened by and returned to the scene of the crime in this wonderful conveyance. Fortunately, road manager Bob Daitz was on the deck of the boat parked next to the club that served as our dressing room—he was actually looking for Goldmark, so our return did not go unwitnessed.

Daitz brought a certain authentic rock and roll road-trip ambience wherever he went. He was like a native guide, giving out with the rock patter, the snappy lines, always with an answer for everything and a tool for anything the occasion demanded. After more than a dozen years with Sammy Hagar, he has undoubtedly become inured to just about anything. Traveling with a busful of authors in search of a real "rock" experience didn't give him much pause. He was first up, last to go to sleep, ready to flip a cigarette in his lip from his waist at the drop of a match.

Daitz talked about sitting in with the band on congas at the tour finale in Miami. He had played in salsa bands before getting honest work in the music business. We told him we'd like to have him join us, but first he would have to stuff a sock in his pants. "For something like this," he replied, "I'd have my wife Federal Express my dick back to me."

We gave press conferences at every stop, and they developed into a routine. Arrayed on bar stools, the band members would exchange quips with the press, who paid no attention to the Critics. In Atlanta, we woke the morning following the twenty-two-hour bus ride from Philly, piled into a couple of vans, and headed downtown to the Hard Rock Cafe, where we duly inscribed a cheap acoustic guitar for display on the hallowed walls. Everybody enjoyed a semiliterate framed letter from Fats Domino discussing his lack of interest in "rapp" music, but the press conference was typical:

This press conference turned into a Christopher Cross Demolition Derby.

PRESS: Do the Rock Bottom Remainders have backstage groupies?

DAVE BARRY: We try to get 'em, but they won't come out voluntarily. We've been hiring them. Our groupie budget is kinda low, so we're not getting top quality. At times, they get a little angry at us and throw their walkers at us and stuff like that. We're an old band anyway. For example, at this moment, I'm wearing Dockers. We were actually offered an endorsement by Dockers, but we decided to go with Hair Club for Men.

STEVE KING: The good side of that is that we're relatively disease-free. Dave is the guy who checks.

DAVE BARRY: These are the Critics. When the Critics were in high school, they would get together and go (*snaps fingers*), "I thought that was pretty bad."

PRESS: Do you tune your own instruments?

AL KOOPER: What do you mean "tune"?

DAVE BARRY: Which ones are the instruments?

KATHI GOLDMARK: No, you see, they tune them at the factory.

DAVE BARRY: We don't even change chords.

STEVE KING: I know that Dave Barry has written whole columns on "I Am I Said," but here we are in the damn Hard Rock Cafe and they got a Christopher Cross gold record on the wall. We may be a lame-shit band, but we never did anything like "Sailing." And here they've got his gold record on the wall. Now it's true that it's outside the ladies' bathroom. But somebody ought to ask the hard questions of management. What the hell is Christopher Cross doing in a Hard Rock Cafe? He is a fern bar. Christopher Cross is a living fern bar. There. That's it. I feel better. I'm glad I said that, and you can quote me.

PRESS: What are you donating to the Hard Rock Cafe? What's going up on the wall?

KATHI GOLDMARK: The guitar.

STEVE KING: I can tell you what's coming down.

DAVE BARRY: We have one thing we'd like to say in closing, one message we'd like to give to the people of Atlanta, besides that they should come tonight to the Roxy to see the show. But aside from that, we have one song that we feel expresses how we feel about literacy and just about every other issue in the world, and that includes Bosnia. Here's how it goes . . .

ALL OF GROUP (*singing in rough approximation of harmony*): Sailin'.

A few of the band members repaired to the television studios at Atlanta's WAGA-TV to appear live on the noon news. The poor news reader assigned to interview the band never had a chance.

TV PERSONALITY: You have a show tonight. Tell us about that.

KATHI GOLDMARK: We're going to do about an hour and a half of old rock and roll, most of which will be us performing the same song at the same time. I'm going to pass the mike over to Dave, so he can tell you more about the guitars.

STEVE KING: But before it goes over to Dave, we're also going to tell you that we're at the Roxy tonight, tickets still available, so come out by the billions.

DAVE BARRY: We've gotten so good technically that sometimes, by the time we finish with a song, many people in the audience are able to identify it in only two or three guesses.

TV PERSONALITY: I understand there's a video in case people just want to take this home and enjoy the moment forever.

DAVE BARRY: I want to stress the video angle here, as opposed to the audio. We don't recommend actually listening to this tape so much as just looking at the tape.

TV PERSONALITY: Amy, real quickly, what did they have to do to get you to do this?

AMY TAN: Chains. Blackmail and chains.

Tabby King and wardrobe mistress Lorraine Battle spent a far more productive morning, haunting some sleazy downtown women's clothing stores, where they drummed up a bridal grown and bustier for Marsh, who by now had taken to donning Kathi Goldmark's wig for his ritual interruption of King's "Teen Angel" finale. That night, covered in catsup, Marsh made his resplendent entrance, only to have King wrestle him to the ground, feign a full physical assult on the hapless Marsh, and then turn back to the audience. "Sometimes they come back, you know," he said.

Whatever overcame Marsh the other members of the band watched grow in him incrementally as the trip progressed. When a blissfully ignorant Greil Marcus finally turned up that afternoon in Atlanta, the rest of the band was busy doing a sound check at the Roxy and Marsh was backstage trying on his new trousseau. Marcus made his way backstage and turned a corner in the wings only to come face-to-face with Marsh in the white wedding outfit, hairy chest exposed. "I might have expected something like this," Marcus deadpanned.

Sweaty and practically giddy, the band assembled after the Atlanta show in the downstairs dressing room, a large basement with no windows, hugging each other and slapping each other's backs. It had been a great show. The crowd started out sitting on the floor in front of the stage and wound up standing, screaming, yelling and, in general, giving a good impression of genuine pandemonium. Whether they were simply being generous, showing us some southern hospitality or going along with the spirit of the event didn't matter. To the band, it felt like an authentic triumph.

After a half-dozen shows and ten days on the road, including two long bus rides, the band, if it was not entirely seasoned, had attained a certain amount of seasoning. And the show was beginning to go over big-time. Even the Critics were getting the crowd off. "Double Shot," our introductory number, was a surefire crowd pleaser, although that early in the set, the audience didn't really know what to make of us. But we had taken to performing as our second number "Short Shorts," in a kind of tribute to Maestro Kooper, who began his career as a member of the Royal Teens and hit the charts with that idiotic song in 1958. Or, at least, that is what Kooper claims, and it's hard to imagine anybody making up a credit like that. With the Critics providing the call to the Remainderettes' response, we improvised a few lyrics of our own: "Who *eats* short shorts?" And the Remainderettes answered, "Eat *my* short shorts." At which point, we spun around and slowly pulled down our pants to reveal garish, stupid-colored underwear, then danced through the instrumental break like that. With our pants down around our ankles, we hobbled back to the mikes, finished the final chorus, and bunny-hopped off stage like complete fools. Of course, the audience loved it. That's how they wanted to see their critics.

We were hot. We were happening. We were on the road, headed for Music City U.S.A. to perform in a steamy bunker called the 328 Performance Hall. Guest critic Jay Orr of the Nashville *Banner* took Greil Marcus and myself on a spin through the sites, including a stop at the George Jones Gift Shop. You never saw such refrigerator magnets. Back at the hall, the band attracted some distinguished backstage visitors. Roy Blount attended his college reunion that night, and one of his Vandy pals, who happened to be a former governor of Tennessee, turned up, a charming gentleman, even if he looked somewhat out of place in his suit and tie at this dingy hell-hole. Wayne Kramer of Detroit rockers MC5 called on his old friend Dave Marsh.

Barry and King decided to lighten up the Acuff-Rose abuse in view of the publishing firm's elevated station in Nashville. Even so, the show went over the top. Flushed with the intoxication of our newfound prowess, I took to the microphone as Dave Barry paused to adjust his tuning. "David Crosby tunes because he cares," I told the crowd. "David Barry tunes because he can."

At the end of the show, I stood by the edge of the stage. My anonymity allowed me to pass through the crowd without being accosted. But tonight someone was screaming my name from the front row on the other side of the barrier—some long-lost acquaintance, I thought. But no, it was a fan. "Hey, Joel," he hollered, once he finally got my attention. "Is it true Todd has to hire Keta to get a good review?"

Ah, the magic of bootlegging and the obsessiveness of Todd Rundgren fans was at work. The previous fall, Rundgren had appeared at a benefit concert in my honor and joked to the crowd that night that in order to earn my good graces, he had to hire my wife, Keta Bill, to sing backgrounds on his recent album. Now, months later, someone was repeating his wise-crack to me thousands of miles away. I had been recognized, complete with details of my personal life. A heady warmth stole through my being. For the moment, at least, the Remainders seemed to be the center of the world.

So off we winged to Miami, Steve King flying coach for the first time in ten years or more, to visit our grace on the American Booksellers convention, our performance sure to be a highlight of the grubby little sell-fest. Even the Palladium, the South Beach gay club where we would be performing, appeared regal, a large, well-maintained theater crowned by balconies. An electricity hummed through the room that afternoon as the band alternately ran through some numbers and signed an apparently endless stock of posters and T-shirts. We were no longer a ragtag troupe of writers, pieced together haphazardly in an Anaheim basement and hoping to struggle through an hour's performance at a cowboy bar. Now we were road-tested soldiers, ready to play the conquering heroes. After mowing down civilians who'd paid real money, not publishing-company expense accounts, to buy tickets all along the eastern seaboard, wouldn't these book-convention patsies be little piranhas in a barrel?

Selvin finally finds that Double Shot.

At the ABA press conference, the Critics Chorus was introduced as "the Rough Consensus" and "the League for the Singing Impaired." "Their goal is to make us look nearly marginal," explained Dave Barry. "I mean the rest of us, by contrast."

Stalwart bassist Ridley Pearson, who studied his music sheets and practiced his parts on his own in hotel rooms during the tour, admitted to the press conference that if he watched Barbara Kingsolver's left hand carefully, he knew when to play his bass. "That's crap," said Steve King. "He's looking down the front of her dress."

Dave Barry quoted Roy Blount as describing the Remainders' music as "hard listening." Blount admitted that when he came on the tour, he was a writer, and now he couldn't even read.

"We have a lot of inside writer-type talk," Barry said, describing the atmosphere on the tour bus. "Like I'll say to Steve, 'Steve King, where do you get your ideas?'"

"I'll say, 'Dave, buses—what a subject. Is that funny?'" said King.

"It's just nonstop writer talk on the bus," said Barry.

"Dave will say, 'You want a real horror story, you oughta see where I work,'" said King. "It's technical talk."

My wife flew in from San Francisco for the weekend. She was not amused. Keta works every week, singing sixties soul songs in a sequined dress in a professional party band or cooing blues and jazz with her own trio. She is a journeyman craftsman, a highly talented vocalist who labors without enormous fanfare, bringing humble entertainment to the parties of the corporate world, like a doctor in the ghetto. It didn't strike her as funny to see a bunch of witless half-musicians—or in the case of her husband, nonmusicians—enjoying the aroma of stardom, even on the relative basis the Remainders enjoyed it. In fact, I think the congratulatory atmosphere pissed her off, although she did a good job disguising her disgust.

With the town flooded with other authors, backstage now attained a near-luminous aura. Opening the show was a well-intentioned skiffle band composed of two Brit best-sellers: gentle, gray Ken Follett and Douglas Adams, a hulking, grinning behemoth. They warbled the Beatles' "Blackbird" with more enthusiasm than precision, managing, instinctively, to catch the spirit of the Remainders. Erica Jong paid her respects. The foremost imprimatur of what the Remainders meant in Miami was the presence of Larry King, who was to introduce the band. He oozed snake-oil-salesman charm and cozied up to Steve King, who, as always, displayed an admirable tolerance for ass kissing.

Roy Blount bought a Rastaman hat and shirt from a store around the corner from the club. My wife brought the tuxedo shirt I had had tie-dyed specifically for the Miami festivities. Matt Groening finally showed up, sporting a Ren and Stimpy T-shirt. Barbara Kingsolver, after missing the Atlanta and Nashville dates, returned to the fold. Robert Fulghum, the forgotten Remainder, arrived, mandocello in hand. All present and accounted for at the gala denouement.

Hit the spots, light the lights, strike up the band. It only remained for my dear wife to bring me back down to earth with a thud. Once again, regaled by Roy Blount's glowing introductions, we sang our small part—"That's what I want"—and danced like Temptations on crack (Blount often said critics do not dance in lockstep) before dashing offstage after the set-opening version of "Money." The die was cast. The show was under way; our final glory unfurling.

As I rested on an equipment box, my head purring with the splendor of the moment, Keta emerged from the crowd. Did she want to tell me how great I looked? Did she want to compliment my practiced microphone technique? Was she going to gaze star-struck into my eyes, her love renewed at the sight of the father of her child sparkling in the spotlight? No. She prodded the roll of flesh under my shirt. "At least you could have sucked it in," she said.

Keta Bill demands that her husband suck it in—to little avail.

Amy Tan

MID-LIFE CONFIDENTIAL

As the daughter of hardworking Christian immigrants, I was given little opportunity to cultivate a misspent youth.

Ours was a family that rarely went on vacations; during the first sixteen years of my life, we took only two, one when I was six, one when I was twelve, and both of them three-day trips to Disneyland. Most of my summer vacations were spent in Bible classes or in school cafeterias, where I wove lanyard, or planted sweet peas in milk cartons, or made maps of South America out of dried kidney beans, split peas, and lentils. Common amusements during my childhood included riding my bike around the corner, going to the library, mowing the lawn, staring at the candy counter, feeding leaves to caterpillars that eventually died, or watching cocoons that never hatched.

I count as the most memorable moments of my life those that were laced with heart-pounding terror—times when I was so scared out of my wits I could not even scream. For example, when I was two, my mother took me to a department store where I saw one man without limbs and another with legs as long as ladders. When I was three, I stood outside an apartment window and heard the echoing screams of a girl my age whose mother was beating her nonstop in the bathroom. When I was four, I desperately clung to the rails of a hand-pushed carousel, forever it seemed, until I let go and landed facedown in the

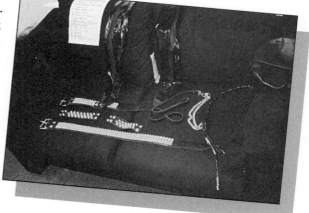

No fun, no freedom. The road to bondage is paved with Nancy Sinatra records.

sand. When I was five, a nurse in a hospital yelled at me for wanting my doll to accompany me to the operating room. When I was six, I stared at a playmate lying in a coffin, her hands crossed flat over her chest. When I was seven, I watched people's skin blister and foam in the movie *The Angry Red Planet*. When I was eight, I flew down a hill on a boy's bike only to realize, at the bottom, that it had no brakes. When I was nine, I caught a snake in a creek—and the scary part was *not* telling my parents that the snake had slithered between the seats of the Rambler right before we drove to the airport to pick up my grand-aunt Grace. The last experience also counted as one of the most fun car rides I ever took.

Actually, the word "fun" was not commonly used in our family, except, perhaps, in the following context: "Fun? Why you want have fun? What's so good about this? Just wasting time and money." In our family, "fun" was a bad f-word, and its antonym was "hard," as in hard work. Things that were hard led to worthwhile results; things that were fun did not.

Another bad f-word was "freedom," as in "So, you want American freedom to go wild and bring shame on your family?" Which brings me to another f-word, "friends," those purveyors of corruption and shame whose sole purpose in life was to encourage me to talk back to my mother and make her long to go back to China, where there were millions of girls my age who would be only too happy to obey their parents without question. The good f-word, of course, was "family," as in "go to church with family," or "do homework with family," or "give your toys to your poor family in Taiwan."

Lest you think my parents were completely feudal in their thinking, let me add that they did adopt some important American precepts—for instance, the notions that "time is money" and "a penny saved is a penny earned." As a consequence, they also were very fond of the word "free"—which should not be confused with the other word "freedom," or the like-sounding "free" uttered in useless expressions such as "free time" or "free to do what you want." I'm referring to the sort of "free" that conveys valuable ideas, such as "You are free to go to summer school because they don't charge us any money there."

Actually, I exaggerated in saying we never had fun. My parents did allow certain versions of *family* fun, like walking around the campus of Stanford University, a form of entertainment that was not only free but served to remind me of a destination and a reward second only to getting into heaven. Both rewards could be attained *only* if I listened carefully to my parents, meaning no boys, no pizza, and of course, no rock 'n' roll.

A few months before my fortieth birthday, I found myself suffering from a bad attitude aggravated by chronic neck pain—symptoms that are common among authors who are on book tour. In my case, I had been on the road nationally and overseas for the better half of a year. The irony is, most people think that when writers go on tour they're having loads of glamorous and exciting fun. Those people have good imaginations. As a touring author, I had lost mine.

I was now spending the productive years of my life not writing but eating hot dogs at airport chuck wagons and obeying signs to "fasten *your* seat belt while seated." I was depleting supplies of brain power trying to figure out which city I had awakened in or how to act spontaneous as I answered the same questions ten times a day for twenty days at a stretch.

Although happily married, I was spending more nights alone than with my husband. I had been sleepless in Seattle, Cincinnati, St. Louis, and Boca Raton. In hotel beds, I would obsess over dumb answers I had given that day, how inarticulate I had sounded, how I was a complete disgrace to American literature. After reviling myself, I would listen through thin walls to what sounded like a woman having her tonsils removed without anesthesia, to a man who was either auditioning for Falstaff or suffering from explosive gastrointestinal problems. To help lull me to sleep, I would recall science facts—for example, that the biggest source of room dust, something like 99.87 percent, is sloughed-off human skin. I would imagine years and years of skin particles from happy and sad strangers who had slept in this very bed, who were now recirculating in the very air I breathed.

This was my mental state when I returned from my latest book tour. This was my attitude on November 6, 1991, when I heard the fax machine churning out what was sure to be a request to do yet another author appearance.

It was from Kathi Kamen Goldmark, the media escort who'd taken me to numerous book-related publicity events around the Bay Area. As I can best recall, her fax said something to this effect: "Hey, Amy, a bunch of authors and I are putting together a rock 'n' roll band to play at the ABA in Anaheim. Wanna jam with us? I think you'd have a lot of fun."

I pondered the fax. Do I look like the kind of writer who has time for a lot of fun? As to singing in public, could there possibly be anything more similar to a public execution? Furthermore, how could I, the author of poignant mother-daughter tales, do something as ludicrous and career-damaging as playing in a rock 'n' roll band? Amend that to a *mediocre* rock 'n' roll band.

Two minutes later, I faxed Kathi back my answer: "What should I wear?"

The very next day, I began exercising my middle-aged body back into stamina strength. And soon after that, Kathi and I went on a shopping spree at Betsey Johnson, the choice of every respectable fourteen-year-old. We perused the sales racks and tried on a half-dozen skintight dresses. There I found it, spandex and sequins, a version of my lost youth, also known as Every Mother's Worst Nightmare.

Being a rock 'n' roll singer presented only one small obstacle: namely, the fact that I couldn't sing. I am *not* being modest. My mother once took me to a voice teacher when I was thirteen. She thought I could learn to accompany myself

Liberace-style on the piano. The voice teacher had me sing progressive scales: "Do, re, mi, fa—*oops*." After twenty minutes, he gave his verdict to my mother: "My dear Mrs. Tan, your daughter has no vocal skill whatsoever."

Suffice it to say, I woke up one night, about two months before our first gig in Anaheim, drenched in sweat. I called Kathi the next morning. "Kathi, Kathi," I panted. "Kathi, I can't sing at ABA."

"Oh no! A conflict came up in your schedule?"

"I mean I *can't sing.*"

Kathi's brilliant solution was twofold: I could practice singing into a live mike at a sound studio that belonged to David Phillips, a friend of Kathi's who was reportedly a very sweet guy. Second, I could overcome stage fright by performing at a karaoke bar filled with festive patrons who, Kathi assured me, couldn't even hear me above the clinking din of cocktail glasses.

At the sound studio, it took me forty minutes before anything resembling even a squeak came out of my mouth. My vocal cords were literally paralyzed. David, as promised, was a sweet guy—a sweet guy who also played in a real band called the Potato Eaters. Plus, he was cute. I had been sort of counting on humiliating myself in front of a dweeb.

As my lips moved voicelessly next to the mike, David would cast knowing but worried looks at Kathi before gently coaxing me for the twentieth time: "Okay, that was a good try. We'll just . . . well, try it again."

At the karaoke bar, I sang with horrible stiffness, but was comforted to find I wasn't the only egomaniac foolish enough to think I could sing publicly. The following week, I left for my vacation in Hawaii. For five hours a day, I sat on the beaches of Kona, wearing headphones while singing harmony on "Mammer Jammer" and lead on "Bye Bye Love." To an audience of porpoises and turtles frolicking in the waves, I sang my heart out, loud and strong, bouncing my head in rhythm to the background instrumentals Ridley Pearson had recorded for the benefit of the musically disadvantaged. My husband later reported that whenever beachcombers came within earshot of me, they retreated with the same deft haste people employ for avoiding sidewalk hell-and-brimstone preachers.

When I was fourteen, I used to go to the beach on the weekends, supposedly to recruit kids for Christ. That was the only way my parents would let me go. By then my hormones were raging to sin. I was no longer content to sing hymns in the church choir as my only excitement. I fantasized shrieking at the top of my lungs while running down the beach—not too quickly, of course—as lanky bad boys chased me, threatening to pick me up and toss me into the ocean. The real boys did not chase me. Nor did they accept my offers to come to a "youth fellowship shindig."

Every afternoon, while practicing the piano, I mourned that I was not a popular girl. I was not the kind who got invited to after-school garage parties where 45s were played at top volume and 7-Up was laced with vodka. I hated myself for being perceived as the "good girl," unlike the "bad girls" who ratted their hair, slouched around in their fathers' white dress shirts, and stole nail polish from K Mart.

That same year, I actually discovered something good about my parents, and that is that they didn't know a thing about bad words, not the real ones at least. While they forbade my brothers and me from saying "gosh," "darn," "gee," and "golly"—those being variations of "God" and "damn"—we could utter "bitch," "pissed off," "boner," and "hard-on" with impunity. My parents were blissfully ignorant as to what those words actually meant. And because English wasn't their native language, they didn't catch on to puns, either. My older brother, Peter, had bought a Fugs record, and when my mother asked me what this word "fug" meant, I said it stood for "happy-go-lucky," and that "fug you" was an American way to greet someone. Well, it was.

By using my parents' naïveté to my advantage, I discovered how to be a popular girl. For one thing, I ran for freshman class secretary, which my parents interpreted as my natural Christian desire to do public service. To increase my very slim chances of winning office, I painted butcher-paper banners with the following campaign slogan: "Amy Tan Has Sec. Appeal." As I already said, my parents didn't understand puns. But the school's vice-principal did. Just as I had hoped, he ordered the banners to be torn down, which then incited protests of unfair censorship from not just the freshman class but *all* the students. In short order, my name became widely known.

This photo will do nothing for Tan's children's book career.

To clinch the election, I made a campaign speech in which I promised to raise money for school dances through the sales of kazoos, which I knew students were not allowed to play on campus. In my speech, I passionately reasoned that there was no rule against the *possession* of kazoos. "Stop censorship," I said. "A vote for me is a vote for kazoos."

I'm happy to report that I won the election and kazoos became the ubiquitous symbol of freedom waved at every basketball and football game. Unfortunately, my newly elected social status did not confer upon me actual sex appeal. Instead, I became the confidante to girlfriends who confessed that their lips were bruised from kissing too much the night before or to boys who wanted to know what to do when girls got mad at them for going too far.

As freshman class secretary, I also had to help organize the dances. I argued persuasively with my mother about the necessity of my going to the dances as well: "Come on! I have to be there to make sure everything goes like planned. Like, you know, what if someone doesn't pay to get in? That's like stealing. Of *course*, I'm not interested in actually *dancing* with a stupid boy. Of *course*, I'll get my Ph.D. before I even *think* about dating. Duh, I'm not *that* dumb."

Before going to the dance, I used masking tape to shorten my dress and I asked my girlfriend Terry to lend me her tube of white lipstick. Neither measure had any effect on the boys. At the dance, I stood near the punchbowl, mortified as Terry, then Janice, then Dottie were asked to dance. The flick of a rotating mirrored ball beat into my brain with hypnotic force: "Nyah-nyah . . . nyah-nyah . . ."

At the end of each dance, Terry did her best to console me: "Did you see that creep who asked me to dance? The one with the great big zit at the end of his chin? I was freaked he'd drip it all over my shoulder. And then I could feel his boner pressing into my hip. God! I'd rather die a virgin. . . ."

Over time, at other dances, a few boys asked me to dance. You know the ones I'm talking about: guys who belonged to the United Nations Club, whose attempts at shaving left them with bleeding pimples, who always raised their hands in class, smug that they knew the answers. In other words, they were dorks like me, and through natural selection we, the dregs of the school, had found each other.

More often, I stood alone, unasked. Well, a girl can go to the bathroom only so many times before she has to concoct another reason why she's not dancing and otherwise thoroughly occupied. I pretended to be fascinated with the band, which was always a bad version of the Beatles, the Beach Boys, or the Lovin' Spoonful—and sometimes all three rolled into one. I fantasized that the lead singer would finally spot me and beckon me with his surly lips—"Yeah, you, the Chinese girl with the moon face. Come up here and do primitive movements with me on stage."

That would show them, all those guys who asked the other girls to dance instead.

And then reality would set in. That would never happen, not in a million trillion years. The lead singer? Singing to *me*? Get real.

It's now May 1993, on a dark road somewhere between Northampton and Cambridge, Massachusetts. I'm in a van with Barbara Kingsolver, Ridley Pearson, Tad Bartimus, and Al Kooper. We're sprawled out over rows of bench seating. Bob Daitz, our road manager, is at the wheel. It's probably close to one in the morning, and we've just finished performing to a thousand screaming middle-agers. We should be exhausted. But instead, we're pumped full of adrenaline, steaming up the windows. Bob turns on the air conditioning full blast to keep down the body-odor factor.

Al slips a tape into the deck. The music is a compilation of his favorite oldies, including "Short Shorts" from his days with the Royal Teens. The song baits us: "Who wears short shorts?" Barbara, Tad, and I answer back: "We wear short shorts!" Forget napping on the way back to the hotel. Our teenage hormones are surging with full force now.

Another song comes on and Al turns up the volume. I don't know the lyrics, but magic and miracles are floating in the air, and my voice somehow finds the harmony. A third above lead, a third below—I can switch back and forth effortlessly. Or perhaps I can't do either, but I'm so elated I actually *believe* I can sing with the best of them. *Ooh-wah, ooh-wah.* I could do backup for Carole King. Another song comes on. Al is singing lead and clapping. *Ooh-wah, ooh-wah.* I could be backup to Aretha Franklin. As if on cue, all of us place our feet on the ceiling of the van and begin to dance. Hot damn, I could be an Ikette. I'm dancing. I'm dancing to the moon. I'm bebopping the night away. I'm putting dirty footprints on the ceiling of a rental van. At last, finally, I'm doing primitive movements with the lead singer.

Come to think of it, on a couple of songs, I *was* the lead singer.

Al was actually the one who suggested I sing lead on "These Boots Are Made for Walkin'." When I first saw my name written on the song list next to this Nancy Sinatra classic, I was filled with the same sort of outrage I once felt seeing my high school picture defaced with a mustache.

I called up Kathi. "Tell Al to forget it. Of all the songs in the world, I hate that one the most. It's a joke. I wouldn't sing it in a million years."

Kathi, ever so diplomatic, broke things to me gently: "Actually, I think this could be a great song for you. You know how you always worry about whether you can really sing? Well, with 'Boots,' you don't need a great voice, just a lot of attitude."

"Attitude?"

"Yeah—you know, a bad-girl attitude. You could look cheap and sexy. You could smoke cigarettes and have all the guys fall all over you. Then again, you could do 'Bye Bye Love' again. That's always cute."

For my "Boots" outfit, I carefully combed through a Frederick's of Hollywood catalogue and found a pair of zip-up patent-leather booties that would transform an ordinary pair of black business pumps into awesome, man-stomping, thigh-high intimidators. At a local S&M shop, I bought a biker's cap and a leather dog leash, as well as studded cuffs, collar, and belt. Like any girl vying to be prom queen, I fretted over which of three outfits I should actually wear. The see-through leopard? The tawdry fishnet lace? Or how about the classically simple little black bustier?

At the risk of sounding maudlin, I must confess I felt

Goldmark looks on enviously as Tan brings out the biker slut in us all.

just like Cinderella going to the ball. And like the birds and squirrels who dressed Cinderella with garlands of flowers and such, various well-wishers bestowed finishing touches upon me.

Lorraine Battle, the roadie who helped me do my two-minute costume change each night, thoughtfully gave me tattoos, a dragon on my biceps, a heart and dagger on my shoulder. In Atlanta, Tabby King handed me a plain brown wrapper; in big-sister fashion, she told me no respectable dominatrix should ever be seen without two essential fashion items: a choke chain and rubber titties with erect nipples. The manager of a lesbian bar where we played shyly asked for my autograph and, as a token of her appreciation, bequeathed upon me a slightly frayed bullwhip that had seen a lot of action at a recent B&D ball. Barbara found me cigarettes each night, which I smoked in dark stairwells to help get me into the proper politically incorrect mood.

And then the boys provided moral support on stage. Each night Roy Blount, Jr., went down on bended knee and in wimplike fashion flinched as he tried to flick my Bic. When I growled, "Are you ready, boots? Start walking!" the other Remainder boys would fall supine and quake. Dave Marsh was especially sweet. As I started to stomp on him, he begged me—to no avail—not to stub out my burning cigarette on his chest; the hotel ashtray he had purloined and strategically placed was not visible to the audience. And each night the guys unselfishly volunteered to be the coup de grâce of my number.

"It's just not fair," Stephen King blurted one night after the show. "Dave Barry got the whip jammed into his mouth *two* nights in a row! When's it going to be *my* turn?"

The roadies and ringers also offered in similar ways to boost my confidence. I remember in particular what happened on our flight in Miami. Hoover, Mouse, and Jim were sitting in first class, while we band members had been relegated to coach. Hoover (a.k.a. Chris Rankin) must have been flirting outrageously with the flight attendant; after takeoff, she swept through the first-class curtains and handed me a Virgin Mary. "Compliments of Mr. Rankin, who is begging you please to whip him tonight," she said in honeyed tones. "If I were you, I'd whip him good, whip him till he *bleeds*."

Just remembering this outpouring of friendship brings tears to my eyes. It also reminds me that I forgot to tell the boys where the butt of that whip had likely been before it was given to me. What a bad girl I am.

Around my fifteenth birthday, I truly became a bad girl. My father and older brother had died recently, which I was not willing to accept as God's will, bad luck,

Hoover, a god.

Blount, with a beverage in the red color spectrum. (Parasol cropped out.)

Barry even
wakes up
funny.

That Selvin kid—
Marsh's scapegoat.

a test of my strength, or any other gloss on grief that adults wanted to hand me. I was pissed off at the world. That was the only way I knew how to grieve. I rebelled against everything that had been taught me. There were no miracles. Goodness was a veneer. Hope was for fools.

My forays into wickedness began with some low-grade sins. I started reading forbidden books, including *Catcher in the Rye*, which I had to buy twice because Christian family friends confiscated it from me three times. When a busybody caught me reading the Krafft-Ebing classic, *Psychopathia Sexualis*, he told my mother that the contents of the book would corrupt my young mind and possibly cause me to go insane. My mother, not wanting to see me go insane, called in the minister. The minister, whose son had once turned me down when I asked him to go to a Sadie Hawkins Day dance, came to our house to give me good counsel. He said, "If you can just be patient, if you can keep your virtue, one day, God willing"—and here he swept out his arm, envisioning the heavenly promise—"hundreds of young men will be lined up around the block, waiting to ask you out!" And I thought to myself, Exactly what kind of fool does he take me for?

Six months later, my mother took my younger brother and me to live in Switzerland, away from the reminders of our double tragedy. There I promptly took up smoking Gauloise cigarettes. I progressed to smoking hashish while walking along the lakefront, listening to a tape deck blaring out the Rolling Stones' "Sympathy for the Devil." The tape deck was a gift from my secret boyfriend, Franz, a long-haired German army deserter with nicotine-stained teeth and fingers, a twenty-four-year-old man who had already fathered an illegitimate child.

Former American Baptist scholar Amy Tan.

Franz, by the way, did not desert from the regular German army but from its psychiatric unit. He had been hospitalized for attempted suicide, a tendency he later demonstrated to me one night by throwing himself on the train tracks when I tried to break off with him. Not wanting to see him lose life and limbs before my very eyes, I made up with him, but before we could hop the train and elope to Austria, the Swiss police came and stopped me for being underage. A few weeks later, thanks to a detective my mother had hired, we were arrested for drugs, along with my other friends, who, unbeknownst to me until then, were international dealers.

In the end, my friends were jailed, then deported. Being only sixteen, I was allowed to appear before a Swiss magistrate and plead incredibly stupid. I had to promise in front of my mother that I would never ever disobey her again, nor would I ever put anything evil to my mouth again, not even cigarettes.

Four months later, I was chosen as one of two hundred outstanding American Baptist Scholars, a model of academic excellence and high moral achievement. But deep down in my heart, I knew what a sham I was. I was bad, bad, bad—bad to the bone.

In Washington, D.C., I did a very bad thing. The members of the band were supposed to attend a preshow reception to meet and greet those fans who had bought hundred-dollar tickets. There they were, just as the minister of my youth had promised: hundreds of young men lined up around the block.

For the reception, the Remainderettes donned the wigs that Tabby had bought us that day to give us a new look. Kathi received a long black Morticia-style wig. Tad had a Diana Ross–style Afro. Mine was a perky blond number à la Carol Channing. And then Kathi and I put on sunglasses, exchanged laminated passes, and entered the dimly lit lounge.

We were sitting on bar stools, sipping rum and tonics, when a woman approached Kathi and inspected her laminate. She gasped, her hand pressing her chest in pledge-allegiance fashion. "Amy Tan! I've loved *all* your books."

"Thanks," Kathi grunted, swishing the ice cubes in her drink. We waited for the woman's eyes to adjust to the dark and recognize her mistake, but instead, she took a seat and continued to lavish praise on me—or rather Kathi.

"Really," she gushed, "your books are so wonderful they inspired me to write my own story."

Kathi gestured toward me. "By the way, did you meet Kathi Goldmark? She also sings with the band."

The woman gave me a perfunctory hi, then turned her full attention back to Kathi. "Actually, I have my manuscript in the car," she said. "I was wondering if maybe you could give me some advice—you know, about getting it published. If you'd like to read it now, I could go get it. . . ."

After a few minutes, I stood up and said to Kathi, "I'll see you around."

I found out later that Kathi gave her good advice: how to find a writer's group and an agent and so forth—the same suggestions I would have offered. But we both felt guilty, knowing that when the show started, the woman would instantly recognize that we had fooled her and then become angry. While getting changed in our dressing room, Kathi and I felt like teenagers who had let a silly prank go too far, not quite knowing how to retrieve it. I was thinking specifically about Steve's book *Carrie* and how hurtful girls can be.

Then again, as Kathi pointed out, I had to endure being completely ignored while sitting next to someone more in demand—rather like being back at the high school dance. *Not* that this social oversight on the woman's part justifies what we did.

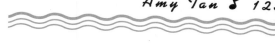

Anyway, just in case the woman we wronged is reading this, Kathi and I would like to say we're sorry. It was Tabby's fault for buying us wigs in the first place.

Right about now, I can hear my parents lecturing me: "You see? Having fun is bad. More important is family." And in a way, I discovered they were right. Because ultimately, the best part about being a Remainder was the fact that we became a family. We had family fun. . . .

Our life together included getting neck cramps while sleeping on the bus. Waking up and seeing how haggard we looked without coffee, without makeup. Teasing Dave Barry, who still looked as if he were perpetually sixteen years old. (I'm referring to his wrinkle-free skin, not his immature behavior.) Going to truck stops for $1.88 breakfasts, cheese-and-bacon hash browns plus grits. Propping food into Ridley's half-open mouth while he was sleeping. Taking a picture of same. Swearing on an oath of death to never reveal to each other's spouses who among us had taken up smoking again. Opening up our laptops, then not writing a single word. Gleefully telling the angst-ridden who had missed book deadlines how many novels, collections, essays, and movie scripts we had finished last year. Buying postcards of road kill and other trucker paraphernalia. Standing in line to go to the movies and noting how many people thought Steve almost looked like Stephen King. Getting Tabby to name all the slang and literary words for "vagina." Spreading rumors that Mouse had legally changed his name to Mouse. Trying on clothes with Barbara and assuring her she really did look cheap and tawdry. Looking at Mouse's driver's license and finding out his legal name really *is* Mouse. Listening to Bob Daitz on the phone, schmoozing nightclub owners into turning over a higher percentage of the take to us. Reading outrageous stories aloud from the *Weekly World News*, including the one that said illegal Chinese aliens were digging tunnels through the center of the earth.

Among the most memorable moments I count those that were laced with heart-pounding terror. Our first day of rehearsal, for example. Also our second day of rehearsal. As well as our third day of rehearsal. Not to mention our first show. Our second show. Every show. The capper was doing what I feared all along: forgetting some of the lyrics to "Boots" one night, which all the Remainders were kind enough to say was an omission I covered with absolute grace.

As to the most fun moments, I count going to an Atlanta disco and learning Tina Turner dance steps from Bob and Lorraine. Dancing cheek-to-cheek with Joel Selvin during sound check in Northampton. Flinging hash browns in Dave Barry's face. Listening to everyone singing oldies at two in the morning on the bus, especially that rocker classic "Catch a falling star and put it in your basket." Posing vixenlike with Kathi on Al's waterbed in Nashville. Watching Tabby demonstrate the transcolonic massage, her surefire method for eliminating constipation on tour.

And among the special moments that bound us together as Remainders forever: gathering around Tad when she confessed she was a bit off-key because she had to go in for scary medical tests the next day. Hearing Steve's recollections about his single mom and the fact that she knew before she died that his first book (*Carrie*) would get published. Attending Roy's fancy college reunion in Nashville and assuring him afterward that he hadn't turned into an old fart. Receiving before each show a huge floral arrangement and personalized cartoon from Matt Groening. Closing our eyes and holding hands as Ridley's cousin Dodge, who is chief of exhibitions at the National Gallery, led us to a room containing a Matisse masterpiece. Walking through the Vietnam War Memorial with Tad, a former war correspondent,

crying as we all sank lower into the valley of death. Listening to Dave Marsh talk about his love for his daughter Kristen. Hugging Barbara when she thought she had lost a piece of jewelry I had lent her. Hugging Tad after she called her mother in intensive care. Hugging and being hugged by everybody in moments of sadness and triumph, because hugging is something that never came naturally to me, and now it does.

To all those people who've been asking me why I joined a rock 'n' roll band, I've been telling them this: I wanted to have fun. I know the answer sounds superficial. But how else should I explain this irrepressible urge shaped by my childhood? Should I confess I wanted to waste my time and money? To be with friends who were purveyors of shame and corruption? To believe once again that miracles could happen?

No, this is the only logical answer: I simply wanted to have fun. And I finally learned how.

Dave Marsh

I DREAMED I DANCED WITH STEPHEN KING IN KATHI GOLDMARK'S MAIDENFORM BRA

I never intended to become known for cross-dressing. Packing for the tour, I didn't bring a dress, let alone a wig or falsies. Yet, in the annals of the Rock Bottom Remainders' Three Chords and an Attitude Tour of 1993, this is how I will best be recalled: appearing during rock 'n' roll's ultimate teen death fantasy, "Teen Angel," while wearing a hideous transvestite getup, stalking Stephen King from beyond the grave into the wilds of imagination, covered in taffeta and fake blood.

"Who the fuck is this?" asked King.

It was a heist. A heist of the conventions that Steve's novels regularly explode by exceeding them, a heist of the death-rock genre, a heist of the spotlight. There are links between this travesty and Jack Benny, Brian Jones, Robin Williams, Larry Johnson, and Kurt Cobain, links of which I am proud (despite Milton Berle, Mick Jagger, Dustin Hoffman, and Evan Dando). But to be honest with you, while we were touring, no thought so elevated ever crossed my mind. I wound up wearing Kathi Goldmark's bra and Amy Tan's wig for a whole bunch of reasons: because I was bored, because I felt I belonged and worried that I didn't, because show business is in my blood (and being a fifth wheel is *not*), because it would shock people and confirm their suspicions, because it made them laugh, because it made me laugh (although not as hard as stuffing the earplugs up my nose did), because I wanted to see the look on Steve's face (which in any case wasn't nearly as good as the look on Dave Barry's and Kathi Goldmark's faces). Or maybe I did it because *whenever I hang around that Selvin kid I get into trouble*.

But mainly, I did it because I had nothing to lose.

There are many ways to divide the Rock Bottom Remainders, but the simplest division comes straight to the point: the split between the eager and the hesitant, those of us who understood immediately why this would be a nifty thing to do and those who had their doubts and, for the most part, kept them. In the first camp dwell most of the musicians—Dave Barry, Ridley Pearson, Al Kooper, Kathi Goldmark— although the doubters claim piano player Barbara Kingsolver.

All the Critics had misgivings, and no wonder. It was merely their expensive public personas that King and Tan and the other more famous writers stood to ruin. But what we Critics threatened to disintegrate was the very essence of our livelihood.

Now, one of the stupider ideas afloat in the world is that you have to be able to do a thing well in order to evaluate its merit and meaning properly. In rock 'n' roll, it's especially easy to see why this is so idiotic—as a rock critic (me) once told a record executive, "Well, only sell records to *musicians*, then." I'm a good critic for a bunch of reasons, but the principal ones stem from being a good listener and knowing how to verbalize what I hear. When I write, I'm not a surrogate player, I'm a surrogate audience.

But just because it was illogical to feel threatened by standing on that stage didn't eliminate the emotion. Joel, Greil, Matt, Roy, and I knew one thing about our performance going in: It was going to be musically abominable. Roy once called us the League of the Singing Impaired, and that's about right. We could not harmonize. In order to create harmonies, we would have to carry a tune, and in order to carry a tune, we'd first have had to be able to locate one, and then hit at least a few of its notes simultaneously, and not one of us ever came closer to that than the breadth of a barn door.

Marcus reads weight-loss tips to Marsh and Selvin.

Still, I bet the Critics had fewer illusions about their talent than anybody else in the band. Even if wanting to be a musician had nothing to do with our career goals—take it from me, our frustrations don't come from not rocking (or even not starring), they come from the difficulties of *writing*—we possessed abundant skills with which to assess our shortcomings, and ample vocabulary with which to savage them. None of us needed Don Henley to tell us where we went wrong, and anyway, as the much (and quite unfairly) maligned Henley would be the first to tell you, *so what*?

So what were we doing up there? More to the point, what was I?

It had to do with my principle of never backing down from a potential embarrassment, and with my sense of loyalty to Kathi Goldmark, and with a slight sense of responsibility for having helped rope in Steve King (though *that* was discharged the minute I saw him with the guitar strapped round his neck and the drums at his back, happy as a pig in shit). It also had a lot to do with underestimating how hard it is to really do this work.

For dozens of people I know, and thousands I do not, singing is as much a job as any factory or office work, a means of livelihood as well as (or instead of) art and fun. Yet, in our culture, singing is defined as play: i.e., not work. No matter how many times you've seen the sweat pour off a singer who's not even moving much, you're inclined to write it off as "Boy, those lights sure must be hot." It's only when you try to push your own voice above the drums and guitars, across the smoke and into the back of the room, that you can feel the pressure, the ache in the chest and the rawness in the throat, the concentration and stamina required just to stay on the mike, let alone worrying about the nuances of pitch, timbre, and phrasing.

Go up on stage for two one-hour sets on a single night, and you'll feel all those problems for the rest of the week. If you sing *just so*, it'll feel like someone's tried to give you a tonsillectomy with a dull knife and no anesthetic. The Remainders' conversations after the show in Anaheim sounded like they were being conducted by frogs; after Miami, we sounded like frogs with epiglottal malfunction.

For a critic, it's good to have a reminder, occasionally, of the difficulties behind the task. I'm not saying it's anything like essential, just that there's some useful information imparted along the way. I don't know exactly what I'm going to do with it, but then I don't know why I'm about to have five hundred channels on my cable box when there's nothing on sixty-seven of the seventy-six it now carries, and I don't let that stop me from turning the stupid thing on once in a while.

Anyway, that's not why I agreed to join the Remainders. I signed up for the same reason I've done so many screwy things in my life (taking LSD comes to mind): because of something I read.

In this case, it was *Music of the Common Tongue: Survival and Celebration in Afro-American Music*, a book by musicologist Christopher Small. The book wound up in my reading pile because its back cover claims it "show[s] how, in contrast to the now degenerate European classical tradition, Afro-American music can become for all people a tool for the exploration, affirmation and celebration of identity, and a weapon of resistance against the increasingly oppressive power of the modern industrial state."

For me, that sentence expressed a dream as fondly held as Kathi Goldmark's fantasies about the world's great all-inclusive rock band. Amazingly enough, Small, a New Zealander who taught in England, delivered on his promise. The final two chapters of *Music of the Common Tongue* incarnate my rock critic's dream. They present a theory that makes sense of the worldwide dominance of black music from the Americas, and of that music's connections to political and personal empowerment. (I wish I knew some sillier way of saying this, but I don't.) What Small wrote isn't only what I wanted to know, it's what I wanted to believe.

Christopher Small and Kathi Kamen Goldmark share a vision. Kathi thought that everybody had a song they could sing, and that they should sing it. Small writes that "the central musical culture of the west in our time . . . despite the commercialism and the star-making inflicted upon it remains a music of participation rather than of spectacle, in which all are invited to join, and through which even the most downtrodden members of industrial societies can come to define themselves rather than have definition thrust upon them."

Small offered more than a rationalization for being a Remainder. He made joining up imperative by arguing that music is a verb, not a noun. For him, music is a *doing*, and he proposes that we refer not to "making music" but to "musicking."

If you find this argument persuasive and try to incorporate it into your theory of how music works and why it changes so many lives (including, periodically, your own), then you can be sure that, almost immediately, some crazy dame from the Coast will come to town, buy you dinner, and suggest that you ought to join her in this new rock band she's just dreamed up. At least, that's what will happen if you're me. At least, that's what *did* happen.

In Anaheim, I lost my inhibitions enough to get up on stage, and I'd lost my

mind enough to think that we sounded passable, Critics included. But that wasn't why I said I had nothing to lose.

In October 1990 my younger stepdaughter, Kristen Ann Carr, a nineteen-year-old whom I'd helped raise since she was three, had surgery for a large growth in her pelvis. It proved to be malignant—a very rare form of cancer called liposarcoma. We were told that this kind of cancer did not often prove fatal, though treating it could be complicated because it tended to recur. But our doctors at Memorial Sloan-Kettering Cancer Center were the leading sarcoma experts in the western hemisphere. Kristen remained on the dean's list at New York University, and she continued her active and altogether wonderful life with her boyfriend, Michael Solomon. Her mother, Barbara Carr, fretted, consoled, prayed, and looked for alternatives. I counseled trusting the doctors—that was my role, and despite how things turned out, it was the best thing I had to offer.

The doctors' advice was to do as little as possible, because more surgery would cause greater harm than the tumors that they had no way—not through surgery, or radiation, or chemotherapy—of preventing from returning to their site atop Kristen's bladder. Generally, this kind of cancer develops fairly slowly. A final resolution would probably not be achieved for years.

Kristen tried a very gentle experimental chemotherapy. It left her well enough to work with Michael and Barbara on Bruce Springsteen's summer 1992 tour of Europe. It also did nothing to halt the progress of her disease. When Kristen came home, she wasn't sick. But she was literally bulging with tumors. Every biopsy showed them as low-grade, thus not metastatic, and therefore not life-threatening in the short term. But we were all freaked anyway. When the Remainders played the Bottom Line that September, I begged off to spend the evening with Kristen and her new puppy.

It was the last time we ever spent an evening alone. On Monday of the last week of October, Kristen began to cough. On Thursday, the doctors took an X-ray and found multiple lesions—too many to remove—in her lungs. They immediately hospitalized her and began a very rigorous round of chemotherapy, with side effects that cost her hair and her energy, even as the explosive growth of the tumors restricted her mobility and her breathing.

Barbara, Michael, and Kristen's sister, Sasha, immediately went to Kristen's bedside and stayed with her, in urgent communication with doctors, alternative healers, psychiatrists, nutritionists, and most important, with *Kristen.*

I cracked up. Not for long—for four days, from Thursday through the following Monday night. But in that time I learned everything there is to know about despair, including, finally, why it is a sin. I allowed myself to know already what the rest of my family had not accepted: Kristen's disease had become fatal and it would kill her very quickly. Egotistically, I blamed myself, for having trusted the doctors and dissuaded Barbara from seeking radical, non-Western alternatives. I felt as if (as I told someone in a very vivid dream), "my life is a complete and total failure." When you raise a child from age three, she is yours, and to hell with biology. If you're a parent and your kid is going to die, you have failed. Period. That was how I saw it. Now all that was left was to prepare for what might, perhaps, if we focused hard enough on it, be an appropriate, even transcendent death.

On Tuesday morning, I went to the hospital (where Barbara and often Sasha slept) and apologized to my wife, who merely embraced me and said, through the blur of her tears, "Good. I need you back." Then, without relinquishing my knowledge of the outcome, I helped out in the dozens of different ways required, as Sasha and Kristen showed me how you get an appropriate, transcendent death: not by focusing on death at all, and certainly not by surrendering to it, but by centering all your energy, attention, and imagination on being alive.

I'd preached this for twenty years. It was the reason I loved rock 'n' roll so much—that capacity for finding the spark of life *everywhere*, even, or especially, in the trash. But it took my own kids to show me how the lesson really applied. Sasha in particular took Kristen over, and she brought to her so many things that were beyond my ken—most of all, hope right until the very last minutes of her life. Nine weeks after her metastasis, Kristen died, peacefully, gracefully, with Barbara, Sasha, Michael, and me holding on to her hands and arms, as if lifting her up to the light.

These are the reasons I had nothing to lose.

The Remainders' tour began five months after Kristen's death. I'd just returned from a vacation in Spain, which had been restful and restorative. As a result, I was the last to show up for rehearsals. Boston, a city I loathe, was just about the last place I wanted to be, but I came anyway, largely because of my commitment to edit our book.

It felt as if nobody could understand what I'd been through in those past few months. (As this book's dedication shows, that was dead wrong.) Besides, all my reservations about musicking made the exercise seem more frustrating. What were the Critics going to do for the next three weeks—stand there and let Dave Barry and Kooper insult us? *Sing?!* And what would we do when we weren't "singing"? A waste of time and energy, at a time when I felt there was an insufficient supply of both.

Fortunately, I have the world's lowest threshold of boredom. If you were going to be in the Remainders, part of the Critics Chorus, and basically sober, your back-stage hours would be many, your tasks few, your options limited but—given a certain cast of mind, and, as Stephen and Amy would surely remind me, an idle mind *is* the devil's playground—the temptations would be enormous.

Here, I part company with Professor Small, at least a little bit. Musicking is also a theatrical experience. So on the second night, in Northampton, when some addled Dave Barry fan presented him with a whole, raw beef tongue, I sat it in my lap and played with it all through dinner, then encouraged Dave to use it on Steve that night during "Teen Angel." He agreed to do so, but he just laid the damn thing on King's shoulder, quickly and sloppily, with no setup at all. The tongue flopped to the floor. Steve gave it barely a glance and went back to his song. I knew there was a better way.

The next night in Cambridge, as Dave announced, just before the Critics' first number, that the Surgeon General required the band to throw earplugs to the audience "or the bodily orifice of our choice," I set about slowly unwrapping a pair, then plugged one in each nostril. "The music *stinks*, too," I declared. This got a laugh, but the real reward was Barry's stare. He clearly did not know that I spent a formative year hanging out with Iggy and the Stooges. Once you've seen someone cut himself with glass just to see how folks react, using your body to shock is easy.

Backstage, I spotted some Remainderette's leopard-print robe and slipped it on. It looked suitably ridiculous, so I wore it onstage. Meantime, the Critics didn't sing for so many songs in a row that we had time to order barbecue from the rib joint downstairs. Ribs mean, among other things, bones—bones with shredded meat, dripping blood-red sauce, that could be presented to Stephen King during "Teen Angel." The restaurant didn't even charge me for the platter. "This is all we could find of 'er," I told Steve solemnly. He didn't look too annoyed.

In Washington, after our first hideous bus ride and an utterly unrefreshing night at the Inn at Foggy Bottom, the world's most hostile hotel, we played the Bayou. Its stage stands about fifteen feet above the dance floor (or what would be the dance floor if people other than guitarists doing the butt dance and Roy Blount with a Zippo still danced to rock), pitched at an angle so steep that it seems like bands playing at this club wouldn't so much bomb as defenestrate. You reached the stage from the dressing rooms by walking along a hallway so narrow it became a catwalk, then clambering down a flight of stairs and entering through a curtain draped at the back.

During sound check, I found an empty box that had contained a gross of earplugs and slipped it over my head. Tabby King, my sartorial conscience, told me how much she liked it, so I figured I'd just wear that onstage as my statement for the night—which I did for the Critics' first number. Then, standing around in the girls' dressing room (probably looking for that robe), I noticed that somebody had left her aquamarine bra lying on the couch.

"Whose is this?" I asked Lorraine Battle. "Kathi's," she replied in her best don't-fuck-with-me-son voice. But she didn't lift her eyebrow—when Lorraine Battle raises her one eyebrow, the world is nearing an end and *you better not push*. This time, the brow stayed down, so I just said: "Well, I think I'm going to put it on and wear it for 'Teen Angel.' And I guess I'll borrow a wig, too." I slipped off my jeans and went out just like that: wig, an extremely empty bra (its front-closing clasp held together with a chain of half a dozen safety pins, as many as Lorraine could find on short notice), my gut hanging over a florid pair of boxer shorts. I was barefoot and probably appeared pregnant, and sure enough looked ugly. When Roy Blount took a gander, he seemed ready to puke, and as I passed the Remainderettes on the catwalk, they just about lost it, too. I could hear Kathi behind me, saying to Lorraine, "Is he going *out there* like that? (*Beat.*) Is that *my* bra he's wearing?"

Stephen told me later that he couldn't figure out what was going on when the crowd started hooting as I came through the curtain and picked my way across the cords and around the amps toward him. Ridley and Barbara rolled their eyes; Al gave me one of those "You critics!" stares. Dave Barry's jaw dropped so that he looked like the cover of *Dave Barry Turns 40*. Stephen's first impulse, he said, was to look down—he figured his zipper must have broken and exposed him. Only then did he look back over his shoulder.

His eyes popped, but Steve's a trouper. He pulled himself back together and embraced his "Teen Angel," this nightmare come to life. That was it. I had a new job. Dave B. looked at me with new respect; Roy kept his distance; Kathi complained about the ruining of her bra, but clearly *her* wildest expectations had moved a step closer to being realized; Selvin, my personal imp, clapped me on the back and gave out one of his great haw-haws. I sacked out at two A.M., then got up and took a shuttle flight back to New York to meet Barbara, who'd just arrived from London for a meeting to set up a Madison Square Garden benefit concert in Kristen's memory. By six P.M. I was on a Metroliner headed to Philly, and by six-thirty, I'd arrived at the Katmandu Club, sick as a dog, but for the first time eager to carry out the night's program.

A lot of people will tell you that the Remainders were at their best in Atlanta, and a few claim that we were at our worst in Miami, but that Philly show, despite a really great audience, felt the shakiest to me. I decided it would be better to come out during Steve's other big death-rock number, "Last Kiss," since there was already so much business taking place during "Teen Angel." It didn't work at all. Part of my theory had been to keep Steve off-balance, but this time the move just felt disruptive.

Before the tour began, I'd taken a look at the schedule, seen the *projected* eleven-hour bus ride from Philly to Atlanta (it took seventeen), and told Kooper, "Well, everybody will be sick in Georgia." That was only partly true: Stephen, Tad, Joel, and I could barely function, but everybody else held their own.

Lousy as I felt, it cheered me up when Greil Marcus turned up backstage in Atlanta. He arrived just as I was being fitted into the long white prom-style dress and huge falsies Lorraine and Tabby had picked out for me that afternoon. Greil, who's known me since 1970, took one look and grinned. "I might have expected this," he said.

Nashville proved more of a test, not because I was afraid to act girlish within such a redneck citadel but because just before showtime, somebody told me Wayne Kramer was looking for me. I've known Wayne since about '68, when he was the lead guitarist for the MC5 and I was their teenage fan, occasional fill-in MC, and chronicler in the pages of the Motor City rock review *Creem*. The Five were probably the most macho band ever to stalk the Earth, Kiss included; and in front of Wayne, whom I hadn't seen in exactly twenty years, cross-dressing seemed a little . . . embarrassing. But he'd done his time down at Stooge Manor (as we dubbed Iggy's house), too, so he reacted with much more aplomb—and way more approbation—than I'd expected.

It was seeing Wayne, I think, that snapped the Remainders into focus for me. He'd played lead guitar in one of the flashiest and most powerful bands of all time, a band that disintegrated in a morass of failed revolutionary politics, drug addiction, and the overall collapse of the counterculture. The MC5 took down with them much innocence and many dreams, including some of my own. The Remainders reflected only a shadow of that kind of promise, yet even shadows create a kind of beauty. That is the strangest word anyone has used to describe what our band did, and yet the beauty was there.

It did not have anything much to do with the music. Our instrumentalists had essayed competence, which was one hell of an improvement over Anaheim; but what made our shows exciting, fun, and, yes, a little magical happened between and around the notes. It happened, in my opinion, not in the music but in the *musicking*—the fact that we did it meant more than how well. We could go off In Search of the Fourth Chord, but if we'd lost our attitude, we'd have entirely missed the point. Once I'd found my slot, once I'd found a way to give to the band something of what it deserved (which, Christ knows, I wasn't about to offer by singing), I loved being part of the Remainders. I loved it because, no matter how we may have sounded, our band consisted of people making music because they loved those sounds—and through that, had come to know and love one another.

Our audience may have come to witness a creative footnote to the career of Stephen King, Dave Barry's best-ever standup act, Amy Tan's deliverance from the kitchen gods, or the humiliation of rock criticism. If so, it came away with a lot better than it bargained for.

Myself, I think these days that if I hadn't taken this journey, I'd be both poorer and sadder. It does not redeem my failure of nerve in Kristen's crisis that I wound up (as Kathi pointed out) dressing up like a dead teenager. But it shows that I did with that experience the only thing I've ever wanted my children to do with their failures: learn and grow from them. This is what I preached to them that they could do, and what I have preached to everybody that rock 'n' roll could help them do. Now I know for certain that I was telling the truth. To find that out, I'd have been willing to pay a far higher price than a few snapshots of my aging carcass in drag.

Dave Barry

NAME OF THE CHAPTER— BROADWAY CHAPTER

As a boy, I never wanted to be President of the United States. I wanted to be Buddy Holly.

I loved Buddy Holly, and not just because he was young and famous and hip and wrote great rock 'n' roll music. I loved Buddy Holly because *he wore glasses.*

I wore glasses, too. I got them when I was young, way before any of the other kids in my class. Sometimes I felt as though I had them at birth; as though I came into the world wearing thick little lenses framed in little plastic fake-turtle-shell rims, which had been damaged somewhere in the birth canal and consequently were being held together by a little strip of white adhesive tape; and Dr. Mortimer "Monty" Cohn, who attended all the Barry births, looked down at me, then looked up at my mother, shook his head, and said, "I'm sorry, Marion. It's a dweeb."

Kooper and Barry offer interim keyboardist Jimmy Vivino two different approaches to finger-picking.

But actually I didn't get glasses until the third grade. I was the first kid in my class to get them. This was in 1955, Whippoorwill Elementary School, Armonk, N.Y. One day we were studying how Eskimos make igloos, and Miss Kennelly was writing on the blackboard, and I realized that I couldn't read the words. (I *still* don't know how Eskimos make igloos. My guess is, they wear gloves.)

So Mom took me to the optical department of Macy's in White Plains, where I got my first pair of glasses—Model 786-J, "The Weenie." It could have been worse: I could have been a girl. This was the era when the popular style in women's eye-wear was "harlequin"[1]-style glasses, the kind where the frame swoops up at the sides, winglike, so that it looks as though the woman is being attacked by some kind of alien transparent face-sucking bat. This is the style always shown on large, comical housedress-wearing women in "Far Side" cartoons, but back in the fifties women wore it for *real*.

Anyway, as a kid with glasses—a *puny* kid with glasses, not to mention a kid who was doomed to reach puberty about twenty-three years behind the rest of the class[2]—I was not what you would call a romantic threat. I had virtually no success with the Kissing Girls, a gang of girls who ran around the playground at recess, threatening to kiss boys. We boys naturally pretended that we would rather eat live earthworms[3] than be kissed by these girls, but in truth we all secretly wanted them to catch us. At least *I* secretly did. I ran away from them as slowly as possible, moving like the actors in those love scenes where the man and woman are running toward each other in slow motion, except I was running away from the Kissing Girls, with a look of feigned disgust on my face, and hope in my heart.

Dave Barry, Pig in Heaven.

But they never chased me. They chased larger, cuter boys with perfect eyesight, and left me out there slo-mo-ing across the playground, all alone. Nearly forty years later, I can still remember every single Kissing Girl's name.

Not that I am bitter.

My point is that in those days I was not overly fond of my own self. Low self-esteem is what I had, way before it was popular. And the focal point of my unhappiness was my glasses. So you can imagine how excited I was when I discovered Buddy Holly. Here was a guy who had glasses at least as flagrant as mine; a guy who did *not* look like a teen heartthrob, but more like the president of the Audiovisual Club, the kid who always ran the projector for educational films with titles like *The Story of Meat*. In a word,

[1] French word, meaning "ugly."
[2] I *still* don't have any forearm hair.
[3] Actually, some of my friends *did* eat live earthworms.

Buddy Holly, let's be honest, looked like a geek. And yet he was *unbelievably* cool.

The first song of his that I ever heard was "That'll Be the Day." I heard it on the radio, and it became the first record I bought, a 45 r.p.m. costing forty-nine cents at the Armonk Pharmacy. I cannot tell you how much I loved this song. We had a primitive 1950s-style Extreme Low Fidelity record player that seemed to be actually *designed* to scratch records, with a tone arm that had about the same weight and acoustical characteristics as a ball-peen hammer, and a spindle that slapped the records violently down on top of each other, as though it had a personal grudge against them. If you didn't put a new record on, it would play the same one over and over, and that's how I listened to "That'll Be the Day." I'd set up the record player in my room, and I'd get out my pretend guitar, and I'd face a large imaginary worshipful audience of cute girls, and I'd sing:

When Cupid shot his dart
He shot it at your heart. . . .

Words cannot describe how irresistible I imagined I was.

I loved all of Buddy Holly's songs. I thought "Every Day" was the most wondrous artistic accomplishment of any kind in the history of the human race, including anything you might find in the Sistine Chapel.

I was *really* blue when his plane went down. Not blue enough to write a 374-verse, fourteen-hour song about it, the way Don McLean did, but blue.

Nevertheless Buddy Holly, in his short time on Earth, had taught me an important lesson: namely, that you didn't have to look like Elvis to be popular and attractive and cool. All you had to do was work hard and use your God-given talent. So even though I appeared, to the casual observer, to be merely a puny four-eyed insecure bantering wiseass, there was nothing standing between me and international fame and adulation except the fact that, compared to Buddy Holly, I *had* no God-given talent. God had chosen to deposit the majority of this particular brand of talent in Buddy, and then he had chosen to put Buddy on a small plane in a bad storm in Clear Lake, Iowa. (And yet Fabian is still performing. Go figure God.)

At the time, however, I didn't realize that what I needed was way more natural ability. What I thought I needed was a guitar, and I nagged my parents relentlessly until they got me one. It was a four-stringed, El Cheapo model, and it came with a little booklet that showed you how to make different chords, although for quite a while, all my chords sounded like this: THWUD. Also, every time I changed chords in a song, there was a thirty-second pause while I repositioned my fingers:

Every (thirty-second pause) (THWUD) *day,*
(thirty-second pause) (THWUD) *It's a gettin'*
(thirty-second pause) (THWUD) *closer. . . .*

If I had ever had an actual cute girl around to sing this song to, she would have died of starvation before I finished it.

But I kept practicing, strumming alone in my room for hour after hour, day after day, until, inch by painful inch, I had scaled the steep musical slope from the Valley of the Really Terrible to the Scenic Overlook of the Still Pretty Bad. Along the way I moved up to a six-string acoustic guitar, and then, on a glorious Christmas morning when I was in the ninth grade, to a candy-apple-red solid-body electric guitar that was built in the Orient according to the same exacting standards of musical craftsmanship used to make kazoos. It was a heavy, clunky, squarish chunk of wood, like a coffee table with strings, and it came with an amplifier that had the kind of sound quality we associate today with the drive-thru window at Burger King. But I loved this guitar, because now, instead of strumming quietly in my room all alone, I could strum REALLY LOUD in my room all alone.

That's what I did for several years: lie on my bed, strumming and humming, waiting for something to happen. And then something did. It was 1964, and I was riding in a crowded station wagon with some really old people—some of these people had to be at *least* twenty-five; basically, as far as I was concerned, they were walking, talking Easter Island heads—in the front, and me and several of my friends in the far backseat, the one that faced backward, and the radio was tuned to WABC in New York, and the DJ said here they are, the new band from England, the Beatles. And then we heard the opening guitar chords to "I Want to Hold Your Hand," which sounded *nothing* like Frankie Avalon and all the other small-curd musical cottage cheese that Top 40 radio had been spewing out for years. In the back of the station wagon, we thought this sound was *amazing*. We were bouncing in the seat, drumming on the window frame, yelling at the driver to turn it up. But the old people in front had their noses all wrinkled up: they *hated* it. So we *knew* we were right.

I loved the British Invasion, all these groups of skinny wisecracking guys making raucous new music and making girls crazy and being even cooler than Buddy was. Plus, John Lennon *sometimes wore glasses*. Now I knew exactly what I wanted to do: I wanted to form a garage band with my more musically talented friends and grow my hair long and make wisecracks and play raucous new music and make girls crazy. The problem was that (a) none of us had a garage (Armonk was more of a carport community, and there are real problems with being a carport band, especially in winter); and (b) none of my friends had any musical talent, either. Just as Lennon inevitably found McCartney, and Jagger inevitably found Richard, I have always had a knack for making friends with guys who cannot clap their hands without the aid of detailed color diagrams.

So I had to wait until I got to college to find some musical guys to be in a band with. I went to Haverford, a small all-male college near Philadelphia, which had a very good academic reputation, by which I mean it had—this could be proven

mathematically—the worst football team in the United States. We lost games to *Swarthmore.*

I got to Haverford in 1965, when what we now call the sixties were really starting to explode, and *everybody*[4] was starting bands with names like the Catatonic Sturgeon. The first band I was in was called the Guides, because we had read in some hip underground newspaper that "guide" was a hip underground slang term for a person who took people on an acid trip. Unfortunately, it turned out that nobody except the person who wrote this article had ever heard this particular term, so people had a lot of trouble grasping what our name was.

"The Guys?" they'd say. "You're called the *Guys?*"

The original Guides were a four-piece band—bass, guitar, organ, and drums. I was the guitar player; I had gotten rid of my coffee-table guitar and moved up to a white one that, because of the material it appeared to be made of, everybody called "the toilet seat." The bass player, Freeman Cottrell, didn't have a real bass amp; he had part of his hi-fi system hooked up to a speaker, so that it looked as though his bass was plugged into a science-fair project. Our organist, Ken Stover, had also built his organ, and he had covered the cabinet with some kind of orangeish vinyl-like material, similar to what is used to cover seats in diners. The only band member with a normal instrument was our drummer, Tom Pleatman, who had a regulation drum set, and who taught the rest of us the basic musical rule of being in a rock band, which is that *you* better play loud, because the drummer can't help it.

If I were asked to describe, in six words, the genre of songs that the Guides played, the words I would choose are: "Songs involving three chords or fewer." Our best song was "Land of 1,000 Dances," because it had only one chord, and basically only one important word, specifically, "na" (as in: "I said a na, na na na na, na na na na, na na na, na na na. Na na na na"). We also did "Satisfaction" (it was against the law *not* to do "Satisfaction"); "Twist and Shout"; "Wipeout"; "Money"; "Hanky-Panky"; "Louie Louie"; "Wild Thing"; and "Hang On Sloopy," which I am still fond of today because of the following line, which demonstrates just how far a lyricist will go to find a rhyme for "you": "Sloopy, I don't care what your daddy do."

The Guides' first public performance was at the big end-of-the-year bash in the freshman dorm. We were able to get this coveted gig because we had exactly the type of sound that the social chairman was looking for—namely, a sound that cost fifty dollars. This price was a flagrant, unconscionable ripoff—for the audience. Or it would have been, if the audience had been capable of rational judgment. Fortunately for us, the audience had consumed several kegs of beer—I am talking per capita—and therefore was highly receptive, or at least as receptive as guys can be when they have passed out facedown in the world's largest indoor spilled-beer lake.

---

[4]Except Bill Clinton.

Most of the guys who *weren't* passed out decided, at some point, that they should come up and sing with the band. This was a phenomenon that I was to see repeated many times in my band career: drunk guys staggering toward me, determined to get the microphone and demonstrate their vocal prowess and maybe puke on our equipment. I learned to play Defensive Music, fending the drunks off by thrusting my guitar at them, rapierlike (unless they were really large guys, in which case I would step aside and, if necessary, sing harmony).

In the succeeding years the Guides acquired new personnel and more instruments that enabled us to play at a new level, by which I mean louder. We also changed our name to the Federal Duck. We selected this name one night when our new bass player, Bob Stern, became briefly, but very seriously, concerned that some ducks in the Haverford College duck pond were in fact government narcotics agents. Bob Stern is now a respected dentist in New Jersey, so I am not about to suggest in this book that the use of illegal hallucinogenic substances had anything to do with this incident.

Musically, we became more sophisticated, sometimes attempting songs with four or even five chords, and parts in the middle where everybody was supposed to stop simultaneously. Like many suburban white guys, we thought the blues were really hip, and we'd sing, with great earnestness, about how we had our mojos working, despite the fact that we had *no* idea what a "mojo" was, and the only blues-inducing experiences we'd had in our young privileged lives involved, for example, getting a C in poli sci. Our favorite band was the Blues Project, which we worshiped, because its members were hard-rockin', blues-playin' suburban white guys like us, but they were *good*. (If you had told me back then that I would one day be in a band with Al Kooper, I would have assumed you had ingested illegal hallucinogenic substances.)

The Federal Duck worked cheap, so we played a lot, all over the Philadelphia area, mostly at colleges. We learned to play through *anything*—people hating us; musicians' union guys hassling us for not being in the musicians' union; people in the crowd wanting to fight us or each other. Once we were at a University of Pennsylvania frat house, and an entire sofa came crashing in through a large front window. We just kept playing, which is what I am sure other professional musicians, such as Lionel Hampton, do when this kind of thing happens to them.

The worst thing was requests. Show me a band member who likes requests and I will show you a band member who has been messing around with illegal hallucinogenic substances. The frat boys always wanted us to play Motown, which of course we did not do, because it requires skill and talent. And some old asshole was always walking up to us, after we had just finishing playing, say, "Under My Thumb," and asking us to play "My Funny Valentine."

Our standard answer to this type of request was: "We'll get to that in the next set."

(Another very common request we got was: "Can you guys *please* play quieter?" To which we would answer: "WHAT?")

I hope I'm not giving you the impression that I disliked being in the band. I *loved* being in the band. I loved practicing; I loved driving to gigs; I even loved schlepping all the equipment around. I loved when we'd be playing somewhere, and somebody in the band, frequently me, would mess up, maybe in a way that nobody in the crowd would notice, but the band knew, and we'd catch each other's eyes and laugh and give each other the finger in cool musical ways without missing too many notes. But above all, I loved it when—this sometimes happened, if the conditions were just right—the people actually *liked* us, and the dance floor was jammed and throbbing and the strobe light[5] was flashing and we knew exactly where the song was going, to a high place, and we were taking the whole crowd there.

It wasn't *exactly* the same as being worshiped by cute girls, but it was pretty good.

You will perhaps be surprised to learn that the Federal Duck actually made a record album. This was in 1968. We loaded all our stuff into a U-Haul trailer and drove up to New York City. Not all of us fit in the car, so two of us—Jack Bowers and I—squeezed into the U-Haul trailer with the equipment. It was a strange ride, because, for one thing, it was very dark inside the trailer. There were other reasons why it was strange, but I cannot discuss them without using, for a tedious fourth time, the phrase "illegal hallucinogenic substances."

(I want to stress to you impressionable young readers out there that everything I'm talking about here was illegal and stupid and I now deeply regret it.)

So Jack and I were riding back there, talking, and suddenly Jack said, "Whoa."

And I said, "What?"

And Jack said, "I'm seeing upside-down pictures over your head."

And I said, "What?"

And Jack said, "I'm seeing pictures, and the pictures are *changing*. And some-times there are upside-down *signs*."

And I said, "*What?*"

The nineties—you had to be there.

So I moved over to Jack's side, and he was right: there *were* upside-down pictures and signs on the trailer wall. For a long time I assumed, logically, that this was a miracle; but eventually, using our four working brain cells, we figured out that the images were caused by light shining through a tiny rust pinhole in the trailer wall over Jack's head, causing the famous "pinhole camera" effect.

[5] Of *course* we had a strobe light.

When we stopped at a service plaza on the New Jersey Turnpike, we told the rest of the band about it, and of course *everybody* wanted to ride in the U-Haul. Nobody wanted to drive.

The sixties: you had to be there.

For me, the trailer ride was the highlight of the album experience. We spent a few days practicing a new batch of songs in a Lower East Side recording studio. I didn't like the record producer, who had never heard us play but who kept telling us what our "sound" was, and I didn't like the new songs, so I decided to drop out of the record project. The other band guys tried to talk me out of it, arguing that I was missing a chance at fame, but I was stubborn, and I went back down to Haverford. This proved to be one of the dumbest mistakes of my life, because the Federal Duck, performing music that I had been so contemptuous of, produced an album that went on to sell, worldwide, by a conservative estimate, including sales to relatives, maybe nine copies. I think it might be, in some ways, the worst album ever made, if you disregard the *oeuvre* of Jim Nabors. To this day I regret that I'm not on it.

The Federal Duck played for another year after that. At the end of our senior year, in 1969, I sold my guitar—I had worked up to a Fender Jazzmaster—because I needed money to get married and go out into the real world and try to find something that people would pay me to do, which was clearly not going to involve guitar playing. I would also have sold my amplifier, but it had suffered some damage when, at a major end-of-college party, a friend of mine and I accidentally drank bourbon from a shoe and decided that we needed to know what an amplifier sounds like when you throw it out of a second-floor dormitory window.[6]

And that, for a long time, was the end of my organized musical career. The Federal Duck was the best thing that happened to me in the sixties (and a *lot* of things happened to me in the sixties). And although Haverford is a fine educational institution that taught me many important life lessons,[7] I remember playing in that band far more vividly, and more fondly, than I remember anything that happened in any classroom.

So anyway, after I graduated, a number of years passed, in chronological order, and I became an older person with a wife and a son and a writing career and a mortgage and (finally) contact lenses and certain gum problems and two dogs so stupid that they are routinely outwitted by inanimate objects. I also eventually got another electric guitar, which I pick up and play whenever I am desperately trying to think of a punchline but nothing is coming, and I have progressed *way* beyond writer's block, to a *much* more terrifying condition called Writer's Gonna Have to Get a Real Job. This can happen to me as often as nineteen times per day, so I play

---

[6] It sounded pretty cool.
[7] Such as, "Never take any course that meets before noon."

the guitar a lot in my office (just ask the dogs). It reassures me to play old rock songs, because I know how they're supposed to end, which is something that I cannot say about anything I am trying to write.[8]

But diddling around with a guitar in an office is not the same as being in a band. So when Kathi Goldmark called to ask if I wanted to be in a rock band consisting of writers who met the tough musical criterion of saying yes when Kathi called, I said yes.

And when she called again to say that Al Kooper had agreed to be the musical director of this band, I wet my figurative pants. I mean, *Al Kooper*. The man is a rock icon. A giant. A defining musical force. A *really* weird guy, it turned out. But that is not surprising. Al has been a professional rock musician since his early teens; this is an experience that, in terms of social development, is comparable to being raised by wolves, except that people raised by wolves are more comfortable in a social setting.

Don't get me wrong: I have come to love Al like the older brother I never had.[9] But he made me nervous, the first day that the band got together in Anaheim to start practicing for our performance at the 1992 American Booksellers Association convention. I walked into the rehearsal room, and there, behind the organ, was this big, brooding, bearded guy, dressed all in black, staring balefully out from the world's deepest set of eye sockets, looking like the leader of a group called Billy Goat and the Gruffs. I later realized that even when he's in a good mood, Al looks like a man whose toes are being gnawed by rats, but at the time I was intimidated. I thought, Whoa, what am I *doing* here, presuming to play guitar next to this guy, a guy who has jammed with Mike Bloomfield, a guy who was in the Blues Project, a guy who co-founded Blood, Sweat and Tears, a guy who backed up Bob Dylan, a guy who worked with the Rolling Stones, a guy who—very few living musicians can make this claim—performed on the original Royal Teens recording of "Short Shorts"?

I think all of us writers were intimidated the first day. But Al was surprisingly gentle with us, listening nonjudgmentally as we'd fumble through a song, then offering insightful suggestions for making it sound better, such as:

- "Don't play so loud."
- "Don't play at all."
- "I don't think we should do this song."

Using this technique we were quickly able to develop a fairly large repertoire of songs that we were definitely not going to do. We also got to know each other better, and got to share our ideas about the craft of writing. For example, on our first

[8]This book chapter is a good example.
[9]Thank God.

lunch break, Stephen King, whom I had never met, walked up to me, leaned down to put his face about an inch from mine, and said, in a booming, maniacal voice, "SO, DAVE BARRY, *WHERE DO YOU GET YOUR IDEAS??*"

Stephen was making a little writer's joke. He *hates* this question. Like most writers, he has been asked this question nine hundred squintillion times.

The truth is, the Remainders hardly ever talked about writing, and that was one thing I liked about being in the band. When you're a writer, and you go out in public, on book-promotion tours or to workshops or whatever, people are always asking you about writing: not just where you get your ideas, but also what kind of word-processing program you use, when you write, how often you revise, how long you take, what you think about, what your *system* is. And the truth is that most writers—I firmly believe this—have *no fucking idea* how, or even why, they write. They just *do* it. I also believe that many of us, deep inside, fear that at any moment we could suddenly *stop* being able to write. That's why we tend to write all the time, compulsively, shutting ourselves away and pecking at our keyboards, trying to crank out *something*, to reassure ourselves that we still can.

Or maybe that's just me.

Anyway, I found it liberating to be hanging around with a group of writers, and knowing that they already knew that there was basically no point in talking about writing. And we hardly ever did. We spent a lot more time talking about issues such as the chord changes to "Leader of the Pack"; and whether Elvis was bald;[10] and where was the most interesting place that anybody in the band had ever had oral sex.[11]

After we got on the bus and started traveling, we hardly talked about anything except band-related stuff, such as where we were playing, what songs we were going to do, what the audience was going to be like, and—above all—what bus travel was doing to everybody's hair. Al Kooper had warned us about Bus Hair, which is a disgusting medical condition that strikes you after you have spent a night attempting to sleep in a bus with your head smooshed up against a seat coated with a mixture of old hairspray, spilled beer, and potato-chip grease, and your hair is being relentlessly exposed to a bus atmosphere consisting of 2 percent oxygen, 17 percent nitrogen, 39 percent diesel fumes, and 42 percent bodily vapors. You'd be rolling down I-95 in some place like South Carolina,[12] and you'd wake up at dawn, having slept for maybe two hours, and you'd look around, and there, in the other seats, instead of your fellow band members, were these horribly deformed creatures with bloated faces and red eyes and green moss visibly growing on their teeth and big sectors of hair sticking straight out sideways, looking like

---

[10] Dave Marsh and Joel Selvin claim he was. I am still trying to deal with this. [We were lying, or at least bluffing.—Ed.]

[11] Roy Blount, Jr., definitely had the most interesting place, but out of respect for his privacy I will not discuss it here except to say that it involved a trampoline.

[12] Such as North Carolina.

Bozo the Clown, but with pastier skin; and they'd be laughing at you, and you'd realize that *you looked even worse than they did.*

A major insight that I had on the Remainders bus tour, after maybe the ninth straight day of getting almost no sleep and not eating any green vegetables except for the ones that come in a Bloody Mary, is that traveling rock bands do not have a healthy lifestyle. I believe the reason why so many rock stars elected to die young is that, basically, it was better for their health.

After we'd been on the road for a while, the Remainders drifted into a collective, surreal state of mind that I think of as "Bandland." Bandland was our little separate cocoon-bus world, whose residents had little direct contact with the normal human race. We developed our own verbal communications system, which was based on saying only the punchlines to inside jokes. For example: Early in the tour, we were riding through New England on our way to play in Northampton, Mass. We had been riding through the New England countryside for maybe two hours, with traditional scenic New England vistas both sides of us as far as the eye could see, and suddenly our saxophone player, Jerry Peterson, an incredible musician with an enormous hairstyle that, I believe, enables him to receive signals from another planet, looked out the window and said, quote:

"New England. Check it out."

Apparently Jerry had just then noticed New England, and wanted to make sure the rest of us didn't miss it. We all thought this was wonderfully funny, and for the rest of the trip, many dozens of times per day, we urged each other to check things out, as in: "Popcorn. Check it out." And "Marcel Proust. Check him out." It became virtually impossible for any object, person, or abstract concept to come to our attention without somebody urging everybody to check it out. I am not saying this was good; I'm just saying this was the way it was, in Bandland.

Another example was the "Funky Broadway" All-Purpose Question-Answering System. We developed this one night on the bus. We were talking about songs with great lyrics, and somebody brought up Wilson Pickett's "Funky Broadway," which goes roughly like this:

Every town I go in, there's a street
Name of the street—Broadway Street

Now on Broadway, there's a nightclub
Name of the nightclub—Broadway Nightclub.

Later in the song a woman appears. Name of the woman? *Broadway* Woman.

So we were pondering these lyrics on the bus, and suddenly we realized that the song was basically presenting a simple formula for answering questions on a wide variety of subjects:

Q. What was the name of the inventor of the steam turbine?

A. *Broadway* Inventor of the Steam Turbine.

Q. What do you call the part in an automobile engine that mixes the air and the fuel?

A. *Broadway* Part in an Automobile Engine That Mixes the Air and the Fuel.

Q. What is the sum of 678,987 and 87,024?

A. *Broadway* Sum of 678,987 and 87,024.

Perhaps this seems stupid to you. I'll be honest: it seems pretty stupid to me, now that I've been back in Reality for a while. But it never failed to slay me when I was in Bandland.

And the thing is, the Remainders were together for only a couple of weeks. Some bands travel together for *years*. No wonder so many rock musicians are weird. Not that I am specifically referring to Kooper.

Speaking of Kooper, one of the best things about the tour was playing with him, Jerry Peterson, and drummer Josh Kelly, the professional musicians who had been everywhere and played with everybody, and who kept the Remainders from being really horrible. It made me feel as though I had been allowed, just briefly, inside a secret and exclusive club. There'd be times when we'd be on stage, playing, and I'd look over at Al, and he'd give me some musical hand-signal reminder, like quickly touching his hand to the top of his head to indicate that we were supposed to go to the "top," or beginning, of the song, and I'd think: "Here I am, on stage, getting cool secret hipster-musician hand signals from Al Kooper!" I'd be so excited, thinking this, that I would not necessarily remember to go to the top of the song.

We were not, it goes without saying, a very good band. Fortunately the audiences didn't expect us to be one. They seemed to be satisfied with the novelty of it, with knowing that very few bands have novelists of the stature of Amy Tan singing "Leader of the Pack," or have Stephen King singing his special version of the immortal teen-tragedy song "Last Kiss," featuring such sentimental improvised lyrics as:

The Throwbacks—looking and sounding like a mid-sixties frat band without even trying (left to right: Barry, King, Pearson, Fulghum).

I saw my baby lying there
I brushed her liver from my hair.

And no normal band has a weapon anything like the Critics Chorus. This is a group of men who make their living criticizing professional musicians in print, so it goes without saying that they were, in terms of raw musical skills, probably the least talented group of individuals ever assembled. We practiced for many hours and performed a total of ten shows, and I don't believe we were ever in a situation where all the critics managed to clap their hands simultaneously.

Naturally the audiences loved the Critics Chorus. They loved it when respected critic Joel Selvin took his now-legendary Scream Solo in "Louie Louie"; they loved it when respected critic Dave Marsh came out during "Teen Angel" wearing a ketchup-stained wedding dress; they loved it during "These Boots Are Made for Walkin'" when Roy Blount, Jr.—three-time winner of the coveted "World's Whitest Man" title—attempted to dance and light Amy Tan's cigarette at the same time. There was not a dry set of underwear in the house.

I myself treasure those moments. I treasure everything that happened in Band-land, even the things I hated at the time, such as when we arrived in Miami, beyond exhaustion, wanting desperately to go to sleep, but instead we had to go to a beach and pose for the *Vanity Fair* Magazine Photo Shoot from Hell, which lasted for what seemed like seventeen hours, during which the main instruction we got from the photographer was, "OK, I need you to have an idea." ("Where do we get our ideas?" said Stephen King.)

After we played our last gig, I had a hard time coming back to Earth—having to trudge back into my office and spend my days staring at the computer screen again; having to communicate with people in complete sentences; having nobody to play music with, and no audience to play in front of except the dogs.[13] I realize that, for my career and my health,[14] I had to get back to Reality. But I miss Bandland. When you get to be in your forties, heading directly toward (can this *be*?) your fifties, you tend not to do stuff like this—make new friends, go out and have wild adventures, risk making a fool out of yourself.

Actually, we did more than just *risk* this, but you get my point: it was worth doing. My advice is, if you are, like so many people these days, getting older, and you get a chance to do anything like this, you should. I'm not talking necessarily about being in a band; I'm just talking about doing something that you have no rational business doing, except that you always wanted to. That's a good enough reason. That's the *best* reason. Because life is pretty much finite. I bet Buddy would tell you the same thing.

---

[13] Name of the dogs: *Broadway* Dogs.
[14] Especially my hair.

Tad Bartimus

CHAIN OF FOOLS

t was a dark and stormy night struggling to turn into a sodden, dreary day when the Rock Bottom Remainders—at least those of us who were semiawake—voted for a pit stop off the interstate in southern Virginia. There was just enough light to see a diner, a gas station, and a mostly empty convenience store.

I was pitifully grateful for the break. We were a week into the Three Chords and an Attitude tour and I was exhausted, struggling with bronchitis and laryngitis, and mired in doubt about even being on the road with nearly two dozen people I hardly knew.

I loved the music, the crowds, the adrenaline rush. But the superficiality of being part of a movable media event noteworthy only because of its megastar authors was depressing. Especially since, at the same time that I was on the road worrying about my eye shadow and the lyrics to "My Guy," my mother was lying pale and still in a hospital intensive care unit, perhaps never to wake up. What am I doing here? I asked myself a hundred times a day. Even though I always answered, "I am doing this for me, I need this more than anything else in my life right now," most of the time I was emotional bouillabaisse.

When I get on the bus, I vowed, I will leave everything else behind me. But I have never been able to separate events from context. So, for six hours spent mostly prone in the seat of a huge vehicle with bad shocks careening down I-95 twenty miles an hour over the speed limit, I had brooded.

Besides, Aretha Franklin's toilet didn't suit my behind.

Our bus was rented from Ms. Franklin, and just a few hours out of Boston on the way to Washington, D.C., I knew I would never again look at the Queen of Soul without picturing her on her throne. I'd sit there, rocking back and forth in the tiny bathroom, holding on to the door handle and the window frame just to stay upright as we jounced and bounced along the pavement, and I'd wait. And wait. And wait. Nothing would happen. I'd wait some more. And then I'd get worried, sitting there waiting, that a line was forming on the other side of the door. I'd worry that impatient people were crawling over Dave Barry's head as he slept jackknifed in the aisle, that they would step on him, maybe even crush his skull as they crossed and uncrossed their legs.

So I'd wait just one minute more and pray that something would happen fast. But nothing ever did. Never mind that I'd had a beer and two Cokes and a quart of Ruby Red (requesting gallons of fruit juice for the bus was an early tip-off that this would not be a typical rockers' road tour). My insides were splitting and I *had to go now!* It didn't seem to matter how much liquid I drank. The minute I sat on that tiny little seat surrounded by mirrors, so that two dozen of me looked back in identical misery, all motivation vanished. Clearly, my problem was mental. No matter. I couldn't talk myself into relief. Eventually I'd give up and go back to my seat, my need greater than ever, but Dave Barry's mop head still thankfully intact.

Fortunately, I had a companion with a similar handicap. Perhaps it was the look on my face that tipped him off, or the frequency of my trips to the back, but Steve King figured out that we were having the same problem. So between the two of us, if we saw a decent-looking rest stop every three or four hours, we'd both yell "*Stop!*" and everybody else quickly caught on that we really meant it. *Stop now!*

Which is how we came to be at a truck stop outside Bracey, Va., at 5:30 on the morning of May 25th.

Those of us awake enough to decide we wanted a blue plate special breakfast, heavy on the biscuits and gravy, were straggling into the empty restaurant when I saw it.

Ranking in artistic merit alongside Jesus on black velvet and Elvis woven into a five-and-dime bath mat, the T-shirt featured a pack of eager hounds racing across its front, headed for the left armpit. A single stray stayed behind, watching his buddies take off without him.

"If you can't hunt with the Big Dogs," proclaimed the airbrushed warning, "STAY ON THE PORCH!"

I was off the porch. But what the hell was I doing on the bus?

I am the unknown Remainder, the last member chosen by Kathi Goldmark. I am the most artistically obscure, the least financially successful, and the most physically unstereotypical author in the group. Which is to say, I have never known an "Uh-Huh!" girl in size 16 sequins. This did not bother me in the beginning. Towards the middle it did.

"When I examine myself and my methods of thought," said Albert Einstein, "I come to the conclusion that the gift of fantasy has meant more to me than the talent for abstract thinking."

Eventually, that is what the Rock Bottom Remainders gave me—the gift of fantasy. But learning to accept it was a bitch. My learning curve was more concave than the rest of them. Most of the people in this band already knew how to have fun, to be silly, to let themselves go, to make fools of themselves and each other, to enjoy being frivolous. More important, they knew it before there *was* a band. I didn't.

For twenty years I had been a reality junkie. It wasn't that I had wanted to turn into someone who looked at life through a photojournalist's lens, darkly. It was just that the direction of my life had taken me through too many shadowed valleys, and I had lost the habit of looking up, toward the light.

Once I left high school I never had ego problems. Through nearly twenty-five years with the Associated Press I rose to the top of my profession. I covered Vietnam and Belfast and Guatemala and stopped being funny at parties. I attacked people for telling ethnic jokes and felt guilty at Thanksgiving. I came to believe that I was my work, that my work was me. I stopped separating the job from the person. My creed became my lifestyle.

As a veteran journalist I had twice served as a Pulitzer Prize juror and twice been a finalist for the prize itself. I had been a foreign correspondent, war correspondent, AP bureau administrator, and, finally, a special correspondent who tried to find stories nobody else had found yet. I was co-author of a serious nonfiction book chronicling the effects of the atomic age on westerners. I believed I had credibility and status. I did—but in a very narrow world.

I was ripe for a fall.

Being in the band gave me a chance to become narcissistic, to focus on myself, to kick my "oldest child syndrome" into oblivion. I finally had an excuse to cut loose, raise hell, and regress. Instead, my ego imploded.

Suddenly, I was right back in high school, wanting to be cool but not wanting to be cool, consumed with self-doubt, physically awkward, restlessly standing on the outside looking in, wanting to be anywhere else but never wanting to be anywhere else, watching—twenty-five years later—the exact same cast of characters who peopled the Class of '65: the Nerd, the Nice Guy, the Brain, the Cool Dude, the BMOC, the Cheerleader, the Girl Most Likely to Succeed, the Cutup, the Hood. They already knew how to have fun. Hell, they were having it, weren't they?

And where was I? I was Miss American Pie tethered to a monthly paycheck suddenly delivered unto Beverly Hills 90210. In a nation where money and fame define status, the Rock Bottom Remainders instantly became the fastest pack in publishing. From the first rehearsal, I wondered if this old dog would ever hunt.

Kathi's invitation to be a Remainderette was extended just days after Toni Morrison had said no. Kathi was one singer short for the female trio that already consisted of herself and Amy Tan. I got Kathi as my San Francisco media escort on my tour for *Trinity's Children*, my book about the nuclear age and the West, and as we were circumlocuting about the Bay Area on a crystalline January day I propitiously tapped my foot to her tape deck. "Do you like rock 'n' roll?" she asked innocently.

By that evening, flying home to Colorado, I was a member of something called the Remainders. I did not take it seriously, for, as usual, I was worrying about my latest AP investigative story, starvation in Somalia, and whether I should stop at Sam's Wholesale Club to buy a case of paper towels for Shining Mountains Inn, the bed-and-breakfast lodge my husband, Dean Wariner, and I owned. I almost forgot about the band until the first bulging manila envelope of "Kathigrams" arrived two weeks later.

As Kathi remembers it, she recruited me because of a scattering of laminated rhinestone hearts and stars I had pinned to my purple coat. She liked them, thought they had pizzazz, and believed they conveyed my personality and style. But just because I wore glittering stars didn't mean I knew how to be one. Kathi's casual observation launched me on a personal search-and-destroy mission that even now has not ended. What she saw, barely glancing at me on the first day of our friendship, set me on a years-long course of trying to discover who I *am*, aside from what I *do*.

For Kathi, inviting me to be in the band was a knee-jerk reaction that I know she came, on occasion, to regret. For me, accepting the invitation was like reaching for a life preserver. It was instinctive. It saved me.

By joining the band, I was forced to reclaim my life. For the first time in my memory, I became a participant instead of an observer. Instead of standing on the outside looking in from a protected vantage point, I was in the picture. Not only had I finally looked up toward the light, but I was in the spotlight, and there was nowhere to hide.

Not since I had reached out, in the middle of a war, and picked up an orphan off a Saigon street to take him home (thereby playing God and changing his life and mine forever) had I made such a commitment to and for myself. In retrospect I found this funny. A commitment. The Commitments. Somebody up there has a sense of humor.

The band came to mean more to me than a chance to perform and hang out with interesting people. It started to redefine me. As a gussied-up Remainderette constantly expanding my persona as well as my personality I was learning how to strut my stuff (hell, I was learning I had stuff to strut!), how to howl at the moon, how not to be just the sum of many parts but to recognize and honor each of those parts, too. The day I joined the Remainders I stepped back over the line I'd drawn long ago in Vietnamese dirt, the one that had stopped me from occasionally laying down the heavy burdens of adulthood and picking up childish things again.

It took a year to figure out all the metaphysical stuff. In the beginning, I was stymied by the words to "Da Doo Ron Ron."

Anaheim was supposed to be a lark, a one-time gig pitched to me as a "so what if we make fools of ourselves?" occasion. We would gather in California in late May of '92, do two performances at a bar, and go our own very diverse ways.

I was not awed at meeting some of the hottest literary bylines in America. I had interviewed presidents, prime ministers, royalty, generals, and Robert Redford. Besides, my book had just come out and I was feeling pretty good about myself. But

Kooper's bus hair was bad enough, but worse, Marsh got into Goldmark's unmentionables.

A child of Christian immigrants.

Not only the audiences were overwhelmed by Tan's transformations.

even though I knew volumes about wolves in Yellowstone, nuclear weapons production, the spotted owl, and a thousand other issues affecting my reporting, I had never read a Stephen King novel, knew only vaguely of *The Joy Luck Club*, and had to ask my local bookseller who Barbara Kingsolver was. I was a cultural illiterate. That did not help me make friends in a band full of professional authors.

And Al Kooper, who was he? While Dave Barry, as a fifteen-year-old guitar player, was worshiping the father of the Blues Project and Blood, Sweat and Tears, and Kathi Goldmark was collecting every album Kooper ever made, I was plastering Eugene McCarthy bumper stickers on cars and marching against the war. I'd missed it. I'd missed the whole damned thing. I was one for whom the music had died.

When we gathered for the first time at the Odd Fellows Hall in Santa Ana I got an instant uneasy sense that I'd made a huge mistake. Always professionally prepared, I usually winged the rest of my life, which hardly ever involved actually doing something.

I didn't know the lyrics to all the songs Kathi had sent me. Although I had loved to sing in high school and college, and had sung in clubs occasionally in my early twenties, I had fallen musically mute. I had lost the desire to make a joyful noise. I was tripping over my feet trying to get the "sha na na na" dance steps right. I couldn't even adjust the microphone: I kept banging my teeth on it. After the first hour I knew my voice wasn't up to even that day's rehearsal, let alone a three-hour performance. I felt tentative, ill at ease, was silent between numbers. I'm sure that just as I was wondering how I'd gotten myself into this mess, the rest of the Remainders—especially a chagrined Kathi—were wondering the same thing.

Despite unanimous protests to the contrary, the Rock Bottom Remainders' pecking order is as real as our guitar strings and gold lamé. And why not? If there is curiosity about famous people, there is also deserved respect for those who have accomplished something. The louder the praise and the wider the audience, the greater the prestige. That's human nature.

In this all-author band, Stephen King was at the top of our ziggurat by virtue of writing and selling the most books. At the next level were Amy Tan, Robert Fulghum, and Dave Barry. Then came Matt Groening, Roy Blount, Jr., and Barbara Kingsolver. Ridley Pearson and Dave Marsh followed. An Alaskan musher's truism promises, "If you ain't the lead dog, the scenery never changes." On day one, I was tail-end Nanook.

Steve King kept me from a cut-and-run. He sat down beside me on the grimy rehearsal-hall floor and asked me a few questions about myself. Totally unintimidating in his usual jeans, faded T-shirt, and ragged red high-top tennis shoes, he wanted to know more about me than my name. Later that day his wonderful wife, Tabby, did the same thing, going even further by visiting with my husband, who also felt out of place.

It was Steve's and Tabby's tacit blessing that set the tone for acceptance by the rest of the band. Because wherever Stephen King goes, metaphorically, so go the Rock Bottom Remainders. This is the man who, after all, displays in his office a photo of the Berlin Wall with the spray-painted message "STEPHEN KING RULES!"

I couldn't share in the megastars' talk about problems with agents and publishers and movie producers and TV moguls and foreign reprint rights and too many interviews and arduous book tours and intrusive, adoring fans. I didn't have those problems. But the Kings' continuing kindness, and the dawning realization that I loved singing again, kept me in Anaheim.

So did Barbara Kingsolver, a journalist-turned-novelist whose warm greeting was leavened with humor and curiosity. We immediately established common ground on social and political beliefs, and our conversations leapfrogged far beyond band talk. By performance night we were sharing secrets and makeup, and our friendship later blossomed into one of soul mates.

Dave Marsh and I were starting to become friends, too. Perhaps we sensed common pain. Later he would say, with a wry laugh, that we were friends in part because "as journalists we are both suspicious, looking for the hidden meanings."

Which is one reason I started noticing everybody's feet. The diversity of personalities and styles was reflected in the shoes each band member wore.

Steve favored his high tops; so did Barbara. Dave Barry wore pure white, unscuffed "don't tread on me" tennis shoes. Ridley Pearson's deck shoes were heavily worn, their leather sides soft and pliable. Amy and Kathi, already fast friends from numerous San Francisco rehearsals and costume shopping expeditions, sported identical black cotton flats, the two-pairs-for-ten-dollars kind you find at discount stores. Al, the man of a million raunchy T-shirts, wore beautiful black lambskin boots. Looking down at my own sandals, I started to take heart. Nobody in this band looked, sounded, or dressed the same. It was okay to be different. In fact, I had a hunch our differences were going to be essential to the band's ultimate success as a unit. (I was right.)

From a very lonely beginning, alliances started to form. By the time the blonde from "Entertainment Tonight" asked me, "Where's Dave Barry? Where's King or Tan? Where are the real authors?" I was suffering through a comeuppance unlike any I had ever experienced, but I was hanging in there. I had decided not to quit.

"How potent cheap music is," marveled Noël Coward. The night we played the Cowboy Boogie I was so drunk on the magic I would gladly have stopped time forever between the opening number and the finale.

Sweating in the heat and energy generated by two thousand bodies packed into a tight space, my stomach roiling from fear and Coronas, I reconnected with life's goodness. It happened—*snap!*—just like that. But like a limb severed from the body and then reattached, my reawakening was accompanied by nerves and twitches. When Steve hugged me backstage in the euphoria after the first set, he asked, "Are you all right?" and I answered, truthfully, "I have never felt better in my life!" But it was an odd sensation, one I'm still getting used to.

Don Henley, for all his bum raps on the other band members, nailed not only my off-key performance but my state of mind that night: "The background singers moved like white women with tight shoes and even tighter libidos (although Ms. Bartimus did, at times, exhibit a bit of soulful joie de vivre.)" In your ear about libidos, Don, but you got the joie right. Like Kathi with her hunch about the sparkling rhinestone pins, Henley sensed a glimmer of something I thought had burned out forever.

Changed by cheap music (left to right: Bartimus, Goldmark, Tan).

Suddenly, even though I was the most "other" of "and other rockin' authors," I wanted to stay in the Rock Bottom Remainders more than I'd wanted anything since my husband. It made me *feel* good. It made me happy. I was singing, and laughing, and being an exhibitionist (in an awkward and tentative way—Henley got the tight shoes part right, too), and I wanted to keep on keepin' on.

How it happened, or why it happened, no longer mattered. At forty-five, with life dealing me body blows, I wanted to keep on being a Remainder for what it meant to *me*, for how the experience was changing *me*.

William Shakespeare said it through Puck: "And those things do best please me/That befall preposterously."

I started paying attention.

"Don't take it seriously," all the band members emphatically agreed, in unison and individually, that first day.

Right. So why did Amy Tan buy her own karaoke machine and lug it on vacation in Hawaii just to practice? Why did Kathi increase her visits to her voice coach? Why did Ridley work so hard on a rehearsal tape for everybody? Why was Stephen taking hours away from his media empire to rehearse "Teen Angel" over and over and over?

There is a line from the action film *Air America* in which Robert Downey, Jr., the rookie CIA pilot who has just arrived in Laos to fly clandestine missions against the Communists, looks around at his grizzled, veteran cohorts and says: "I'm used to being the weirdest guy in the room and all of a sudden I'm not even in the running." That was me in the Rock Bottom Remainders.

Before I got into the band I thought I worked hard. But watching the others—particularly Amy, Dave Barry, Steve, and Ridley—I realized these writers were in a different league. Despite self-deprecating wisecracks to the contrary, they were hard-chargin', laser-focused, market-savvy Type A's who seemed incapable of *not* taking anything seriously. If it is true that "the rich are different from you and me," then it is equally true that the (already successful) creatively blessed are relentlessly self-disciplined, determined, and driven.

In my own postmortem after Anaheim, I realized that if I was going to put aside my fear of failure I had to, as Kathi scolded me one afternoon when I was singing too softly at rehearsal, "step up to the plate and swing at the ball!"

Heading into the bus tour I knew the celebrity pecking order was not the band's problem but mine. When the (mostly shallow, superficial, and ill-prepared) journalists who covered the tour stampeded through three Hard Rock Cafe press conferences in three cities gang-banging the bestselling authors and ignoring everybody else in the band, I told myself that this groveling adulation had nothing to do with my own self-worth or, for that matter, anybody else's.

Besides, the media-wise band members were so good at handling the press that everybody who thought they got something really got nothing but were still happy. Right away, Dave Barry and Steve King developed their comedy routine, and it never varied, from Boston to "Good Morning, America" to *USA Today*. Kathi got her pat answers down cold at the first press conference, and the variations on the same theme just kept coming. Amy, despite near cattle-prod techniques from the press, mostly said nothing, smiled, and charmed their socks off.

I started to understand why bad interviews with famous people all had the same quotes, the same anecdotes, the same descriptives. These author folks were in control of the game, and it stayed that way through eight cities. No reporter ever laid a glove on 'em.

By Atlanta—ten days and nearly two thousand miles into the tour—"the band" had come to mean people who mattered to me for themselves. In fact, their celebrity was mostly in the way of friendship, because the richest and most famous among us had, through their metamorphosis from unknown to icon, become extremely wary of letting interlopers penetrate their plexiglas.

On some days I just knew I loved Dave Barry best. But I don't know him. I never got past his shtick, and during the tour, out of respect for the very private person I came to sense behind the public persona, I stopped trying.

Amy, too, was guarded. An overnight sensation when *The Joy Luck Club* was published in 1989, she now is besieged with demands for her endorsement, or blessing, or participation in events that bear no relevance to her own life. Yet Amy, who is not physically demonstrative and is modest in the most old-fashioned and genteel of ways, hugged me several times when I was crying with despair over my mother's numerous ICU crises or my own recent diagnosis of systemic lupus erythematosus, a chronic and incurable disease. She was always a comforting and sympathetic presence, and she took great pains to include me in any spur-of-the-moment fun. If I was the band's Job, Amy was its conscience, as well as its mischievous sprite.

It was actually Amy who gave me the key to unlock the terrific performance I believed I could give, and finally did.

"Attitude," said the always socially correct superstar who donned thigh-high boots, a leather dog collar, and leopard tights to knock 'em dead on "These Boots Are Made for Walkin'." "You've got to have attitude."

I started to get it in Boston. As we were boarding the bus for Washington I heard a woman yell out several times, "Rock Goddess! Rock Goddess!" Trailing the cotton leopard-print robe Amy had given each Remainderette and Barbara for the bus, and which we had adopted as our encore costume, I turned to see which of the other band women she was calling for.

There was no other female in sight. When I looked at her, she eagerly waved me over to the rope barricade and thrust a small leather book into my hand.

"Rock Goddess," she gushed, "would you please give me your autograph?"

Stunned, I complied. When I looked up, Tim Warren, a fine writer for the Baltimore *Sun*, was grinning at me.

"Take note, Tim, that I can now die happy," I said. "I am officially a rock goddess!"

That silly little incident did, in fact, profoundly change me. A complete stranger had seen me in a light so different from the one in which I cast myself that I started to take a deeper look.

In tandem with that incident, Tabby King and Lorraine Battle (the band's official Miss Fixit, who could instantly produce anything from cough drops to safety pins to suspenders to Twinkies) had decided to "loosen you up, girl!" The minute we'd hit a new town, that pair went combat shopping. By the time we got to Atlanta I had an outfit straight out of Whores "R" Us. The real hurdle was convincing me to wear the black peekaboo chiffon baby-doll pajama top, the black lace teddy, the Diana Ross wig, the shoulder-length gold earrings, the purple eye shadow, and the hair mousse.

"Attitude," said Amy solemnly.

"Cool!" gushed Kathi, who immediately started to demonstrate how to keep our nipples from showing through sheer fabric by putting flesh-colored Band-Aids over them. (Lorraine, of course, had the adhesives in her medical kit.)

"Sexy," pronounced Tabby, who had lavished all these luxury goodies on me at her own expense, thereby contributing to my sense of guilt if I refused to wear them.

OK. I'll do it.

And then a weird thing happened. When I looked in the mirror and didn't see myself, I didn't sing like myself, either. I sang like that person I wanted to sing like—that old rocker with the belting voice who was always on key, always able to hit the high notes, able to project out over the crowd and hit the rafters.

When I walked on stage in Atlanta even Kooper noticed I was different. He smiled. As I took the microphone for my solo, I did something I'd never done before—I spoke to the audience.

"When I started this tour," I yelled to the crowd, "I was a Brooks Brothers woman, but now I'm just a Frederick's of Hollywood girl." As they roared their approval, Kooper hit the opening chords and I started singing "Chain of Fools." Later, Kathi told me that she was horrified that I had chosen that song as my solo for the tour, "because it's sacred, you know? Nobody else is supposed to do it but Aretha. None of us thought you could pull it off." But in Atlanta that night I gave it everything I had, and that was, finally, enough. Performing that song was pure joy: I sang the last verse reluctantly, sad that it was almost over. The applause rolled over me like healing waves. Steve gave me a high five, Dave Barry kissed me, Kathi hugged me, and Kooper pinched my ass (he is truly a macho Neanderthal, but he's our Neanderthal and I love him).

By the time we got to Miami, *USA Today*'s reviewer said, "'Chain of Fools' rocked the house." But I no longer needed somebody else's validation to know that I had earned the right to be in the band. I belonged in the Remainders, because I belonged to the Remainders.

The Rock Bottom Remainders, collectively and as individuals, are cradled in my affection like beloved pets and toys. They have taught me great lessons, mostly in throwaway lines.

"You're just one book away, kid," Steve King told me, meaning that I should go on writing until I get it right.

"Hell, *none* of us belong in this band," Dave Barry told me, thereby assuring me that there was room for everybody.

Ridley Pearson likes my fly-fishing stories and nods knowingly when I start talking about the West—"our real world," he calls it—where he also finds solace in the last of the great places.

Blanket of Fools (Peterson, Pearson, Battle, a little of Bartimus).

Dave Marsh tells me all the time that "life is a bitch but what can you do?" and reminds me that none of us get away clean, that we all pay, but the trick is to have some fun in-between.

Barbara—sweet, funny, wise, and gifted Barbara—has appointed herself my writers' group of one and exhorts me, always, "Be yourself. It's the best."

Roy Blount, Jr., that gentle humorist whose unerring sense of timing applies to kindness as well as comedy, understands the journey I took to get here, and says, "We are fellow travelers."

Al, who forgave me for not knowing who Van Morrison was, and in fact got into the spirit of my ignorance by sharing with me rare

tapes of musicians he admires but I had never heard of, endeared himself to me forever by saying to my mystified husband, "You've got yourself one *wacky* wife," and then laughing uproariously, as though we had a private joke.

Kathi came up with the best tribute of all when she called me "a wanton siren." I want it on my tombstone.

Like Rick and Ilsa, who would always have Paris, I will always have the Rock Bottom Remainders. It changed me, made me better, made me happy, gave me attitude.

When I watch *The Commitments*, I understand.

"So, looking back, Jimmy, what do you feel you've learned most from your experiences with the Commitments?"

"Well, that's a tricky question, Terry, but as I always say, 'We skipped the light fandango, turned cartwheels 'cross the floor, I was feelin' kinda seasick, but the crowd called out for more.'"

"That's very profound, Jimmy. What does it mean?"

"I'm fucked if I know. . . ."

Matt Groening

HOW I INFILTRATED THE ROCK BOTTOM REMAINDERS

*I*f you think it's agonizing to read about rock'n'roll, just think how painful it is to write about.

You plug away year after year, covering the latest bogus pop discoveries, dorky new youth lifestyle trends, out-of-it editors' whims, and big-shot authors making fools of themselves.

And after all is said and done, what do you have to show for it?

Chronic fatigue, severe self-loathing, near deafness, beer belly, bucket butt, uncontrollable snideness, a shortened life span, fear of deadlines, a closetful of lousy T-shirts, extreme poverty, a case of herpes picked up from a beer bottle shared backstage with the bass player from the Vicious Young Pinecones, a small pile of yellowing clippings of your blurbs and articles (including your exclusive interview with the lead singer of Destroy All Geezers), and the dull realization that you've spent a major portion of your grown-up life not writing your novel, not writing your novella, not cleaning your navel, not wising up, and not selling all 10,000 of the crummy promo albums you've accumulated in your dinky dark apartment.

How do I know all this?

I was a rock'n'roll critic once.

ASIDE NO. 1:
EARLY MUSICAL TORTURE

I grew up on a dead-end street in the woods near Beaverton, Oregon, with three battered albums and a short stack of scratchy old 78s in the rumpus room, which I played over and over on a squeaky little record player with a tone arm that had eyes painted on it to make it look like a snake. The hippest of the 78s was Paul Whiteman's 1922 smash hit, "The Japanese Sandman." The three albums were *Glen Gray in Hi Fi*, by Glen Gray and the Casa Loma Orchestra; *Exotica*, by Martin Denny; and *Burl Ives Sings "the Little White Duck" and Other Favorites*.

With one exception, I have fond memories of this old stuff. But if I hear the quavering voice of Burl Ives one more time, lilting on about that little white duck sittin' in the water, and how that little white duck's doin' what he oughter, I swear my brains will come bubbling out of my ears and I'll spin around on the floor like Curly of the Three Stooges on horse steroids.

LET'S HAVE AN EPIPHANY

At some point, every rock'n'roll critic has an identity crisis. *Who am I?* he or she asks. *What the hell am I doing? Why am I writing this? What's the point? Why bother? Will anyone read my review of Ooh La La Bink's eponymous debut EP after I am dead, or am I just wasting my time?*

At this juncture, the rock'n'roll critic can go in one of two directions: He or she can sign on with a record company and become a rock'n'roll publicist (not as glamorous as it sounds).

Or he or she can buckle down and make rock'n'roll writing a career, and begin using words like "epiphany" and "juncture."

ASIDE NO. 2:
MY MUSICAL EDUCATION

1957: I fall in love with the woman peeking out from the bamboo curtain on the cover of Martin Denny's *Exotica* album.

1958: I notice that when Elvis is on TV, I can sneak into the kitchen for cookies and my baby-sitter won't notice.

1959: I discover that all 33-1/3 rpm LPs are improved when played at 45 rpm.

1960: I can't get the closing song from my favorite TV show, "Cartoon Corral," out of my head, and I feel like I'm going insane. To this day, I wake up groggily, softly singing, "Sadly now we say goodbye to all our cartoon friends: Felix and Popeye and Mr. Magoo, Spunky and Tadpole all bid you adieu. . . ."

1961: I am scandalized but thrilled by the following playground ditty: "I'm Popeye the Sailor Man/I live in a garbage can/I love to go swimmin'/With bare naked women/I'm Popeye the Sailor Man."

1962: My new favorite song goes, "Tra la la boom dee ay/We have no school today/Our teacher passed away/We shot her yesterday/We threw her in the bay/She scared the sharks away/And when we pulled her out/She smelled like sauerkraut."

1963: My music teacher says the Beatles don't know how to sing. In retaliation, I squirt some water on his piano bench when he isn't looking. He sits down, leaps up, grabs me by the collar, shakes me back and forth, and yells, "You have no future in music!"

1964: I discover that records can sail like Frisbees deep into the ravine behind my house. So long, Little White Duck!

THE ROCK'N'ROLL CRITIC
CONFRONTS THE UNIVERSE

After deep soul-searching, the honest rock'n'roll critic comes to the conclusion that everything in the universe is connected, and that, as the Yingleberries put it so simply on their recent live CD *If You Don't Stop Spittin' on Us, We Ain't Doin' an Encore*, "we are all one."

Sure, we all have different guises, but basically it's all tied together, like a record-company executive's ponytail.

And this goes for rock'n'roll writing as well.

In fact, it's all one big rock'n'roll review when you think of it in the properly profound way. Only the names, hairdos, and video effects have been changed.

Hence this compact but ultimate guide to rock'n'roll writing, which will serve two purposes. First, it will aid rock'n'roll critics who are stuck at their laptops, stymied for just the right adjective to use (see Appendix I for immediate help!). Second, it will enable rock'n'roll readers to delve behind the scenes and maybe even pick up a few tricks of the trade, and other clichés.

HOW TO WRITE ABOUT
ROCK'N'ROLL

It's easy!

THE ROCK'N'ROLL
HEADLINE

First, the headline! A good rock'n'roll headline should have a pun in it, particularly one that plays on the subject's name.

Example: THE RESENTFUL MANURE SHOVELERS ARE OUTSTANDING IN THEIR FIELD. (A near-perfect headline.)

Example: THE FEISTY CREAMPUFFS: FRESH BAKED FOR YOU! (Perhaps too subtle, but still fun. And best of all, it doesn't mean a goddamn thing.)

If no pun comes to mind, a good solution is to make ironic reference to some baby-boomer pop-culture icon such as the Monkees.

Example: HEY HEY, WE'RE GRANDPA BECOMES A FUNGUS.

Example: HEY HEY, WE'RE THAT FETID DUMPSTER SMELL.

Example: HEY HEY, WE'RE REPUBLICANS ON A SKEWER.

With sensitive artists, who seem like they may hold a grudge if crossed, it is best to play it safe.

Example: THE ROCK BOTTOM REMAINDERS: REBELS *WITH* A CAUSE.

Remember! Make it cute, make a pun, make it hip, or better: do all three.

ASIDE NO. 3:
WHAT I REMEMBER OF MY TEEN YEARS,
BESIDES SULKING

When we were thirteen, my pal Joe and I used to lie on the shag carpet with headphones on, trying to grok the deep hidden meanings of *Sgt. Pepper's Lonely Hearts Club Band.* We were especially impressed that "Lucy in the Sky with Diamonds" secretly stood for LSD. "Do you think the Beatles take drugs?" Joe asked. "I wish we had the stereo version of this record instead of mono," I lamented.

Joe formed a garage band called the Imaginary Orgasms, and I asked if I could join. "No," Joe replied gravely, "but you can write our lyrics, if they're psychedelic enough." I ran home and cranked out dozens of pages of ersatz drug-addled poems, all featuring secret messages in the "Lucy in the Sky with Diamonds" fashion. My best song was "Funny Undulating Circling Kaleidoscope, Yellow Omnipresent Universe."

If the band had ever gotten out of that garage, we would've been huge.

THE HARDEST PART OF ROCK'N'ROLL WRITING: THE OPENING SENTENCE

The blank page staring you in the face! Silent! Mocking!

Or is it?

Not really. Beginning a rock'n'roll story is as easy as falling off a log, once you know the secret.

The secret is *The Formula*.

Or actually, three formulas. Take your pick.

You can begin with: 1) the gratuitous autobiographical aside, 2) the seemingly trenchant biographical anecdote, or 3) the pseudo-audacious critical assertion (such as the lead sentence of this very chapter).

The gratuitous autobiographical aside is hard to get away with at a daily newspaper (see Appendix 2: The Deflavorizer), or at a publication with "style" or "standards." But at alternative newsweeklies and all music magazines, a combination of editors who are former rock'n'roll writers, and the sheer embarrassment everyone feels for the paltry wages offered leads to a considerable looseness in editing, which means you can write just about any damn thing you want.

The gratuitous autobiographical opening should get things rolling in a semidramatic way, as well as reveal how hip and soulful you are.

Example: "It was 3 a.m., October 17, 1992, and I was standing in a small, smoky bar in Tacoma, Washington, and even though I'd packed away six too many, I was still alert enough to know a band that would change my life—as well as the course of rock'n'roll history—when I saw one. They called themselves Li'l Buford and the Bulgy-Eyed Boston Terriers then, but today of course we all know them as the Unholy Peabrains."

Example: "I was hurtling down Interstate 80 last year, near Little America, Wyoming, about 3 a.m., when a song came on the radio that damn near made me cry. Not in self-pity, you understand, but in joy—the joy of being young, alive, American, and gassed up. That song, of course, was the Raging Pathetics' Number One summer megahit, 'I Won't Turn My Music Down ('Cause I'm a Royal Asshole),' but even though we've all heard that masterpiece a million times, I've got to ask you: Have you really heard it?"

Then there's the seemingly trenchant biographical anecdote. If you can't find one that suits your purposes, do what the professionals do: Make one up.

Example: "When Little Billy Joel had been taunted about his runtish size for the umpteenth time, the petulant twelve-year-old slammed his tiny fist into his favorite inflatable pool toy and silently vowed: 'Someday they'll never ever call me Little Billy again!'"

Example: "Who would have thought a chance meeting at a Bisbee, Arizona, frozen yogurt shop one cloudless night in 1993 would lead to one of the most meteoric careers in the history of rock'n'roll? Certainly not Fisk Hurfty, the late guitarist of the Southwest's Number One thrash combo, I'm Not High Yet, Let's Shoot Up Some Bathroom Cleanser."

And then there's the pseudo-audacious critical assertion, which says a mouthful, yet says nothing at all.

Example: "They say a rolling stone gathers no moss. Well, try telling that to British rock'n'roll legend Mick Jagger, who just sold a bag of his own bodily waste at Sotheby's to an anonymous buyer for over $7,000."

Example: "If Wolfgang Amadeus Mozart were alive today, you might well find him playing bass with Us R Dimwits."

Example: "A rock'n'roll legend, in order to stay on top, must either re-create the past, or try something new. The great Bob Dylan, after making a mysterious purchase at Sotheby's, is doing both."

Example: "Life has not always been good for legendary rock'n'roller Nork Wilson, ex-keyboardist with I Hate My Parasites."

Example: "Who *is* this guy?"

ASIDE NO. 4:
CONFESSIONS OF AN ASHAMED
ROCK'N'ROLL CRITIC

I've never owned a Bob Dylan album. Most rock lyrics sound like nursery rhymes to me. I think Bessie Smith is a drag. I don't believe that rock'n'roll will never die. I've never done acid. I've never owned a record by Elvis. I tried to dig Robert Johnson, but I couldn't. I've never done speed. I don't know who's in the Rock'n'Roll Hall of Fame. I've never watched the Grammys. I like Bing Crosby. When singers at concerts say,"Put your hands together, people," I don't particularly feel like doing it. I write things I don't believe, just to piss people off. I'd rather listen to accordions than guitars. I hate everything on the radio. I don't want my MTV. I've never filled out my *Village Voice* Pazz & Jop survey. My favorite group at Woodstock was Sha Na Na. I've never owned a record by Bruce Springsteen. Or Roxy Music. Or U2. Or R.E.M. Or The Band. Or the Sex Pistols. Or Prince. Or the Velvet

Underground. Or MC5. Or Nirvana. Or Public Enemy. I've never done coke. I think rock musicians are idiots. I never want to see the same group perform more than twice. I've never written an in-depth analysis of anything. I don't think the Butthole Surfers are as good as they used to be. I'd rather listen to Burl Ives than Rod Stewart. I think rock music is too loud. I used to invent bands and give them rave reviews. You haven't lived till you've heard Chatterbox Punch Gruffy.

THE MEAT

With the opening out of the way, the rest of the piece should write itself. Continue with a brief description of the subject using superlatives whenever possible. This will convey both the importance of the subject and the importance of you, the writer.

Remember, you are not trying for precision. You are trying to create a mood. So write like: "Dave Barry's voice has an aching, romantic tug to it, filled with the muted passion of late-night loneliness."

And: "The Slime Weevils are not trying to be trendy. They're shooting for a truly American experience that is timeless in the purity of its emotion. Needless to say, the new album, *Love Me, Love My Crab Lice*, is a classic."

And: "With no compromise or calculation, the moody yearnings of the sensitive outsider are poignantly portrayed in the thoughtful songs of Bob Dole's Left Nostril—with a pure-hearted integrity that has shot this fledgling group straight to the top of the charts!"

Don't forget to insert references to at least two of the following in your article: Elvis Presley, Chuck Berry, the Velvet Underground, the New York Dolls, U2, Bruce Springsteen, or Snoop Doggy Dogg. Pertinence does not matter.

ASIDE NO. 5:
CONFESSIONS OF AN ASHAMED
ROCK BOTTOM REMAINDER

I can't play an instrument. I can't keep the beat. I can't carry a tune. And I don't mean that in the cute sense. I mean I sing worse than Dave Marsh and Greil Marcus rolled into one. I was kicked out of the Ooga Booga Blues Band in high school for playing the tambourine wrong. I can't remember the lyrics to any of the songs the Remainders have ever done. Even when I'm holding the lyrics in front of my face, I lose my place. I can't believe that the rest of the band hasn't turned on me and yelled in unison, "You have no future in music!"

I didn't go on tour with the Rock Bottom Remainders because I was swamped with work on *The Simpsons*, or so I told everyone. The real reason I didn't go on tour was because I got a whiff of the tour bus that we'd hired when we played the Bottom Line in New York last year.

This bus reeked.

Let me put it this way. When I was fourteen, I had a summer job pulling weeds at a Multnomah County, Oregon, sewage treatment plant. This was a bad job, with few, if any, perks. And the two things I remember most from that long, hot, sticky, smelly summer were the seventy-five cents an hour I earned, and the barfing I endured every morning when I arrived for work.

I assure you that the tour bus smelled worse.

So I bowed out of the big Remainders tour, cackling to myself about the misery these authors were going through while I laid back in Hollywood, living the good life and taking meetings with TV network executives. My plan was to swoop into Miami for the final show of the tour, fresh as a daisy, and nod my head sympathetically at the tales of woe and odors that the rest of the band would regale me with. Certainly a fistfight or two would have broken out on the bus, and no doubt the whole group would be completely alienated from each other. My job would be to soothe every-one's jangled nerves and egos, let whoever felt like it weep on my shoulder, then get everyone together for a big California New Age Hug of Forgiveness.

But something went wrong. At the last minute, just before hopping on the plane, I decided to autograph a hundred Simpsons posters for fans. I sat at my drawing table with a stack of posters, doodling a Bart on each one as fast as I could, then twisting to my left and dropping the finished poster on the floor. I started sign-ing faster and faster, pleased with my demon signing speed, when suddenly, while twisting to the left with poster number seventy-three, I felt a sort of *squinch* in my lower back and found myself doubled over in a TV-sitcom-style contortion, unable to straighten up and in severe agony.

A quick painkiller prescription later, I was on the red-eye to Miami, moaning in discomfort. I'm in serious trouble, I thought to myself. I could barely writhe in my seat, much less rotate my pelvis in lewd abandon onstage, the way I knew the rest of the Remainders would expect.

I found, however, that by accidentally slightly overdosing on the painkillers, I could make the plane trip not only tolerable but the best goddamn flight I've ever been on. And when I leaped off the plane in Miami at 6 a.m., I was in such a good mood I tried to get the guy running the floor polisher at the airport to let me ride him to the hotel.

The rest of the trip is a hazy, hallucinogenic blur. Not only do too many painkillers make you loopy, I found that when you combine them with beer, the world turns sideways and you have to hold on to the floor to keep from falling to Cuba.

But even in my hampered state of semi-drooling goofiness, I noticed that the rest of the Remainders were not at each other's throats, as I'd expected. They were all lovey-dovey and huggy-wuggy, as if they'd somehow bonded on that fume-filled tour bus. I realized then that my special healing powers were not at all needed, which was just as well, because it took all my concentration to perform small tasks like walking across the room without flapping my arms and getting my fork from my plate to my mouth without stabbing myself in the eyeball.

I must say that being out of my gourd felt like the appropriate way to perform. Sure, I couldn't keep the beat, carry a tune, or remember the lyrics, *but it didn't matter, man!* It was rock'n'roll! I could sing! I could dance! I could scream gibberish into the microphone!

And everybody cheered!

I made a fool of myself that night. I minced, I cavorted, I wiggled my curvy butt. I did the Worm, the Hully Gully, the Mashed Potato, and the Charleston. I hogged the microphone whenever I could, and stuck my tongue out like that jerk from Kiss. I ogled Amy Tan, Barbara Kingsolver, Tad Bartimus, Kathi Goldmark, and Joel Selvin. I beat my chest, flexed my muscles, fondled myself, and humped an imaginary dance partner. I lifted my shirt and exposed my belly, pulled down my pants and pranced in my boxers, squirmed on the floor like a legless dog, and winked lasciviously at out-of-focus human shapes in the audience.

Of course, so did the rest of the band, so I fit right in.

HOW TO CONCLUDE
A ROCK'N'ROLL ESSAY

Three ways. Take your pick.

The innocuous closer: "No doubt we'll be hearing more from the Rock Bottom Remainders. Soon."

The reportorial info conclusion: "You can decide for yourselves whether all the fuss is hype or not when the Rock Bottom Remainders make their urban Idaho debut this Tuesday night at the Deer Musk Club in downtown Boise as part of their 'Oh No, the Bus Is on Fire Again' tour."

Or the singer's concluding remarks: "'I'm proud to say that it's become our generation's anthem,' says Stephen King about the Rock Bottom Remainders' current hit, 'Yow! (That's One Body Part I Shouldn't've Gotten Pierced),' before nodding off for an apparently much needed midday nap."

APPENDIX 1:
ASSORTED HANDY ROCK'N'ROLL
WORDS AND PHRASES
(SUITABLE FOR ANY REVIEW OF
THE ROCK BOTTOM REMAINDERS)

Agitated sensibility. Alternative. Angst-filled. Anti-commercial. Artless vocals. Ass-kicking rock'n'roll.

Ballsy. Breakthrough. Brutal.

Catchy. Charismatic. Chart action. Commitment. Crossover.

Danceable. Dazzling. Deceptively simple. Deceptively anything. Def. Deft. Delicate beauty. Demonic drumwork. Down and dirty. Dylanesque.

Eclectic. Enigmatic. Eponymous.

Fierce. Focused. Frantic yet fluid. Fresh.

Graceful yet pile-driving. Grunge. Guitar hero.

Impassioned spirit. Impressive debut effort. Infectiously melodic. Integrity. In-your-face. Irradiated by the unbearable lucidity of despair.

Jangly guitars.

Legendary.

Mass popularity. Meaty.

Old-school hip-hop 'tude. Overdrive.

Packs an emotional wallop. Postmodern. Postpunk. Power chords. Profound.

Radio-friendly. Raw talent. Recently married to actress/model. Righteous authenticity. Ripping solos. Roots-conscious.

Serious. Shatteringly lovely. Silken-voiced. Sly. Solemn. Soulful. Spacey. Springsteenian. Straight-ahead rock'n'roll. Street credibility. Subversive. Synergistic. Stellar.

Taking it to the next level. Tasty licks. Teen anthem. Thrusting. Trippy.

Uncompromising yet commercially pleasing. Urgent.

Videogenic. Vital.

Well-crafted. Willful obscurity.

Youth-oriented.

Zany, devil-may-care attitude that belies a moody, almost suicidal despair about the mistreatment of animals and the sales of their last album.

APPENDIX 2:
THE DEFLAVORIZER

This is an editorial process used to remove troublesome words, syntax, and ideas from a rock'n'roll essay. The aim is to end up with a gentle, pleasing flow of words that is not slowed down by peculiarities of individual style or humor. Sort of like a bowlful of butterscotch pudding, only without the bite. Most professional rock'n'roll writers learn to anticipate the deflavorizing process, and are able to do it to themselves.

APPENDIX 3:
WHAT IF FYODOR DOSTOEVSKY WERE ALIVE TODAY? WOULD HE BE WRITING ABOUT ROCK'N'ROLL? AND WOULD DOSTOEVSKY GET TOGETHER WITH A BUNCH OF OTHER WRITERS AND SIMPER ONSTAGE TO THE POP DITTIES OF THREE DECADES AGO?

"What if" games are a waste of time.

Greil Marcus

THE BOSNIAN CONNECTION

Appearing onstage as part of a rock & roll band, in front of an audience of real people, was not the fulfillment of a lifelong dream for me.

My fantasy had always been to be a disc jockey—a fantasy I'd actually had the chance to realize once or twice. Let others fool with the open possibilities of "I'd like to teach the world to sing"; the fascist imperatives of "I will force the world to hear" are more appropriate for a critic. For that matter, I knew perfectly well I couldn't sing, dance, or play an instrument, but any jerk can pick records and rave about them. Or rage about them: My disc jockey hero was Russ "The Moose" Syracuse, master of "The All-Night Flight" on KYA in San Francisco in the early and mid-sixties. People would wait up until three in the morning for the moment when all the sound effects of the Second World War would be marshaled for Russ's nightly bombing raid on the record he hated most. As the bombs fell, Russ the Moose urging them on, you could hear the record break up: EAT SCREAMING DEATH, CHRIS MONTEZ! And as Chris ate it, all around him played the strangest music, records I'd never heard before and have never heard since: "Need Your Love" by the Metallics, "Drinkin' Wine" by Larry Dale, mixed in with weirdo hits like Jimmy Soul's "If You Wanna Be Happy" or the Day Brothers' "Cleopatra Brown." As a performer, a DJ was a public secret. If you wanted it that way, no one knew what you looked like, what you did outside the invisible box your noise came from, where

you came from, where you went. The DJ was not exposed. The DJ was himself a creature of fantasy—of whatever fantasies he could provoke in his listeners. As a public secret the DJ was every poor kid, alone in her room, dreaming and fearing, wishing and hoping, loving and hating—he alone in his room, you alone in yours.

A voice in the night, without a face—perfect. I had to be dragged into the Rock Bottom Remainders.

Onstage in Anaheim in 1992 at the booksellers' convention for our first and, we supposed, last show, I made a discovery: the thrills of secrecy and anonymity were slightly overrated. There was nothing quite like the feeling of being absolutely shameless in public. Oh, Dave Barry might actually play guitar or Barbara Kingsolver piano; Stephen King might truly have something to offer "Teen Angel," some slime of glee the song had resisted all through the years; but no such argument could be advanced for the Critics Chorus. As a five-person assemblage—Dave Marsh, Matt Groening (former rock critic, anyway), Roy Blount, Jr., Joel Selvin, and myself—we could take the stage with the hope that we might be able to hide amongst ourselves, one clumsy move canceled by another, one nonvoice drowned out by a louder version of the same thing, or rather by Selvin, who *could* sing and reveled in proving it. This sort of subterfuge lasted for about half a song. It was immediately obvious that nobody cared; there were no routines; antisinging or antidancing in the worst way, one was still taking part in some holy rite, joined now to a tradition fated to outlast all who were part of it, "Double Shot (Of My Baby's Love)" *excelsior*.

Unfortunately, you had to be there.

Watching the videotapes of this holy rite was precisely as embarrassing as I'd been sure trying or pretending to perform would be. There was talk of releasing this stuff commercially (it happened); from the evidence before us we were so bad not even relatives were going to make it to the end. At a party, conversations by the persons responsible drowned out the recorded sound seconds into each song. As "Bye Bye Love" played, the weather was suddenly endlessly interesting. And what *is* your philosophy of life, Amy?

The idea of a tour—a heroic barnstorm down the East Coast, Massachusetts to Florida, just a happy-go-lucky troupe of crazy scribblers with their repertoire of sock-hop tear-jerkers and frat-house drinking songs—struck me as utter lunacy, all but criminal hubris, the indulgence of infantile fantasies of mastery and sexiness by those less wise than I. I figured the jig would be up by the third gig at the latest.

As rehearsals commenced, and then the first of the scheduled shows, where ordinary people were supposed to pay real money in order to be part of the audience, I kept waiting for the phone call calling the whole thing off, or at least suspending the joke until the concluding among-friends blowout at the 1993 ABA convention in Miami. I stayed home, having signed on for the bare minimum necessary to sustain friendship and assuage guilt. Rehearsals? For five guys to stand up and shuffle around for "Louie Louie"? If I hadn't learned the words after nearly thirty years (I hadn't), I wasn't going to learn them now.

On May 27, I flew in to Atlanta and took a cab to the Roxy, site of the sixth show on the tour. It was late afternoon; I walked into the club and heard a muffled tape of the old records we were going to butcher. But onstage was the band—lip-synching to the tape?

Of course there wasn't any tape; the band had turned into a music machine. Some people had taken lessons, some people had put in countless hours in the salt mines of karaoke bars; some people had practiced at home. I walked up to the stage, stood in the well before it, looked up, and grinned: this was still funny, but it wasn't a joke. And then it struck me, an obvious thought that was apparently just too big for the previous year: there was a bunch of writers in this band, but also a guy who had made "Like a Rolling Stone." If, someday, we ended up as a footnote to a footnote to that footnote, it would do.

For the next two shows, I was as much fan as bellower. In 1992, there were times when I couldn't bear to look at us; now, some moments were so good I forgot my own bits and stared. The Chorus didn't do much more than rumble "VRRROOOOM, VRRROOOOM" (motorcycle noise) for "Leader of the Pack," but I had problems with that, blinded by the light of three flashing lamé dresses, blond wigs, with Amy Tan as a Shangri-La (and in Shangri-La), drawing one gloved arm across tear-stained face, choking with grief, stretching her hands to the stunned crowd as if it could somehow save her, or anyway the soul of Shangri-La Mary Ann Ganser, who was already dead.

It wasn't clear who made up the audiences in Atlanta or the next night in Nashville. There was the inevitable contingent of Stephen King followers—more or less Trekkies with strong backs, as each one seemed to come factory-equipped with an armful of King hardbacks, always carried loose, never in a sack. They didn't dance much. But otherwise the crowds seemed composed of whoever normally showed up at the Roxy, or Performance Hall in Nashville, on a Thursday or Friday night. "Suspend Your Credibility" was our slogan, and it seemed these people had—it seemed as if they'd shown up actually expecting a good time, not a freak show.

With this kind of energy feeding the stage, we went through the entire history of a band, first blush to cynical fakery, in three shows. Everyone agreed that something clicked in Atlanta, that there was some spirit in the performance that had been missing before: a touch of who-cares nihilism, every gesture extended just a bit beyond melodrama, one note justifying the next. We weren't going through the motions and neither was the crowd. When the Chorus had nothing to do on a song, I liked to get down from the stage and walk through the audience; people were pumped, laughing for the louder faster numbers, not really caring who was playing, but living inside the songs. There was a snap in the sound, in the air; the irony every one of us had brought to the whole idea of the group was burning off. Backstage in Nashville—well, the very word is wrong, it simply meant "through the curtain over there," no doors, stairs, barriers you couldn't blow away—one could have found Lamar Alexander, former governor of Tennessee, secretary of education under George Bush, now already running for the GOP presidential nomination for 1996. But there was no rush, no aura, no importance to glean; he was merely an ordinary-looking guy, and after a minute he started to act like one.

Ah, but it all turned to ashes in Miami. No more scruffy joints, but the biggest, glitziest gay disco in Miami Beach: multileveled, huge batteries of light, VIP rooms, a sound system much too big for us. No more audiences of the curious, the accidental, the fanatical; now it was all publishing people, and we were a hot ticket. If you couldn't get in to see the band you were nothing. If you could get in but didn't have a pass to the after-show party you were nobody. If you had a pass but couldn't get backstage you weren't somebody, and backstage was crawling with somebodies: base preeners on the order of Erica Jong, throwing her arms wide, the women in the band trying to duck on their way to sing.

The crowd was a mass of—it seemed—fifty-year-old Yuppies. All eyes fixed on our stars and then immediately began scanning the crowd for the people they'd come to be seen by. The audience was dressed up, and I think that threw the band; the audience had come not for a good time but for gossip material. They were bored straight off, and we were off, too. Every song seemed slack, too long, as if depending on the next number to keep its promise. We played two sets, added numbers we were better off without, and began to run out of gas. During a break I headed to the dressing room to sit down; the place was jammed with people, not one of whom had anything to do with anyone in the band. To cap it all, Susan Faludi, who had teased us with a promise to completely discredit herself by appearing as a go-go dancer, went to a wedding instead. Really, it was horrible: the next day, after an overdose,

an attempted murder, and refusal of immediate seating at Joe's Stone Crab, we knew it was time to quit.

Out of the several days I spent on the Remainders tour—days when we pretended to be a rock & roll band, and, in occasional moments, were—one odd incident stands out. I met a woman from Bosnia, or, rather, read her T-shirt.

Now, even in the Rock Bottom Remainders, people in the band got treated like rock stars—that is, like children. Someone else told us when to show up where, drove us from there to somewhere else, pointed us in one direction, then in another, opened the door, closed it, handed us towels when we left the stage, told us to watch our step when we went back up on it, said complimentary things, ran errands. Even on the smallest of small-time levels, such treatment creates a wonderful cocoon; on the right night, only good feeling grows within it. You walk around smiling, shaking hands, feeling friendly, knowing, though, that at any given moment you have something more important to do, something more important than what anyone is saying to you. The real world—any other world—is kept at bay.

We were in Nashville, Al Kooper had a solo spot, the Critics weren't needed, I was checking out the audience. In fact I was looking for Stephen Greil, former southern rock promoter, now head of the Nashville Symphony, and a long-lost, never-met cousin, the Greils being from Alabama. The club manager had promised he'd be there. Instead, a small, trim, dark-haired woman of about thirty came up to me. She was wearing a T-shirt with "BOSNIA-HERZEGOVINA" spelled out on it in block letters, as if the country were a football team and she was rooting for it. It was one of the most pathetic, heartbreaking things I've seen in my life.

"My name is Ljerka Vidić," she said. "I'm from Sarajevo. I'm an ethnomusicologist." She kept talking, but I couldn't help thinking back a couple of months to a dinner party in Berkeley. "It'll be very interesting," said the professor who invited me. "There'll be a professor of ethnomusicology from Bosnia." Oh, *that'll* be fun, I thought; I'll probably end up sitting next to her. It wasn't and I did.

We talked for three hours about the destruction of Yugoslavia, the risk of rape while conducting field research in Yugoslavian villages, the way the division of Yugoslavia into ever more narrowly defined groups had after a few months of civil war put Sarajevo's Jews at each other's throats—after all, some had been there a hundred years longer than . . . "I hated communism," Ankica Petrović said to me. "But after the war began, I found a picture of Tito and put it up on my wall. We had a country and now we have nothing." She had left a month before; she was almost certain her mother was dead by now, couldn't imagine that she would have survived; she didn't know about her husband and her son.

"I've been here seven years, teaching," Ljerka Vidić said in Nashville. I realized she had to know Ankica Petrović. "I studied under her, of course!" Vidić said. I'd met two people from Bosnia in my life and they were teacher and student; I figured the chances of that were about the same as finding two Greils in the same room, but of course the odds were much greater, which is why one happened and the other didn't. People in the same field meet each other sooner or later.

And that was what Ljerka Vidić wanted to talk about. "I understand what *you're* doing up there," she said, pointing to the stage. "You're *music*. But why is Stephen King"—he was in the throes of "Sea of Love"—"in this band?" It bothered her. I was about to launch into some disquisition on the malleability of cultural barriers in the United States as opposed to Europe when my eyes went again to the block letters on her shirt and I wanted only to take her by the hand, bring her up on stage, and make her Guest Critic (we sacrificed at least one local writer per show), to prove to her anyone could do it. Instead I just told her about *Christine*, about Stephen King's radio station—the one he bought so he'd have a chance to hear something decent in his own hometown—and then said, "Just listen. Wait till he gets to 'Teen Angel.'"

A while later, I saw Vidić again in the crowd, this time with her husband. Now you could see it all made sense to her. She was less a musicologist than part of the crowd. She was beaming—at King, Dave Barry, the Remainderettes. I stared once more, this time from behind her, but looking right through her, seeing only her version of "GO BOSNIA! PUSH 'EM BACK, PUSH 'EM BACK, WAAAAAYYYY *BACK!*" I realized I was missing the Critics' cue for our last big number. Fuck it, I said, as if one curse would put Ljerka's strange affirmation out of my mind. It didn't, and now that memory is my only real souvenir of the trip, a souvenir that makes every tune we did count for more than we ever had in mind.

Tabitha King

I DIDN'T GET PAID ENOUGH

Somebody had to do photographs for the RBR tour. Since I was going along anyway and had been seen working a camera at the rehearsal for the Anaheim ABA show, I was asked to do it. Let's get it right out front. I didn't get paid enough. As a consequence I have withheld from publication in this book a number of photographs that I plan on publishing when somebody offers me enough money. Or not publishing when somebody offers me even more money.

No doubt there are morons out there demanding to know if I don't have enough money. Well, would you work for diddly-shit? No. You wouldn't. Just what I thought. Probably if you had enough money, you wouldn't work at all. So who's got the work ethic here? I *have* enough money. There's a difference between having enough money and *getting paid* enough to compensate for the work. I knew you'd understand.

Truth: I'm not a good enough photographer to call what I do art. Art you can do for free, because you like, *have to*. Or else you explode or implode or whatever. I sweat over this stuff. I need to get paid for reassurance.

And of course I've earned combat pay. It's dangerous doing the devil's work. It's true that cameras steal souls, a layer at a time. The camera in all its forms is literally—pun—the medium of the celebrity culture, transforming its subjects into public figures. That's not a minor mutation—it is, for instance, virtually impossible to slander or libel a public figure. Being a public figure is like being a bug trapped in resin. It's easy to wind up fossilized in amber, in the posture which is the permanent public perception of you.

Visual animals that we are, we buy the lie that a picture is worth a thousand words. Actually, a picture is worth a picture, and pictures lie all the time. But because sometimes the camera does record some fraction of a second with a high degree of accuracy, we accept all its recording as, often, more real than reality. The photographer knows better but with the devil's tool (well, one of them) in hand, is seduced into giving up respect for the person in pursuit of an arresting image.

I try to work in natural light and when I can, draw in shadow, to break the surfaces. It was no surprise that some of the best stuff I got was in Philly, where sound-check and show took place out of doors. It was there, for instance, that I think I came closest to the real, but elusive, Barbara Kingsolver. Philly, by the way, is where some of us went out on a boat on the river before the show, which was in a club on the riverbank. I never thought about Philadelphia as, like, a *river* town. A river you could put a boat on. I mean, isn't Philadelphia basically the city that made raw eggs famous—*getting strong now!* Actually, I used to eat raw eggs myself, only I beat them up with milk and vanilla. Then I developed a mild allergy to them. (An allergy to raw eggs makes receiving vaccines dicey, because egg white is the nutrient for most vaccines. Unless there's been some changes made. Also, raw eggs can breed salmonella on account of fecal contamination, which means chickenshit, which means steak tartare, combining raw eggs and raw beef, is potentially a mega–bowel bomb. I wouldn't eat it, if I were you.)

The only other time I've ever been in Philadelphia all I saw was the airport while I waited for the weather to clear enough to allow my flight into New York. When I finally arrived at my hotel in Manhattan, it was around one in the morning. I happened to laugh at something the bellman said as we approached my room, and a door opened and John Travolta stuck his head out—evidently summoned by the sound of a woman laughing—and said "Mary Lou?" Since I was obviously not Mary Lou, he slammed the door immediately.

I've always wondered if Mary Lou ever showed and if not, why. Maybe her flight never got out of Philadelphia.

In some clubs there was no place to work out front—I'm five four and weigh too much for a block-and-tackle—and in D.C. working in back meant way higher than the stage. I went for backstage stuff at those shows—besides, those full frontal stage shots of the band are boring. All group shots suck. You get more than three people in the frame, they all turn to cardboard (which is why I cut the original Remainders' group photo from Anaheim into a riser card).

In Amherst, I was able to shoot from the foot of the stage. I happened to be standing in front of some witch who teaches at a college in the area, just as she explained to her companions that she had students telling her Stephen King was as great a writer as Tolstoy. Scandalized (thrillingly so, from the tone of her voice), she reported vowing to her students she personally would never read anything written by Stephen King. I love an intellectual position firmly founded in complete ignorance, don't you? It apparently never occurred to her to be curious about what

it was about Stephen King's work that spoke so strongly to those students. She had her little literary god and she was going to give those kids the revealed truth. She gets paid for, and feels justified, in passing Tolstoy-worship off as intellectual activity. I kept trying to step on her pointy feet but never did quite manage to get my full weight into it. That's all right. We all pay for our sins in the most appropriate manner. I figure her medicine cabinet is full of laxatives.

Mine's not. There's not one in the house. Which brings up the subject of transverse colon massage. Once I found out it was a no-no to actually use the toilet on the bus, I foresaw no end of problems. Not for me—I was born regular. But I was traveling with a bunch of middle-aged writers—sedentary, by and large, and most of them in mid-life crisis. I knew we were talking about staying up past regular bedtimes and a lot of junk food and—well, a fool could see it was a recipe for sluggish bowels.

Transverse colon massage is a simple little non-invasive, low-tech, free and safe method for giving aid and comfort to one's lower intestine. (It's one of the really useful skills I've picked up in my life.)

Lie down flat. *Gently* push the heel of your palm in a diagonal, starting from the left at the top of your hip bone, down to the bottom of your right hip bone. Then reverse directions, straight across, bottom of the right hip bone to bottom of the left hip bone. Voilà. You just massaged your transverse colon.

You can do it a couple of times if you want but you probably won't have to. Amy didn't.

Of course you should also do all the things your mother and Wilfrid Brimly told you to do for your bowels—water, exercise (dancing), laughing, eat oatmeal, don't smoke, don't put your colon on hold when it rings, and so on.

WARNING: *If when you place pressure on your tummy above your belly button, you feel excruciating pain, you really should call your doctor right away. And don't do the colon massage. It doesn't do a thing for peritonitis.*

It struck me, in reading what everyone else had written, how little was reported about the atmosphere on the bus itself. The Hole-of-Calcutta-on-wheels ambience broke down nearly all the social barriers immediately, the way it does at summer camp. We were all the same g-g-generation, packing up our cares and woes (in some instances in lots and lots of layers of tissues) and looking, as usual, for love. The Beatles taught us that was all we need, and we believe it, lately with the word self in front of it. We're great old believers, we boomers, for people who have such high regard for their critical faculties.

Al Kooper sat up front most of the time, and usually Dave Marsh and Steve King and Dave Barry and Kathi Goldmark and Lorraine Battle and Carol Eitingon and Jerry Peterson and Josh Kelly did too. And Bob Daitz when he was with us.

Ridley Pearson hung out in the back of the bus with Tad Bartimus and Barbara Kingsolver and Amy Tan. Lorraine and Carol provided us with pillows and blankets and we all made nests—curled up and crunched up and some of us sprawled—it was a summer camp kama sutra of sleeping postures. People gave each other foot and hand and shoulder massages and swapped around sleeping masks. And germs, of course. Sometimes Al came back and slept on the bench by the toilet and Tad slept on the one opposite. Sometimes I lurched forward and fell over the outstretched limbs of various sleepers.

Carol and Lorraine tried to provide fresh fruit and juice but most of the band was more interested in beer and artery-and-bowel-clogging junk food. Everybody talked, at some point and at length—even the ones who started quiet eventually ran off at the mouth, from the enforced intimacy and the sleep deprivation and the performance highs. You never met a more opinionated bunch of people in your life, except maybe if you dined alone with Dave Marsh. There was a lot of laughing—everyone trying to outsmartass Barry. (You could shock him into momentary silence with sheer outrageousness but nobody ever really succeeded in topping him.) What I like about Dave Barry is he is as short as I am, accepts his hair without complaint, and is fool enough to lift his shirt and show me his bellybutton on command.

The fact is we were mostly a bunch of bare acquaintances who were living in each other's back pockets. The only people who had seen much of each other were the critics—Marsh, Blount, Selvin, Marcus—and the West Coasters—Kathi and her crew and Amy.

Indeed, it would be a mistake to think all of these folks knew each other well even in a literary sense. For instance, I've read only a couple of Joel Selvin's reviews, nothing by Greil Marcus, a lot of Blount, a lot of Marsh, most of Barry, a couple of Ridley Pearson's books, Tad Bartimus's book, all of Barbara Kingsolver's, but of Amy Tan, only her kid's story. My impression was everybody in RBR reads at least as much as I do or more, but I'd expect to find the same kind of spotty survey of each other's work. And I don't think anybody on the entire bus, with the exception of my husband, had ever read any of my books. Which doesn't make them exactly rare. Barbara Kingsolver once blurted her surprise that I was funny. Then she stole my line.

We got along—no actual punches thrown—but some of the people on the bus didn't like each other much and there were arguments about who got performance time and so on. Ridley Pearson withdrew before performances and practiced his scales and focused; I didn't notice the intensity of his preparation marred his ability to have a good time. Al Kooper, who had done the rock tour for real, sensibly bailed out when he had to. Michael Dorris, of course, had dropped out after the Bottom Line, and Robert Fulghum and Matt Groening were able to join the band only at the end of the tour, in Miami. Greil Marcus was along for too short a time.

Whenever anybody split for awhile, as Barbara did, there was a sense of something missing. The chemistry changed.

Since this is my g-g-generation, about three minutes after arriving at rehearsal in Boston, nearly everyone was standing around a piano telling each other tales of youthful drug misadventures. This was a subject that came up regularly on the bus and backstage too—indeed, a careful reading of the preceding texts will reveal just how ubiquitous the drug experience has been among this small but very possibly significant sampling of American writers and musicians.

One of the most disbelieving laughs raised on the trip was evoked by my statement that I had the only virgin brains of my generation, as I never did acid—or anything, in fact, except alcohol. Like Bill Clinton, I didn't inhale. I didn't laugh when Clinton said that, either, because I knew just what he meant. I'm a mild asthmatic—smoke of all kinds clogs my respiratory system promptly and effectively. And I learned early on with booze that it wasn't worth how sick it made me. (Later yet discovering a congenital kidney defect that undoubtedly reduced my ability to process alcohol.) As a consequence, I remember the sixties. They sucked.

One of the best experiences for me while I was on the road with the band was learning how to dress like a roadie. I was born fashion-impaired. When grunge had its brief moment of fashion, I was ecstatic. I was cutting my hair with nail scissors and mixing plaid clothing that was too big for me when I was seven. Naturally, Mouse and Hoover immediately became my idols, though I knew I would never be able to wear my socks with Mouse's élan, or drop my shorts with Hoover's artless grace. Actually, getting my shorts down can't be done artlessly—my booty's too big.

While I was out shopping for wigs and glamour drag for the chicksingers, I found a pair of surfer shorts in a bargain bin. They were printed with safari animals. Big ones. The instant I saw them, I knew Hoover would approve. Hoover also wears shirts from tours that happened, like, in 1979. Collectors' items. Mouse wore Hawaiian shirts. Nothing like those in the bargain bin. But once I was wearing my surfer shorts with the animals on them and I had my band laminate around my neck, I could rest easy that Mouse and Hoover didn't have to be ashamed of me. I could never be just like them but I could make an *hommage*. I will cherish my shorts and my laminate forever.

On that shopping trip I found the rubber falsies for Amy. She spent about an hour posing in front of a mirror with a funny smile on her face. There are pictures but you're not going to see them. I tried on the falsies too but they looked pretty silly perched on a set of 38Ds. They didn't work in Dave Marsh's bra either, probably because the chest hair didn't look right.

When the band played D.C., Ridley took some of us to the National Gallery of Art, where we saw the Barnes show before we went to the Vietnam War Memorial. I got to see the Van Gogh that looks just like my younger brother and the Toulouse-Lautrec that looks like Andrew Wyeth painted it yesterday and also I saw a wonderful abstract so full of color and energy I had to jump up and down a lot. Then Rid took us to the Memorial—instant downer but a brilliant piece of work too. It's just a black wall, you know, that rises gradually, the names of the dead piling higher and higher until they are above your head, however tall you are, and then begin to level out again. It's a perfect quotation of the emotional experience—the war creeping up on us until it overshadowed all our lives.

Thanks, Ripply. And Tad, for taking us to the terrific Vietnamese restaurant that night.

The bus broke down on the way to Nashville and we had a picnic at a rest stop. It was a pleasant interlude but foreshadowed our later exit from rehearsal that afternoon, when we discovered there was no transport to our hotel. The professional musicians assured us this meant we had experienced a real rock tour. Nashville is where Al lives, unless it's Memphis. We went to Al's house for awhile and saw his record collection. I thought I had some Old Shit (a technical term referring to music you've only heard sampled because you're too young but which constitutes the roots of everything you hear. Al made some of that Old Shit, personally.) Duane Eddy Does Dylan, stuff like that. Al's record collection is like the Alexandrian Library of Old Shit.

Speaking of sampling shit, in all the stops we made in the South, I never once got a cup of coffee that *wasn't* shit. Greil Marcus informed me Southerners think the shit they call coffee is coffee. Another surprise were the knickknacks at Stuckey's that came in a wide selection of racist themes—Uncle Tom, pickaninnies with watermelons, and so on. Not that I had to leave town to uncover the cockroach of racism. One of our local coffee shops right here in my hometown of Bangor, Maine, displays a line of greeting cards featuring, among other crudities, a black judge who gives lenient sentences to white women. Hey, we all went to look for America. Whoomp. There it is.

In Miami backstage, there were airkisses among famous people and their hangers-on, and hasty introductions, promptly forgotten, as the sense of the band— *the bandness of the band*—dissipated. It was raining when we came out of the club and I was wide awake the way you can only be at two in the morning. The tour was really over.

Steve and I split off to another hotel in Miami—in retrospect a mistake. Once we were at the American Booksellers Convention, Steve wasn't part of RBR anymore. He was Stephen King, public figure, bug in amber. Nothing happened that wasn't typical of ABA, from the silly bitch who threw herself into the limo to announce she was in love with his mind, to eating with publishers in a restaurant so full of publishers it might as well have been in New York as Miami. The tour felt like it never happened.

If you're looking for scandal, there wasn't any worth mentioning. Except for maybe Roy's side trip with the roadies. Sex and drugs for these folks all happened

PMS is a legal defense, Marsh claimed. (In this case, we're told it stands for Post-Masculine Stress Syndrome.)

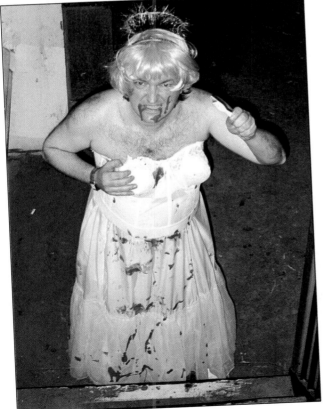

Cool at last.

The Critics Chorus:
Words fail them, too.
(Photo by Keta Bill)

Three bards and an attitude.

Bartimus working on her bus tan.

Four broads and
an attitude.

And it all started
with a little girl and
her fax machine.
(Photo by Dave
Worters)

about twenty, twenty-five years ago. Oh, I guess we should count the consumption of booze and the cigarettes. And actually I did turn down a hit off a number, as did several others, but some people didn't. It was a typical bunch of Americans of my g-g-generation, babbling out both sides of their mouths on the subject of drugs. Mine are okay, yours are bad for you, unless I want to share. We're as good at that piece of doublethink as our parents were.

Oh, all right, there might have been some sex but we're all so past it, I'm sure it hardly counted. RBR is all four-eyed eggheads; they probably all subscribe to that hooha about the brain being the sexiest organ. Except Roy. He's a Southerner. When, in the course of some conversation, I mentioned the practice of watermelon-rape and cited a Cormac McCarthy novel as my source, I was surprised at the swiftness with which Roy identified *Suttree*. Joel Selvin was suspiciously quick, though, to quote a Persian aphorism to the effect that women are sweet, boys are sweeter, but sweetest of all is a melon.

Basically, the fun for the writers who made up RBR was in kicking out the jams. They got off their spreading middle-aged backsides and shook themselves up. They made music together. So fuck the fun police.

Bravo, RBR. May your word processors hum forever.

You should learn some new tunes though. Something that doesn't, like, suck. Heh-heh. Hey, Ramones tapes, coming your way.

Barbara Kingsolver

CONFESSIONS OF THE RELUCTANT REMAINDER

*F*rom my hotel room in Boston I can look down on the Charles River, where white sails zip under a freeway overpass, rippling like runaway laundry against an incongruous backdrop of late-morning traffic and soot-gray bricks.

I have no idea what I'm doing here. It's May 20; I'm two thousand miles away from my six-year-old daughter, whom I miss so badly I feel like I've been shot in the chest, and from my empty Tucson household, where the dust bison roam freely among the piled-up mail and manuscripts and maybe by now are plotting an unopposed takeover. I'm not there; I'm in a hotel, pretending to be a musician on tour with a bunch of authors pretending to be a band.

At this moment I am waiting for two grown men named Hoover and Mouse to come pick up my electric keyboard and haul it to the club in Providence where we're opening our show tonight. Mouse and Hoover are our roadies, hired professionals at my service to tote and tune and do all the dirty work so that I—presumably—can preserve my delicate constitution for the performance. This is a joke; either one of them could play a meaner keyboard than I do, I'm sure, with one or more of his arms in a plaster cast.

I asked them to bring the keyboard back here after rehearsal last night, think-ing that some after-hours practice on my own would render me a passable musician, and then, presto, this very weird scheme would fall into place for me. It didn't. I ran through a halfhearted "Nadine," switched the power off, called my best friend up long distance, and asked: "What in the bejesus am I doing here?" My friend said, as friends do, "I don't know, honey, but you'll think of something." So far I haven't. My keyboard is hulking over there on the table like the remains of some mal-inspired room-service party ordered up at two A.M. and left for dead on its tray.

I'm suffering from sleep deprivation, I know this much. I recognize the signs: life seems baffling and mostly not quite worth the bother. I don't have a musician's sleeping skills, among other things. Our schedule says we stay up very late rehears-ing or performing, then sleep till noon. I've never slept past sunrise, I don't think, not even once in my life, not for love or money or prescription drugs, so these days I stay up till three, get up at six, and then sit around in my room waiting for sched-uled late-morning events like "bag pull" (a new one on me), or the impending visit of Mouse and Hoover.

At last they knock, and I let them in. They are cheerful and embarrassingly subordinate. "Get those changes worked out?" they ask, as if I'd been pacing all night, frowning in my headphones, memorizing modulations and fingering patterns and stunning new chord sequences.

"You guys are great," I tell them. It's the truth. They are kind enough to pre-tend there is work to be done and a show to put on and it's all going to be big fun.

If you ask me, making a fool of yourself on purpose is a scary enterprise. That thought entered my mind right away, when I first got Kathi's letter asking if I'd be willing to get together with a bunch of other authors and play music for the ABA in Anaheim. Her form letter offered three boxes to check, suggesting approximately these alternatives: (1) Yes, wild horses couldn't keep me away! (2) No, I am much too dignified to do such a foolish thing. (3) I might have to wash my hair that night—talk me into it. I checked box number 3.

I'm not dignified at all; that isn't the problem. My friends, under pressure or bribe, will tell you stories about me that involve, for example, food fights, go-go-dancer impersonation, and flamboyant petty thievery. (I once helped relocate the Big Boy from his post in front of the Bob's Big Boy establishment to the front porch of an archenemy.) (The Big Boy weighs a ton.) Dignity has never put any rocks in *my* road. But when I thought over this band idea, it occurred to me that lots of things could keep me away, wild horses being the least of them. I may be fun at parties, but only if I can make it look more or less like an accident; I'm not a *show-off*. To put myself onstage at some kind of ABA crossover talent show seemed a lit-tle audacious.

I received the recruitment letter several months after Kathi mailed it from San Francisco; I was living in the Canary Islands, and so was out of the communicative loop, to put it mildly. After I checked box number 3 and dropped my letter into the bright yellow we-pick-up-mail-when-we-feel-like-it box down the street from my apartment, I thought that would surely be the end of that.

In February '92, when I moved back to the U.S., a mound of mail was waiting for me, shaped something like a faithful dog but much larger. In it I discovered about twenty hot-pink envelopes containing urgent communiqués from Kathi Goldmark. It seemed I was the keyboard player for the Rock Bottom Remainders. Apparently I'd held this position for months. I called Kathi and told her I found it worrisome: maybe all the other people were first-rate musicians, and I would embarrass them. Or maybe we'd sound hideous. She sent me a tape Stephen King had made of himself playing guitar and singing. The first of my worries was expunged, and the second, certified.

So we did our crossover talent show, and made a big hit with the inebriated booksellers and publishers of North America, and somebody got the idea we should do it some more. I pointed out that while hit-and-run is one thing, repeat offenders generally get the punishment they richly deserve. If we kept playing, sooner or later somebody would notice that the Rock Bottom Remainders sound like Hound Dogs in Heat, with the advantage of modern amplification technology. My fellow band members did not think this should pose any significant problems.

At some point that winter, it became clear that we really were going to do it, something big, possibly a *road tour*, in the spring of '93. I felt ambivalent. I was finishing a novel, and knew already that I would have to be on the road way too much in '93, to promote the new book. Also, my personal life had become a protracted crisis.

"So I switched to zoology."

I'm a cheerful person on the whole, but '92 was a rotten year. My marriage of many years had been transferred suddenly from the intensive care ward to the autopsy table. I was single—something I had not been since age twenty-two—and reeling between shock and despair. At the practical level, I was completely overwhelmed with the tasks of being mother of a preschooler, full-time author with big deadlines, carpool driver, chief cook, good citizen, breadwinner, and fixer of all broken things around the house. I'd always watched single working moms with awe, wondering how on earth they did this. Now I was learning. The key to survival is something called "multitasking." You figure out how to combine compatible chores: phone consultations with your editor and washing the breakfast dishes. Writing a novel in the pediatrician's waiting room. Grocery shopping and teaching your child to read. Sleeping and worrying. Sobbing and driving.

The notion of a little bus jaunt down the East Coast pretending to be a rock and roll star seemed, let's say, not very compatible with the other tasks on my list. I didn't see how I could do it.

Tad and Ridley and Amy called up to tell me I needed to have some fun. Steve King sent so many mailgrams, I became a cult figure at my post office. Roy, at some point, offered to write my novel for me. Throughout that very dreary winter and spring, I felt a steady tide of peer pressure and moral support from the Remainders. In April, when I came home from a long hike on my birthday, my message light was having a seizure: every member of the band, I think, had called up to sing "Happy Birthday" into my answering machine. (Al, God of Rock, sang it to the tune of "The Star-Spangled Banner": "Happy Birth-day to you, from A-al Koo-per . . ." When he ran low on lyrics, he worked in "and our flag was still there . . ." Believe me, I have this tape in a safe place.)

In May, I came to Boston for the tour. How could I not?

I'm never nervous when I do readings, I don't care how big the crowd is. But the first day we rehearsed in Anaheim, I was a case of nerve endings, and in Boston my insecurities were back again with interest. I wanted to play well—or at least in the right key. It didn't matter that we created a band persona out of self-ridicule, identifying ourselves publicly as "rhythmically challenged." The truth is, in rehearsal we all paid attention. Dave frowned into space a lot when he played. Ridley sweated and wrote things down. Kathi paced. Tad stayed wide-eyed and quiet. Steve made personal breakthroughs. (The second day of rehearsal I told him I thought he was sounding much better. His face lit up like a carnival ride, and he said, "You know what I discovered? When I'm not sure what chord to play, I don't touch the guitar, I just do this—*air strumming*!")

I tried to be dependable and invisible and watch my little buttons so I didn't come in sounding like a horn section when I was supposed to be an organ, or vice versa. I didn't want Al to roll his eyes at me. (I've found out since, he rolls his eyes even when he likes you.) I wanted to belong to this gang, and I wasn't going to do it by being the class clown or the silver tongue. We were a whole class of clowns, a league of quick wits, but so what? Can a good pig fly? When we got on stage, we were going to have to be a *band*.

Everybody else developed at least a song or two that was his or her own moment in the spotlight—Amy had her glorious black-leather "Boots Are Made for Walkin'," Tad chose "Chain of Fools," Ridley had his "Nadine," Steve specialized in teenage death songs, Dave did "Gloria" and "Money." I supposed I ought to brave center stage too, but the keyboard grows where you plant it, like a tree. It's more of a workhorse than a dance-around-the-stage-and-bite-livestock type of instrument. Think of one single flashy rock and roll band member who plays 'boards, if you can. For reasons partly beyond my control, it was very easy for me to fade into oblivion behind the Hawaiian shirts of the Critics Chorus. (In our video, there's no appreciable evidence that I was *there*.) So I rashly volunteered to step away from my synthesizer and *sing* "Dock of the Bay." I regretted it instantly.

"Dock of the Bay," Otis Redding version, is my favorite song. To my mind, it speaks to the universal human theme of being washed up somewhere with dashed hopes and poor employment prospects and nobody to hold your hand. I've sung it nine million times in private places, mostly tiled and wet. But I don't sing with my clothes on; it's the principle of the thing. I know my limitations—or should, by now.

The first time we went through "Dock of the Bay" in rehearsal, my throat was the size of one of those tiny plastic straws they put in your margarita. The guys faithfully played the right chords behind my soulfully inaudible rendition, but they examined their sneakers a lot when it was over, and I scooted quickly back behind my keyboard like a hermit crab into its shell after a brief interlude of nakedness.

I kind of hoped that song would go away. But Al made me do it again, every day. (He pulled me aside one day and advised that I learn the words. I said, "I *know* the words, I just can't *sing*.") In time I got the volume up, but never to the point of feeling entitled to do it in front of an audience that had actually paid, in cash, to be there.

This band has always been philosophically divided on the subject of music. In rehearsal we worked much harder than any of the guys are going to admit. We didn't want to embarrass ourselves utterly. But in interviews we knocked each other down in the scramble for the title of Lowest Musical Self-Esteem—we are probably still doing that in this book. It's a face saver. Because we all knew no amount of rehearsal could ever make us into a first-rate, or even cut-rate, or irate, or reprobate, rock and roll band. In that case, it's better to pretend you're not trying very hard than to let on that this is really your best effort.

So what *was* the point, exactly? I found myself brooding a lot, those first early mornings in my Boston hotel room. Why make a public show of something you know perfectly well you're not doing all that well? Why should good writers play mediocre music? If this is multitasking, I might as well go home and sob in my car.

My rationale, which came to me long after the fact, has to do with my desire to jump fences and graze a lot of pastures, both greener and thornier than the one where I supposedly belong. Sure, I played in this band because it looked like we could raise a huge amount of money to promote literacy. (We didn't—our production costs ate up most of our profits, but that is another story.) And I did it because I needed a break from an unhappy, hardscrabble time in my life. But I also did it because I want to be allowed to be exactly what I am—a writer who does other things. I've spent my life hiding a closetful of other lives.

When I entered graduate school in evolutionary biology, in my early twenties, my committee looked long and hard down their noses at my interest in creative writing. Now that I'm known mostly as a writer, it's considered comical or suspect that I have degrees in science. When I speak in public, I'm frequently introduced by someone who will make a point of revealing my checkered past: I've worked as an archaeologist, a typesetter, a medical technician, a translator, a biological field researcher, an artist's model. The audience generally laughs, and I do too. Music— don't even bring it up. It seems ridiculous to add that to the list.

But it's on there. In 1973, I went to college on a music scholarship. I studied classical piano performance and music theory and composition at DePauw University, for two years, until it struck me one day that all the classical pianists in the entire nation were going to have a shot at, maybe, eleven good jobs, and the rest of us would wind up with plasticene smiles on our faces, tinkling through "The Shadow of Your Smile" in a hotel lobby.

So I switched to zoology. It seemed practical. I could just as easily have gone over to literature, or classics, or anthropology or botany or math. I'm in awe of those people who seem bent from early childhood upon a passionate vocational path. My father, the M.D., tells me that as a first grader he blew up his toy soldiers for the sole purpose of patching them back together. When *I* was a child, if anyone asked what I wanted to be when I grew up, I would reply first of all that I didn't think I *would* grow up, but on the off chance it happened, I planned to be a farmer and a ballerina and a poet and a doctor and a musician and a zookeeper.

This is not the right answer. I know that now. "Philosopher-king," you might as well say. "Sword swallower–stockbroker. Wrestler–art historian." A business card that lists more than one profession does not go down well in the grownup set. We're supposed to have one main thing we do well, and it's okay to have hobbies if they are victimless and don't get out of hand, but confessing to disparate passions is generally taken in our society as a sign of attention-deficit disorder.

For all the years I studied and worked as a scientist, I wrote poems in the margins of my chemistry texts and field notebooks, but I never identified myself as a poet—not even to myself. It seemed like a private, embarrassing indulgence. Thoreau was unabashedly both scientific and literary; so was Darwin. But something has happened since then. Life is faster and more streamlined, and there is too much we have to know just to get the job done right. To get *one* job done right, let alone seven or eight. And certainly, we are supposed to get it right.

For all the years I've worked as a writer, I've also played piano and synthesizer, bass clarinet, guitar, and lately even conga drums. I have sung in the shower. (I sound *great* in the shower.) I have howled backup to Annie Lennox and Randy Travis and Rory Block in my car. I've played in garage bands and jammed informally with musician friends, and with them have even written and recorded a few original songs. But I have *never* called myself a musician. It's not the one thing I do well.

As I approach the middle of my life, though, it's occurred to me that this is the only one I'm going to get. At some point I'd better open the closet door and invite my other selves to the table, even if it looks undignified or flaky. I *like* playing music. The music I make has not so far been nominated as a significant contribution to our planet, but it's fun.

I've seen those books on multigenre genius: paintings by Henry James, poetry by Picasso. That's not what I'm talking about here. I'm saying I'd like to think it's okay to do a lot of different kinds of things even if you're not operating at the genius level in every single case. I'd like to think we're allowed to have particolored days and renaissance lives, without a constant worry over quality control. If the Rock Bottom Remainders are a role model of any kind, I think that's our department: we're going on record as half-bad musicians, having wholehearted lives.

Thursday night, before our opening show at Shooters Waterfront Cafe, we have all got jitters. The men have turned to alcohol, and the women to makeup. We've regressed to girls-in-the-bathroom mode—sharing hair stuff, asking if this looks OK, relying heavily on each other for fashion advice and kind oversight. This, I imagine, is what other girls did in high school before a big date. I didn't. I skipped the junior prom and read Flannery O'Connor. In 1972 I was into blue jeans and defiance, having found that the best defense, where an uninspiring social life was concerned, was a good offense.

I like my position in this band. I'm not a Remainderette, so I don't do gold lamé and I don't have to be called upon by Al, in rehearsal, as "Girls!" (Always the collective plural.) On stage, I'm a musician. But on the bus and in the hotel and right now in the dressing room I am definitely *girls*. Lorraine is giving me a lesson in remedial makeup. I look in the mirror, blink twice as my glamorous big sister smiles back at me. Finally we leave this war-torn dressing room and crowd out onto the backstage bridge and the guys all hoot at us. I find out what I was missing in 1972 while I had my nose in a book.

We line up and wait for Roy to introduce us so that one by one we can run out on stage and be cheered. I am invulnerable and supremely transformed: I take the stairs by twos, land on the stage in my black lace leggings and long black no-finger gloves, and blow a kiss to the audience. I can't *wait* to sing "Dock of the Bay." I could dance on a table tonight, or roll the Big Boy down the street with impunity. I feel overtly beloved. I lean into my piano and lead out on "Money," and when the bass and guitar kick in I am moving dead center with the In Crowd. I am a river in spring flood season. I may not stop this, ever.

In my fairly short career as an author, I've never quite grown accustomed to public displays of approval, but I've learned at least to behave as if they're normal. I've given readings to many a packed house, and signed books steadily for so many hours that the people at the back of the line, I'm afraid, have had time to meet, marry, and bear offspring. I've been recognized and asked for autographs in restaurants, airplanes, the drugstore, once while I had my shoulder to a truck bumper that was stuck in the snow, and once during a break in a concert, when I realized the restroom I sought was at the end of a line that ran around the block, and I let out a long string of, um, opinions about the situation. (Three women in the line simultaneously responded, "Aren't you Barbara Kingsolver?" I said, "Hell, no!") My point is, I'm not a complete stranger to celebrity. But none of it has ever felt *anything* like playing with the Remainders.

I keep wondering why. Most of the Remainders have said, at one time or another, that the writing life is solitary and this is a chance to be in the bright lights; that nobody throws underwear at a writer. That's not it. People do, believe it or not, throw the equivalent of underwear at writers they love. I sometimes get proposals of marriage in the mail, in plain, business-sized envelopes. I'm not looking for attention. I'm not here for the glitter, the outfit, the roadies, or the instant gratification of dancing fans. I'm not the glitter type. Book tours offer the equivalent of roadies—media escorts whose sole job is to keep you alive and coherent on your way from one interview to the next. And book tours offer enough immediate gratification to support a lifetime of solitary writing.

What they don't offer is the chance to belong to a group. Book tours are as lonely as a prison term. Nobody believes me when I say this, but it's true, nonetheless. Yes, you are continually surrounded by people, and you hear "I love your work" and even "I love *you*" hundreds of times a day, and that never stops feeling amazing. But you're completely isolated from friends and family and intimate conversation and real life. You move from city to city in a strange glass bubble, the psychic equivalent of that aquarium car that is used for displaying the Pope. Nobody knows what you're going through. You are here *for them* at this moment, and afterward you will disappear. My last book tour took me to a different city every day for about two months, and in all that time I can remember only about four moments when some kind stranger looked me in the eye and said, "You must miss your daughter," or "How long since you've been home?" Each of those times, tears sprang to my eyes and I realized the extent of my loneliness. Being adored and lonely is surreal, in the same way that vacationing alone is surreal. If you don't have anybody's hand to squeeze when the taxicab radio erupts into the Hallelujah Chorus at the exact moment you turn a corner and see Notre Dame, will anyone ever believe that really happened? There is a kind of veracity of experience that only comes—to me, anyway—from seeing my own delight reflected in someone else's eyes.

That was the thrill of the Rock Bottom Remainders. I must have sought it out in the middle of my dark winter, like a pale seedling straining for sun, because somewhere in the basement of my boarded-up heart I knew it was what I needed. Tad's enormous eyes, wide and starry with mascara, smiling at mine in the dressing room mirror as we prayed we'd hit our notes. Amy with her chin tipped up, glancing over for her cue on "Leader of the Pack." Steve's little wink when he takes over the whistle reprise on "Dock of the Bay." Dave's grin and Ridley's smiling nod as we look at each other and move, smooth as silk, from A major into the F-sharp-minor bridge that we *always* screwed up in rehearsal.

Look at us, we are saying to each other. This is really happening. This amazing and joyful noise that has got all those people jammed together and sweating and howling and bumping and grinding is coming from *us*. We are here, right now. We are the ones.

Edited and Annotated by Roy Blount, Jr.

THE HENLEY EPISODE AND ITS RAMIFICATIONS

*I*n a letter to his friend Dave Marsh on March 26, 1992, Don Henley, former Eagle and recent defender of Walden Pond, expressed his willingness to "sacrifice my Memorial Day weekend on the altar of sweat, beer, and thrash." This in response to Marsh's suggestion that Henley review, for the *L.A. Weekly*, the Remainders' maiden outing in Anaheim. (Did Henley ever consider that? That it was our *maiden* outing? Amy wasn't even tattooed yet!)

It seemed a good idea at the time.

"To be perfectly honest," said Henley in a second letter to Marsh, which accompanied a copy of the review, "my heart just wasn't in this. It's hard to criticize amateurs in any situation. . . ."

Should the purity of this book be marred by the inclusion of a piece of writing which nobody's heart was in? No. Particularly a piece of writing that spattered our hearts' blood all over. The review's specifics may be inferred from Remainders' responses.

Dear Don,

As you will see from the enclosed correspondence, none of the band members took your review to heart, and some of our husbands and wives laughed so hard that juice came out of their noses. It seems like bad reviews are part of the rock and roll experience.

I thought it might interest you to know, from our point of view, a few details about your much-heralded visit to our show.

A scant couple of hours before show time, I received a phone call from the singularly most obnoxious person in the greater L.A. area. He said his name was Tony, and that he was calling to "advance" your visit to Cowboy Boogie, and demanded "extra security and a roped-off table for Don Henley" at a COWBOY BAR, fer cryin' out loud! I assured him that there would be full security provided by the club, that it was too late to arrange anything special for you, and that in this crowd of bookworms, probably nobody would recognize you anyway. He then asked if Stephen King was the "real" Stephen King, and I said no, he was my brother-in-law, Stephen Irving King from Riverside, and if this was all too much trouble, you didn't have to come. I think we both slammed the receivers down at the same time. (Note: Last night Amy Tan, at a KQED celebrity benefit party, wrote "Don Henley" on her name tag. She wasn't mobbed by a single fan, so after a while she added "You know—from the Eagles." There was still no need for extra security. Go figure.)

Although we understand the spirit of loving fun in which the review was written, and although we secretly think he should stop whining and be glad that, at age forty-plus, he has any hair, we must band together and take exception to your rude remarks about Dave Barry's hairdo. The Remainderettes think his hairdo is sexier than yours (that is, if we could remember what yours looks like).

Best,
Kathi Kamen Goldmark
Tight-Libidoed White Woman

To: Whom It May Concern
Don Henley is a dead man.

Dave "Vito" Barry

Remainders:
What Henley wrote about us was within the fair grounds of rock crit shit. If you don't believe me, I'll send along some of my (or Greil's) Eagles reviews.

Dave M.

To: Dave M.

   Yeah, but did you insult their fucking haircuts?

                                             Dave B.

To: Dave B.

   Of course we did. I'm not saying Henley's right. If he was right, he wouldn't be a rock critic.

                                             Dave M.

To: Dave B.

   While I was out of town, I received a letter from my uncle, T.C., who somehow got it in his head that you know some guy named Don Henley. I'm sending along the letter, since he's my uncle, and he was the one who arranged for all the chains to put my books on the bestseller lists.

                                             Amy

Dear Mister Barry,

   Look like you know man name Don Henley. I very upset hear he written somethin in L.A. Weekly about garbage. Not just me upset—whole Secret Triad Society! Maybe you know this, maybe not, Secret Triad Society we in honorable business, not calling it garbage like this Henley person. Waste disposal. Lots recycled too. All major metropolitan areas. L.A. too. I telling you, Mister Barry, no alley cats in our business. Very clean. Professional. That why I so upset. People saying bad things about Chinese business. Not good for business.

   You do this for me, Mister Barry. You give me Henley person address. My friends at Society we can go see him. We "dispose" of bad image problem. Get it, joke?

   We take care him. You see. You just send address to my niece, Amy Tan, nice girl, write a couple books do well (thanking to me). She let me know. All third person. Your hands not involved. Okay? Okay.

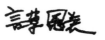

   Most sincere yours,
   T. C. Chun

To Amy:

   I got your Uncle Chun's letter, and as a journalist, I must ask you whether this man is aware of the First Amendment to the Constitution, guar-

anteeing freedom of speech. No? Good. Then he's the man we want to put on this Henley thing.

Not that I am sensitive. Not at all. I thought that a great deal of the Henley review was extremely hilarious. "Ha ha!" I remarked to myself repeatedly. But I think that any objective observer would agree that Henley stepped over the lines of civilized human decency when he made fun of my haircut. I think it would do him a world of good, as a person, to have Uncle Chun explain to him, calmly and reasonably, why it is bad to write these things, in hopes that he may come to a better understanding of his proper role as a critic. Then he should die a horrible death.

Dave B.

Dear Mister Dave Barry,

Okay, this my thinking. We invite this Henley person come for big banquet dinner. He thinking, Mm-hm, good Chinese food, eat up, twenty minute later still hungry. Ha-ha, he make big joke. Only he not so hungry twenty minute later. Not even twenty year later. Get it? He the joke.

You choose "recipe." Two kinds here. One called "Dancing Shrimp." Take live shrimp, wiggling, little legs moving lots. Use long skewer, sharp tip, poke through belly, softest part—ffft!—all way through. Don't kill, see. You kill, don't taste good as live. Put dancing shrimp in hot sauce. You bite, still wiggle in mouth! That good. Very good shrimp this way. You want be nice, put a shrimp in wine first, get a little drunk. Then hot sauce. Still not bad taste.

Second recipe this. Take live monkey. Put little clothes on. Make him dance just for you friends laughing. Then put monkey under table, a hole cut out the middle so head stick through. Everybody seat around table, laughing lots—because just seen monkey dance, remember? Then take out very sharp knife, cut around monkey skull, like cutting cantalope skin around the middle. Very careful now, lift skull. You do right, monkey still living. Brain still steaming. This very important. If already dead, taste not so good. Now pour chili sauce over top of brain. Invite everybody at table, Eat! Eat! Don't be polite!

Or maybe you don't want use shrimp or monkey. Maybe you want try some other kind meat. Invite Henley person for dinner. Not eat dinner. Be dinner! Get it? Ha-ha! Little monkey clothes too! Maybe make him do tambourine dance first.

Sincerely yours truly,

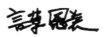

T. C. Chun

To: Uncle Chun

  I like the dinner concept very much. I am especially attracted to the monkey recipe, my big concern being that we might open Henley up, only to discover that his brain is the size of a standard cocktail onion. Then the guests would go home hungry. "Such skimpy portions!" they'd be saying. "Apparently our hosts forgot a fundamental rule of Home Economics, namely that if you're going to serve aging former rock-star brains, you need a lot of aging former rock stars."

               Dave B.

Dear Mister Barry:

  I got a bad news give you. We do everything too fast, make little mistake. You remember you give me address? Thanking you for that. But I see 1 look like 7. My wife she tell me other day, Time for eyeglasses. I tell her, You wrong. Maybe now I think she right all right.

  Anyway we go wrong address, Mulholland Drive. I not recognizing who this Henley person is. To my eyes he not too famous, look like everybody else. So man open door. Small head, bad haircut, big loser type—all like you describe him. And we do fundoo dinner like you suggest it. You right, no nerve that Henley person. Oh, he scream! Climb wall like fly on sticking paper. You be proud.

  I go home, sleep good, call my niece Amy Tan next morning, tell her, "That young man you say be a bad image problem, guess what, no more problem." She tell me, "He's not young man—he's OLD!" Oh, she mad! Of course, this not nice, she get mad at her uncle that way.

         Special regarding to you,

          T. C. Chun

P.S. You next book just write a story about me. Good story. Poor boy in China, then come United States, use a quarter to start business, now successful millionaire. Many good stories in between. How much friends like my dancing, my singing. Some funny parts too.

  So deal go like this. I tell you my story, all you do just it write down. Even though this my story, I be generous. We split fifty-fifty.

Dear Uncle Chun,

  This is an excellent idea, a book by you. I have a feeling that it would sell very well, especially if we pick a catchy title, something like

T. C. Chun: His Life
And Yours Too, If You Don't Buy This Book

Also we could have a Marketing Plan wherein Secret Triad Society sales consultants would be on hand at major book outlets to assist consumers. The consultants could stand near what we call the "point of sale" and explain the benefits of the Bulk Purchase Option. "You buy just one book?" they would say. "This very good book. Maybe you buy some more."

I'm confident it would be a big seller. But we have one problem: we need an agent. An agent is a person who takes your book—your book, Uncle Chun—and gives it to a publisher. Then, just for doing this one little thing, the agent takes 10 or 15 percent of your money. It doesn't seem fair to me, Uncle Chun, but that's the system. Maybe you could get a better deal for us if you talked to an agent. Maybe you could invite the agent for dinner, you know? You could serve a special dish. Maybe Henley Surprise. I know you'll think of something. You're good with people.

Literarily,
Dave B.

Internal Revenue Service
Assistant Commissioner (International)
International Fraud Unit

RE: Tax Returns 1971–1991

Dear Dave Barry:
    We recently received an urgent phone call from a Mr. T. C. Chun of New Patriots for America. He asked for a special agent who could help him reduce his liability to below 10 percent, "same as Mister Barry, good humor writer, laugh all way to bank."

    Of course, we have no such tax bracket, but if we did, to qualify, you would have to be living substantially below the poverty level. Or, to be precise, you would have to be living in a shack in the swamp belt, have black lung disease from smoking corncob pipes, be raising nine children under the age of eighteen, all of whom help you earn a meager income selling pennies squashed on the railroad tracks (the pennies are not deductible).

    Furthermore, according to a computer check of your 1099s over the last five years, we do not see a shred of evidence that you have qualified for such a disgustingly low tax bracket. In fact, the way we see it, you probably owe us millions. For example: your annual $100 charitable contribution to the Disabled Lawnmower Veterans. This organization does not meet our 501(c) *criteria. Moreover, it does not exist. In addition, we have noted on your previous returns the following inappropriately expensed deductions:*

- *"Beer & Wine Coolers" under Professional Supplies*
- *"Amazon Mudfight Series Tickets" under Professional Dues.*

In light of these preliminary findings, we are now initiating a full-scale audit of your tax returns. Normally, the statute of limitations on felony cases expires after five years. But in special cases like yours, we've waived the limitations and will audit for tax years 1971–1991. Please get your documents in order, then call me within two working days at (202) 555-4426 so that we may set up your first interview. Failure to do so may result in a twenty-five-year prison term or $2 million fine.

> *Sincerely,*
> *Ken Barbie*
> *Special Agent*

Dear Mister Barry,

Good news. I use you suggestion, good result. Happen like this.

I ask my niece Amy Tan give me name of agent. She give me name, but I tell her, No, too long, how I can remember! So she give easy one, I-C-M. Later I go home. My mind tired, so can't remembering too good. I-something-something. Sudden I remember. I-R-S. Sound familiar anyway.

So I call. Very hard finding right person. Finally I reach special agent. I tell him what you say—don't want pay too much, less than 10 percentage. Even I don't make millions like you, why I should pay more.

We talking, talking, talking. Sudden I realize, I call a wrong place.

Lucky for me, IRS person, he very kind, very happy talk to me. Then he say I get big reward. 30 percentage. I ask him 30 percentage what. He say 30 percentage what Mister Barry owe U.S. government, lots money, he told me, maybe like hundreds thousands millions.

Course, I feeling bad make money off you. But not right cheat government, United States of America, same place give me new home when my country no longer wanting me.

So this my thinking. You just pay. Good for you next life anyway, don't come back insurance agent. Get it, joke. Anyway, I get good reward. Everybody happy that way. Bad feeling in you heart—gone!

> *Faithful truly,*

T. C. Chun

Fair Acres Federal Penitentiary and Condominium
"Choice Units Still Available"

Dear Uncle Chun,

Hey, don't feel bad. Anybody could have made the same mistake. And the IRS people have been very fair. They have let me keep my spleen, even though it's not medically essential.

So I have tried, as an American, to be as cooperative as possible with them. I told them all about how various best-selling authors [may have engaged in certain legally marginal activities that need not be detailed here—Ed.]. I also told this to the grand jury, so there is probably no cause for concern.

You're right, Uncle Chun: I feel a lot better, now that I got all this off my chest. I owe a large debt of gratitude to you, and if your schedule permits, I'd like to meet with you and thank you personally and get to know more about your life story and current business activities. Anywhere you want to meet is fine with me, as long as there is no radio interference.

Dave B.

At this point Uncle Chun withdrew from Remainder affairs—and Don Henley's brains remained uneaten. The Henley review continued to rankle even as the band discussed whether to play for a second time, at the Bottom Line in New York.

To: All Remainders of All Types, Including Bold Italic

Okay, so we do not all agree about playing in New York. This is all right. This is good, in fact. Because we're a band, and real bands have disagreements. Real bands have factions.

For example, the Remainders are divided into factions based upon the crucial artistic question of whether or not Don Henley liked us. I am definitely in the faction of people he didn't like. I form the entire faction of people whose haircuts he made fun of. On the other hand, I think he liked Roy. Roy has tried to deny this in a weaselly manner, but I think he was secretly pleased by the Henley review, and I would tell him so myself if he had the fundamental human decency to get a fax.

I know *Henley liked Ridley. Ridley* hasn't even tried to deny it. This has been a tough pill for me to swallow. Time after time, I say to myself: "I was a friend to Ridley. I let Ridley buy beer for me. And all that time, he was just sitting there, smiling, being a person whom Henley was going to like, and he said nothing."

So I have as much cause as anybody to be bitter. But I'm not. Because I realize that when people are under the great pressures associated with being in a band that has achieved our level of mediocrity, there is going to be friction. We are, after all, only human beings, except possibly for Al.

Dave B.

To: the Leftovers

I've been trying to remain aloof from this faction thing, but I do need to point out that Don Henley liked me least of all. "Sloppy but heartfelt"? Okay, true, but aren't these the same words you've used to describe your retarded golden retriever, or your most orally fixated high-school boyfriend? I feel sure that Don Henley would also have called into question my libido, racial standing, and haircut, if only he could have seen me. But of course he couldn't since his intimate friend Roy Blount was doing everything within his downhome folksy power to stand in front of me, with his credibility hanging out all over the place, successfully obscuring me from general view and causing me to be consigned to the dustbins of boogie-woogie-triplet history. "Where are all those sloppy but heartfelt keyboard sounds coming from," the audience was probably asking itself, "ROY BLOUNT'S NAVEL?" My life is, not to put too fine a point on it, wrecked because of this, and if I had a fax machine and if Roy did I would tell him so myself.

All of this notwithstanding, I miss you guys and am pining to play with you again in New York. But I've got this novel deadline in October, and 200 pages to go. Daddy Warbucks has chained me to my keyboard (the one that makes weenie clicking sounds, not the other one) and says I can't leave the mansion till I've turned out a draft. And I, for one, still have to keep my day job. (Thanks to Roy.) I'm pretty torn up about this, for real. I'll live only for future reunions.

Steve, I wish you could come and carry me out of here, but I'm chained down pretty good. Can't quite reach that glass of water. . . .

Barbara

Our emcee was late getting into the loop, and began catching up, perhaps to excess.

Dear Other Remainders:

Well, I guess I will have to get a fax. I was going to hold out until someone could prove to me that Solzhenitsyn had one, but I guess if I am going to hold my own in today's highly competitive publishing industry—I wonder if there is any interest in taking up a collection to buy me one. Or you could all send me your starter models that you have outgrown; I would say that you could fax them to me, but if I don't have one already I don't suppose I can receive one in that way.

Anyway here I am resorting to the public mails, via which some of you have been kind enough to forward me your communications. I never did get a copy of the Henley review—can it be that I was singled out as the main thing wrong with the Critics Chorus (which is like being singled out as the main thing wrong with the Congress, or the Russian economy, or the publishing industry) and my feelings are being spared?

How about if I work on my dancing, learn to do splits and the like? Or, alternatively, if I stay most of the time under Barbara's keyboards, na-na-ing quietly to myself and emerging only occasionally to exclaim "You should see her feet!"? I don't want to button up my shirt, though, because it's going to be even hotter under there. In fact I don't want to . . . never mind.

The beat goes on.

                                      Roy

Dear Rest of the Remainders:

It has just now come to my attention that Don Henley liked me. In my defense let me say that he also liked Ridley, and sometimes or somewhat liked certain others. Still I find myself in an awkward position—which may explain why no one has responded to my innocent suggestion that everyone buy me a fax machine.

It may be that all of you, with the exception of Ridley, noticed right away that Henley liked me (right after noticing that he did not particularly like you), and therefore you are assuming that in my heart of hearts I am thinking to myself, "Well, the scumbrained degenerate snottynostril lowlife vicious piss-spraying assassin of my friends does recognize genial downhome humor when he sees it, though; you've got to hand him that."

But no! In the first place, I don't remember making half the reassuringly sane, homespun observations that Henley quotes me as making (in fact I believe Dave B. made several of them, while wearing that hair), and I believe I would feel that way even if I distinctly remembered anything that happened that night after the green manta-ray-shaped thing descended in that shower of bubbles and threw up the dully glistening lozenges in the emperor's lap.

(I did say, as Henley reported, "Suspend your credibility" for the Remainders. But the next day it hit me that what I meant to say was, "Let's have a willing suspension of disbelief" for the Remainders. It seems likely that many of you went through the entire show rocking, yes; rolling, yes; but *also wondering: " 'Suspend your credibility'? What does that mean?" The beauty of writing is that you can change it. Whereas emceeing is carved in stone.)*

In the second place, I wasn't trying *for genial downhome. I was in more of a "Gonna put a SPELL on you" frame of mind. I kind of thought that the audience would pull their children out of any educational institutions I had ever attended, after I got finished working my mojo. It was a wonder to me the next morning that I wasn't in jail.*

So. *I hope that this gracious admission on my part that I am nearly as upset over Henley's interpretation of us as the rest of you are—and more upset than Ridley, if I may name a name, has any right to be—will prevent a wedge's being driven into our esprit de corps by a . . . critic.*

Roy

AN OPEN LETTER TO BARBARA, AL, AND EVERYBODY

BARBARA:

ONE:

THE TRUTH IS THAT DON HENLEY LIKED YOU BETTER THAN ANYBODY ELSE! A LOT BETTER. IF YOU KNOW WHAT I MEAN.

THERE. THE TRUTH IS OUT.

AND THE REASON HE WROTE SUCH A BAD REVIEW OF YOU AND INCIDENTALLY OF EVERYBODY BUT ME AND RIDLEY IS THAT ME AND RIDLEY PROMISED TO INTRODUCE HIM TO YOU IN THE WEE HOURS OF THE A.M. AFTER THE CONCERT AND THEN ALONG ABOUT THE TIME THE WEE HOURS STARTED GETTING MIDSIZE WE REALIZED WE HAD FORGOT AND SO WHILE RIDLEY TOLD HIM THAT THE EAGLES MADE WHAT WERE PROBABLY GOING TO BE REMEMBERED AS THE CLASSIC MAKEOUT RECORDS OF OUR TIME I WENT TO A PHONE AND PRETENDED TO CALL YOUR ROOM AND THEN CAME BACK AND TOLD OLD DON THAT YOU WERE TOO STUCK UP TO COME OUT AT SIX-THIRTY IN THE MORNING (ACTUALLY, I COULDN'T THINK RIGHT THEN HOW EXACTLY TO MAKE A PHONE WORK) AND BESIDES, THAT YOU THOUGHT "YOUR LYING EYES" WAS NOT REALLY ROCK AND ROLL.

I DIDN'T THINK HE WOULD TAKE IT SO HARD.

MEANWHILE RIDLEY HAD RUN OUT OF NICE THINGS TO SAY ABOUT THE MAN'S WORK SO HE HAD BEEN TELLING HIM THAT DAVE B. HAD BEEN MAKING SNIDE REMARKS ABOUT THE WAY HE (DON) DID HIS (DON'S) HAIR, THAT STEVE DIDN'T LIKE THOREAU, THAT AMY USED TO BE A MEMBER OF RICHARD NIXON'S INNER CIRCLE, AND SO ON.

TWO:

I USED TO BE ABLE TO WHISTLE THROUGH MY NAVEL BUT THAT WAS BEFORE THE SINUS OPERATION.

AL:

I WANT EVERYBODY TO KNOW THAT THE REASON I AM HAVING TO MAIL THIS OUT AT A COST OF TWENTY-NINE CENTS (PLUS STATIONERY EXPENSES) PER REMAINDER IS THAT I HAVE NOT YET RECEIVED THE BROKEN FAX MACHINE YOU PROMISED TO SEND ME. I AM NOT GOING TO SAY ANY MORE. A GENTLEMAN SHOULD NOT HAVE TO.

EVERYBODY:

ONE:

LET'S ALL GET TOGETHER AND WRITE THE REST OF BARBARA'S NOVEL! WE PROBABLY DON'T HAVE TIME TO READ WHAT SHE HAS WRITTEN SO FAR, BUT IF WE EACH SEND HER ABOUT TWENTY PAGES SHE WILL HAVE THE 200 SHE NEEDS WHICH IS WHAT COUNTS.

Reeling and thrashing like some obscene parody of a—

OF A WHAT? A . . . PERSON.

Reeling and thrashing like some obscene parody of a person, the—

WELL, THAT DOESN'T HAVE MUCH PUNCH TO IT. WE CAN GO BACK AND CHANGE PERSON WHEN WE GET MORE OF A SENSE OF WHERE WE ARE HEADED.

Reeling and thrashing like some obscene parody of a person, the Rev. Ed—

OKAY, THAT IS NOT A GREAT NAME FOR A PREACHER. SYLVESTER? A BIT TOO . . . LET'S STICK WITH ED FOR A WHILE AND COME BACK TO IT.

Reeling and thrashing like some obscene parody of a person, the Rev. Ed or Something Thread—

THREADNORTON? THREADNEEDLE? THREADGILL IS FLAT. OKAY, LET'S SAY THREADWILLIAM, OR SOMETHING, FOR THE TIME BEING. OR MAYBE THROCK.

Reeling and thrashing like some obscene parody of a person, the Rev. Ed or Something Threadsomething (or Throcksomething) burst into the offices of the Oxhollow Land and Trust Federation like a man—

LIKE A MAN WHAT? HAVEN'T WE ALREADY ESTABLISHED WHAT KIND OF MAN HE IS? DOES HE HAVE TO BE A MAN? WHY DOES HE NECESSARILY HAVE TO BE SO UPSET, ALREADY? MAYBE WE SHOULD WORK HIM UP TO IT GRADUALLY.

Mysteriously—

OR, BETTER:

Noncommittally, the Rev. Ed or Something Thread—

SOMEBODY PICK ME UP HERE.

TWO:

WHY DON'T WE ALL GET TOGETHER AND WRITE ALL 400 PAGES OF MY NEXT BOOK? WHAT IS SO SPECIAL ABOUT BARBARA? ASIDE FROM THE FACT THAT SHE IS BREAKING ALL OUR HEARTS BY THREATENING NOT TO COME? IF THAT IS WHAT IT TAKES TO GET A NEXT BOOK WRITTEN, I WILL BE WILLING TO BREAK ALL OUR

HEARTS BY THREATENING NOT TO COME MYSELF. IN FACT I AM WILLING ACTUALLY NOT TO COME. UNTIL THE VERY LAST MOMENT.

BARBARA, AGAIN:
OH, COME ON.

Roy

P.S. TO DAVE B.:
YOU MAY WANT TO BEAR IN MIND THAT BARBARA MAY ALREADY HAVE A HURRI-CANE IN HER FIRST 200 PAGES.
P.S. TO EVERYBODY:
I HAVE NOT RESPONDED TO THIS THROUGH FORMAL CHANNELS BECAUSE I HAVE NOT RECEIVED AN OFFICIAL FAX TO ITS EFFECT, BUT I HAVE HEARD TALK THAT FUL-GHUM IS ALSO THREATENING NOT TO COME. HEY, WE COULD CATCH FULGHUM UP ON HIS NEXT BOOK IF WE EACH WROTE THREE PAGES.
P.P.S. TO EVERYBODY:
IF STEVE SHOULD THREATEN NOT TO COME, THOUGH, I CAN'T WRITE THAT MANY PAGES.

Finally, an explanation of the entire Henley affair was provided by Henley's favorite:

Remainders:
Okay, Dave has prompted me to reveal this, and this is really something I was trying to avoid, for reasons that will be immediately clear to all of you:
I AM Don Henley.
I knew that no one, except Al, knew what I looked like—I mean, who knows what Don Henley looks like? So Al and I cooked up this scheme: I would play bass in this band, not drums. I would hire a guy to make a big Hollywood stink about coming to the gig, because I make stinks about EVERYTHING and you have to keep up your reputation or disguises like this just can't be pulled off. Al agreed to give me a lot of shit at rehearsals, because that would throw you all off the scent. And, I can say with some authority, at least that part worked!
The trouble is, when I wrote the review my damn ego just couldn't stay out of it. I tried to tone it down, just kind of hint around the edges how fuck-ing genius my performance was.
Don't hate me, okay? I mean I have fucking nightmares about Uncle Chun and my brain—what's left of it—on the dining room table like some cauliflower casserole. Whoa! Calm down, Amy. I'm not that bad. Am I? Maybe I am! Oh, shit, I have these debates with myself all the time.

Don't throw me out of the group please. It's so damn nice to be in a group where they don't use tape for the vocals. Have you ever tried to lip-sync for four hours? We Eagles even lip-synced the dialogue with the audience, because our lead guitar player couldn't get three words out that made sense. Ah, those were the days.

Ridley

But perhaps the moral of the Henley episode was stated best in the following fax:

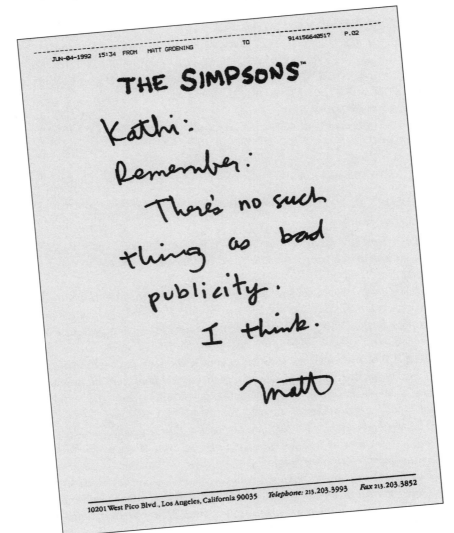

Michael Dorris

THE REMAINDERS: A ROCK 'N' ROLL SAGA THAT'S STRANGER THAN FACT

It really was a dark and stormy night, much scarier than any of the five-year-olds had bargained for when they brought home the permission slips for the end-of-year sleepover. Outside the empty kindergarten classroom, lightning played against the black sky, silhouetting the treeless limbs of the bean trees that lined I-25. The thunder, loud as a nuclear explosion, woke sleeping animals from their dreams and, in one freak accident, streaked through an open window and set a bed on fire, turning the mattress to toast. And then the rain began—a hard, hard fall. It ran into the gutters, causing misery to the nameless things that dwelled therein, sizzling the charred metal again as it struck the ruined frame. Was the rain *accident* or *chance*? Was it fate or just blind luck that brought joy to the members of the club?

"I haven't heard a noise like that since the group burp at last year's Tupperware Convention," laughed little Davey.

"I say we get outta here," warned Roy. "That was the fourth near-miss in a row, and on ball four you walk!"

"Wait'll I finish this drawing," Tomie begged. "It's my best one yet."

Matt looked over Tomie's shoulder. "Too ornate," he said. "Keep it simple." Then he caught sight of the clock. It was nearing eight. "On second thought, let's go. If we don't hurry we're going to miss 'The Cosby Show,' and it's my favorite."

"Make tracks," agreed Louise, and started to get up when the harried teacher, Ms. Goldmark, walked through the door.

"Don't worry, my dears. No matter what happens I'll take care of you," she promised. "I don't care what you need, where you want to go—I'm here to get you there. Just tell me or Mr. Kooper, the principal, and we'll be your parents-away-from-home."

"Ms. Goldmark! Ms. Goldmark!" sang out the new student from Detroit, the one everyone called the Marshmallow, the one who always wrote the lyrics to "Louie Louie" on the blackboard when nobody was looking. "Ms. Goldmark, what's your favorite song?"

"What an interesting question, Marsh—I mean David. I've always had a soft spot for Pink Floyd myself."

"See, what did I tell you?" Marshmallow said to his friend Robert. "Hey, are you asleep? Is that contraption safe to lay down on?"

"If there's one thing I've learned," Robert answered, "it's that if you're tired you should rest. It may have been on fire before, but now it's fine."

"What's for snack, Ms. Goldmark?" Amy begged, her eyes straying to the cafeteria door. "The kitchen," she told her best friend, Michael, "is my favorite room in the house. To me it is God."

"Yeah?" said Michael, his feelings hurt. "Well, why don't you marry it, then?" He played idly with the severed electrical wire that had frayed at the first stroke of lightning.

"Maybe I *will*," pouted Amy, and turned to Davey. "What do you think you'll be doing by the time you're forty?" she asked him.

"All I want is a wife, a child, and a really smart dog," he said, and wrote this thought down in the idea notebook he always kept in his breast pocket.

Suddenly the door creaked again, and at Mr. Kooper's entrance the whole class rose.

"Be cool," Mr. Kooper-Call-Me-Al told them, and they slouched back into their seats. "This storm's doing major damage. We can't stay here, but on the other hand you may not be able to make it home. I suggest each of us head out in a different direction, make his or her own way. I can't promise we'll ever meet again, but I want each of you to look around, remember the events of this night, make them a

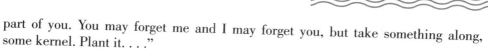

part of you. You may forget me and I may forget you, but take something along, some kernel. Plant it. . . ."

"Don't forget to put a little fish in each hole with the corn," said Louise and Michael simultaneously, as they so often spoke.

"Don't forget to write a weekly report about it," reminded Davey.

"Nothing I learn from now on may be as important as what I've learned here," chimed Robert.

"I hope you burn up at your senior prom," sneered Stephen.

"Children, children! I will not be responsible," cautioned Ms. Goldmark. "There are limits to even *my* patience."

"Maybe, someday, we'll meet again," Mr. Kooper offered. "Maybe we'll all find ourselves one day in some paradise for children, some Tomorrowland, some home-land for children where recess never ends."

"Like a state park with a lake and a raft where you can swim to," said Michael.

"Better," interrupted Roy. "Like hitting a home run and making it to the plate without getting tagged."

"Like writing a best-seller," all the children shouted simultaneously, joyously. "Like making The List and sitting there till cobwebs form."

"I'm never never going to grow up," said Tomie. "I'll only make my drawings for other children."

"Bag that," nudged Matt. "Crossover is the future, man."

"I'm *afraid*," cried Stephen. "I may never get over this."

"Use it, kid," advised Mr. Kooper. "Don't let anything go."

"What's your favorite song, Mr. Kooper?" asked Marshmallow.

And so, at the next break in the rain, the children were sent out into the night, one by one, each in a different direction. There was no good in their goodbyes, but they promised that they would see each other in September. "Bye bye, farewell," they said, each one holding on to one primal memory, one image that would draw the world for their future. For some it was a verbal cue; for others, visual. For all, the night would prove to be formative.

And so the years passed. Childhood melted into adolescence. Adolescence phased into mid-lifescence. Each man, each woman had dreams—unexplained, disturbing dreams—at night. Who were these phantoms that haunted their sleep? What were these three or four chords that played, broken and otherwise, in their mental quadraphonic speaker systems? Why couldn't they relate to Bach, to the Bee Gees? Why did they drive their Chevys to the levee and just sit there, discon-solate and glum?

And then, one day, the call went out unto the land: Ms. Goldmark, like Rachel, sought her scattered kinder. "Whither thou goeth, I . . ." she said to herself, Ruth-like, wed to the idea of a great reunion, a coming back together of the class of '67, Wordsworth Pre-School.

And they answered, one by one, two by two. Syncopating, percussing, doo-wopping. Thunder was their anthem, lightning their illumination. "Come-a, come-a, come-a, come-a, come, come, come-a," the siren song that drew them back, unknowing, unsuspecting. Until the night they remet, compared verbal SATs, jammed for good causes.

"We learned all this in kindergarten," Robert reminisced.

"Speak for yourself, Roundeyes," quipped Amy. "My mother taught me."

"I learned it in the hills," asserted Barbara. "And yet there's something familiar, something—"

"I know what you mean," Stephen interjected. "It's weird, strange. I don't know where I get my ideas, and yet—"

"I always *thought* it was baseball . . ." Roy mused.

"Bombs," added Tad.

"Chippewas," said Louise.

"It was *me*, you turkeys," announced Ms. Goldmark. "Everything you ever knew you learned from me, and now I demand 50 percent of all your royalties."

"Ms. Goldmark!" cried the no-longer-children. "You've became an agent!"

"Play," said Ms. Goldmark.

"Play, play, play," said Mr. Kooper.

"Residuals," said Mr. Kooper and Ms. Goldmark. "Finders' fees. Points. Grosses."

"But but but but," protested the Remainders.

"Grow up," advised Ms. Goldmark. "This is the nineties. This is L.A.—or almost. If you can't cook, get out of the kitchen. If it weren't for me, your fingers would still be sticky with paste."

And so the Remainders played. Played, played, played. It was a sound to hear.

And to forget.